Politics in Fantasy Media

Politics in Fantasy Media

*Essays on Ideology and Gender
in Fiction, Film,
Television and Games*

Edited by GEROLD SEDLMAYR
and NICOLE WALLER

McFarland & Company, Inc., Publishers
Jefferson, North Carolina

LIBRARY OF CONGRESS CATALOGUING-IN-PUBLICATION DATA

Politics in fantasy media : essays on ideology and gender in fiction, film, television and games / edited by Gerold Sedlmayr and Nicole Waller.
    p.   cm.
Includes bibliographical references and index.

ISBN 978-0-7864-9510-8 (softcover : acid free paper) ∞

ISBN 978-1-4766-1755-8 (ebook)

1. Fantasy in mass media.   2. Politics in literature.
3. Politics in motion pictures.   I. Sedlmayr, Gerold, editor.
II. Waller, Nicole, editor.
P96.F362P86   2014
809.3'8766—dc23   2014037062

BRITISH LIBRARY CATALOGUING DATA ARE AVAILABLE

© 2014 Gerold Sedlmayr and Nicole Waller. All rights reserved

No part of this book may be reproduced or transmitted in any form or by any means, electronic or mechanical, including photocopying or recording, or by any information storage and retrieval system, without permission in writing from the publisher.

Cover images © 2014 iStock/Thinkstock

Printed in the United States of America

McFarland & Company, Inc., Publishers
  Box 611, Jefferson, North Carolina 28640
    www.mcfarlandpub.com

Table of Contents

Introduction: The Politics of Fantasy • GEROLD SEDLMAYR and NICOLE WALLER — 1

I. IDENTITY

"It's all a big show": Constructing Identity in Suzanne Collins's *The Hunger Games* Trilogy • STEFANIE FRICKE — 17

Gender and Racial Roles in Computer Role-Playing Games • ANDREAS BLÜML — 31

II. THE POLITICS OF FANTASY

Conservative and Countercultural Elements in *Tim Burton's The Nightmare Before Christmas* • BEATRIX HESSE — 43

Subversive or Conservative? Vampires and Ideology in the *Twilight* Series and *True Blood* • CHRISTIAN KNIRSCH — 57

From Hyper-Male Aardvarks to the Female Void: Gender Politics in *Cerebus* • SEBASTIAN DOMSCH — 72

Fantasy as Politics: George R.R. Martin's *A Song of Ice and Fire* • RAINER EMIG — 85

The Politics of Post-Apocalypse: Interactivity, Narrative Framing and Ethics in *Fallout 3* • MATTHIAS KEMMER — 97

The Atheist Believer: *Harry Potter* and the Politics of Religion • BÄRBEL HÖTTGES — 118

Political Rhetoric as a Structural and Ideological Instrument in *Star Wars* and *Harry Potter* • CHRISTINA FLOTMANN — 137

Haven't I Been Here Before? China Miéville's Uncanny Cities •
  DIRK VANDERBEKE   150

III. THE FANTASY OF POLITICS

Fantastic Body Politics in Joe Abercrombie's *The First Law* Trilogy •
  GEROLD SEDLMAYR   165

The Fantasy of Politics: The Past and the Future of Object-
  Related Fantasy • SLADJA BLAŽAN   179

Tolkien's Baits: Agonism, Essentialism and the Visible in
  The Lord of the Rings • DIRK WIEMANN   191

About the Contributors   205

Index   209

Introduction:
The Politics of Fantasy

GEROLD SEDLMAYR and NICOLE WALLER

In their contribution to *The Cambridge Companion to Fantasy Literature*, Mark Bould and Sherryl Vint claim that "[a]ll fantasy is political, even—perhaps especially—when it thinks it is not. From the abstruse literary confection to the sharecropped franchise series, a fantasy text at the very least functions like any cultural text to reproduce dominant ideology" (102). While this statement is likely to trigger immediate consent, its commonsensical generality may still beg a couple of questions. If fantasy, politically, functions "like any cultural text," does it accordingly lack specificity? In case of a positive reply, to inquire after the politics of fantasy would be a somewhat vain endeavor, since the answers yielded would be synonymous with those produced by any investigation into the politics of (popular) culture. Secondly, in what way exactly must we take for granted that fantasy "at the very least [...] reproduce[s] dominant ideology?" If fantasy indeed functions to reproduce and stabilize power and thus operates as an essentially conservative genre, the quote nevertheless also seems to allow for other options, such as the opposite claim that fantasy can serve to subvert dominant power structures. In consequence, must we tailor our readings of the politics of contemporary fantasy to an endless back-and-forth between interpretations of fantasy as conservative and subversive? While many of the essays collected in this book participate in this important debate, they also point to the possibility of moving beyond the dualism of this critical gesture by complicating both our definitions of fantasy and of the political.

Precisely because "fantasy" is used so often—and so often without theorizing—its semantics have become extraordinarily wide-ranging, unspecific, and, often, self-contradictory. Lucie Armitt, when defending fantasy fiction against the allegedly more valuable realist forms of fiction, writes: "What is it about literary realism that endows it with this innate privilege over fantasy? In essence, the advantage seems to reside in the perceived proximity between realism and 'the real.' [...] And yet, [...] there is no more a genuinely direct connection between realism and the real than there is between fantasy fiction and the real; fiction is fiction is fiction" (2). Since all fiction *per definitionem* is fictive, a realist novel or film cannot claim more "truthfulness" than a novel or film with fantastic elements. Still, for our purposes, such an argument, though unquestionably of critical importance, might turn out to be too general again. Although hybrid modes, like "magic realism," clearly demonstrate the difficulty of drawing a clear line between realism and fantasy, there still is a difference between, say, Ken Loach's social realist films and Peter Jackson's Tolkien adaptations. Although both kinds of film are fictive representations, there is a difference in their ways and strategies of representing. Tzvetan Todorov has explored such differences of representation in his work on *The Fantastic*. He places the fantastic as an aesthetic strategy in between the uncanny, which is ultimately explainable by rational laws, and the marvelous, which participates in a discourse of the supernatural (see 41–57). According to Todorov, it is exactly the hesitation between rational and supernatural explanations which characterizes the mode of the fantastic, producing an aesthetics of ambivalence (see 25–33). The fantastic as a literary mode, then, both enacts and points to the space where lines are blurred and decisions must be made. It seems to us that many definitions of the genre "fantasy," although covering a much wider range of literary modes than Todorov's "fantastic," keep returning, in their most productive forms, to exactly this ambivalence. In an extension of Todorov's fantastic, however, fantasy literature often does not stop at evoking and cultivating the hesitation between different models of explanation or sense-making. Rather, fantasy tends to offer narrative resolutions, many of which—such as the fulfillment of fate or the restoration of naturalized hierarchies—seem to reduce complexity and ambivalence in rather reactionary ways. These two options (hesitation, resolution) return us to the debate about fantasy's subversive and conservative tendencies, a debate which still remains dominant in discussions of the politics of fantasy. However, as a third option, the resolutions offered by fantasy can also serve to emphasize the very act of choosing between conflicting worldviews and ideologies. In this reading, fantasy addresses the ambivalence involved in making sense of differing interpretations of the world by depicting the process of making sense as a process of making decisions, a highly political undertaking. While ambivalence is resolved, this resolution remains temporary, the result of a decision instead of an essential truth. As the essays show, fantasy covers the entire spectrum of these approaches.

We would like to propose that the politics of fantasy are closely related to genre politics. Indeed, the tension between unresolved ambivalence, easy resolutions, and complex explorations of sense-making and decision-making processes resurfaces in many definitions of fantasy as a genre. According to Lucie Armitt, for instance, the specificity of fantasy lies in its psychological functions. Just as the supernatural elements in traditional Gothic literature, for example in Coleridge's "Ancient Mariner," can be interpreted as exteriorized symbols of interior processes, contemporary fantasy is likewise nurtured by a "need to construct narratives to explain the utterly inexplicable, what terrifies us and why, and what our greatest desires may be" (Armitt 3). Arguably, then, fantasy fictions assume functions that, in pre-modernity, were fulfilled by mythical tales. They try to be *ersatz* mythologies in that they propose alternative, "otherworldly," lenses through which to view this world and judge the nature of our own predicament in it, although—and this is the point of hesitation—it is never easy to decide where or when precisely the purely fantastic assumes real-world relevance, be it psychological or other.[1] "Fantasy enjoys," Armitt claims, "a greater freedom from that overdetermination to order, organize, and package the chaotic set of experiences we call 'real life' than classical literary realism can" (3). In other words, like mythological tales, (post)modern fantasy productions, in spite of their more or less ostensible disconnectedness from "real-world" affairs, do after all deal with "the chaotic set of experiences we call 'real life.'" And precisely because they do so, they can and must be measured by the exigencies of their real-world social and political contexts. If it were otherwise, we would ban them into a purely esoteric realm, which would not do them any justice. As Rosemary Jackson has claimed: "Like any other text, a literary fantasy is produced within, and determined by, its social context. Though it might struggle against the limits of this context, often being articulated upon that very struggle, it cannot be understood in isolation from it" (3).

Brian Attebery has suggested to "use the term *fantasy* [...] for the genre, letting *fantastic* designate the mode" (11), and influentially proposed to approach fantasy as a genre in terms of a *fuzzy set*. This means, on the one hand, that it is "defined not by boundaries but by a center" (12); on the other hand and somewhat paradoxically, however, "there may be no single quality that links the entire set" (13). In other words, at its fringes, fantasy is an extremely open genre: it "edges into science fiction; science fiction impinges on mainstream fiction; mainstream fiction overlaps with fantasy" (13). When it comes to the center, fantasy as a genre is *not* structurally fixed either, but nonetheless coheres around certain productions that are deemed to be prototypical of the genre, although their specific features might not correspond in each and every case. For Attebery, the most central text in this sense is *The Lord of the Rings*: "Tolkien's form of fantasy, for readers in English, is our mental template, and will be until someone else achieves equal recognition with an alternative conception. One way to characterize the genre of fantasy is the set of texts that in some way or other resemble *The Lord of the Rings*" (14). This resemblance, Attebery claims, can be boiled down to three aspects. The first refers to content: fantasy, in some way or other, has to deal with "the impossible" or "some violation of what the author considers to be natural law" (Attebery 14). Another pertains to the reader: fantasy is meant to produce "wonder" or "estrangement" (Attebery 16); it is bound on producing a defamiliarizing effect. And last but not least, there is a structural requirement: "the characteristic structure of fantasy is comic. It begins with a problem and ends with resolution. Death, despair, horror, and betrayal may enter into fantasy, but they must not be the final word" (Attebery 15). This is what Tolkien, in "On Fairy-Stories," circumscribes with the help of the term "*Eucatastrophe*" (153), which combines the Greek syllable *eu*, meaning "good," with *catastrophe*, a term taken from the Aristotelian theory of drama and of course referring to the final resolution of the plot. *Eucatastrophe*, then, very literally, is a "good ending" in that a "sudden and miraculous grace" (153) is bestowed on the characters. As the ending of *The Lord of the Rings* illustrates, though, this sudden and miraculous grace is usually not provided by a "deus ex machina," an external and unaccounted-for savior; on the contrary, it is the protagonists themselves who bring the eucatastrophic ending about, by way of their own efforts and their own integrity. Fairy tales—or, rather, fantasy tales à la Tolkien, since this is what he actually seems to define—hence create "the joy of deliverance" (Tolkien, "On Fairy-Stories" 153), the joy that is felt when being saved. Indeed, if this is true, then fantasy narratives will indeed be always *utopian*. However, their utopianism, according to Tolkien, is not of an impossible kind; rather, they provide "glad tidings," which is one possible translation of the Greek *evangelium*. In this manner, fairy stories give "a fleeting glimpse of Joy, Joy beyond the walls of the world," indicating that "Escape from Death" ("On Fairy-Stories" 153), as part of Tolkien's Christian ideology, may take on a wholly different meaning as well. It does not have to refer to never-ending life in this world; rather, it might as well refer to the possibility of eternal life in another, a better, world.

It is likely that the charge against fantasy to be either non-political or starkly conservative is connected to this last feature, fantasy as providing resolutions associated by Attebery with the comic mode, precisely because such resolutions can easily acquire an essentializing force. In this light, the above differentiation between an ending brought about by a "deus ex machina" and a solution based on a character's integrity may only serve to obscure that fantasy's depiction of personal integrity is itself based on the assumption of an underlying, naturalized set of ethical standards which must eventually persist in the end. In a related vein, by allegedly recreating an "authentic" "medieval" setting, many works of sword-and-sorcery fantasy pose patriarchal gender models, hierarchical class relations, and a static metaphysical orderedness of the world as "natural" and desirable. Acts of violence are often glorified as heroism and, particularly in the context of (computer) fantasy role-playing games, intertwined with an allegedly value-free consumerist logic: the more enemies you kill and the more objects you collect, the more experience points and status you receive. In this way, war is constructed along binaries of friend and foe, and peace becomes naturalized as the restoration of a conservative order. Does that leave any place for the political?

In theory, at least, it does. It might be stressed, for instance, that even Tolkien insisted on the fact that "the joy of the happy ending [...] does not deny the existence of *dyscatastrophe*, of sorrow and failure" (153). In his view, eucatastrophe, in an irreducible manner, dialectically implies its opposite, its antithesis. Even fantasy in Tolkien's vein, hence, is not naïve, as Attebery remarks: "Much fantasy does not have what we would call a 'happy ending.' Indeed, the fantasist often seems to start with the idea of such a resolution and then to qualify it, finding every hidden cost in the victory" (15). Attebery's conception of "resolution" is thus adjusted to include ambivalence and ambiguity. If we take Attebery's definition a step further, applying the idea of the comic mode to fantasy would not only imply stabilized endings or even the more unstable binaries of thesis and antithesis, but could serve to delineate how fantasy questions conceptions of greatness, heroism, and integrity, conceptions which tragedy puts center stage but which comedy often serves to undermine. As Dirk Wiemann suggests in his essay on Tolkien in this volume, Tolkien's work can be read as simulating several such de-essentializing moves, but may ultimately not be the best place to look for the realization of this potential. In consequence, although Tolkien remains formative for Anglophone fantasy in particular, the authors collected in this volume have extended and at times moved beyond Attebery's idea of using *The Lord of the Rings* as definitional template to branch out into more contemporary forms of fantasy and into debates which approach the question of fantasy's conservative or subversive functions from new angles. In doing so, they participate equally in debates about fantasy as a genre and in debates about defining the political.

In the context of fantasy culture, one approach to the political is suggested by the work of Fredric Jameson on the romance. Since some of fantasy's most important "taproot texts" (cf. Clute, "Taproot") are romances, it is possible to ascribe to it a fate similar to that of the older genre. As Jameson has remarked, "[i]t is in the context of the gradual reification of realism in late capitalism that romance once again comes to be felt as the place of narrative heterogeneity and of freedom from that reality principle to which a now oppressive realistic representation is the hostage" (91). Its utopian potential, however, can only be released and realized if the notion of genre, including the notion of fantasy as a genre, is radically historicized so that the "'essence,' 'spirit,' 'worldview,' in question is revealed to be an ideologeme" that, in itself, ultimately may turn out to be nothing more than "a private or collective narrative fantasy" (102). Therefore, we should abstain from considering fantasies as narratives of otherworlds that are essentially timeless but historicize them, not least in order to find out in which ways generic "forms are reappropriated and refashioned in quite different social and cultural contexts" (127).

Accordingly, it is one thing to explain or interpret certain political ambiguities in Tolkien's works within the context of his own times (as Dimitra Fimi, for instance, has done so impressively). It is another to explain or interpret adaptations of his works in other times and other places, since within these new texts, Tolkien's semantic system necessarily becomes invested with new meanings while being prone to retain the old ambiguities. This is particularly problematic with a view to the issue of race. Sue Kim, who expressly exempts the novels from her criticism, attacks Jackson's films as "cringe-inducing in terms of racial coding" (875). Kim presents various reasons for her judgment. One set of charges goes against the way in which the filmic language strengthens the story's semantic system of oppositions, another against the films' context of production. Regarding the first, the intratextual, problem, Kim writes: "In the films, goodness correlates to whiteness, both racially and as a color-scheme, and is associated with Europe, particularly England and the Scandinavian countries, the West, and the North. Evil is invariably black, savage, Southern (or 'Southron'), and Eastern" (875). While with Tolkien, arguably, the opposition between light and darkness, between white and black, carries mainly symbolic and theological meanings, the visualization of these elements in the films is carried out via signifiers whose signifieds clearly refer to present-day contexts. For example, the Haradrim and the Easterlings, Sauron's human mercenary allies who come to his aid from the South, are plainly depicted in the films as orientalized others: they have olive complexions, their garb, especially their turbans, seems exotic, some ride on giant elephant-like creatures, and so on (cf. McLarty 185). Worst of all, they lack individuality. Especially in the epic battles of the third part, they simply merge with the rest of Sauron's dark army, only to be finally defeated by the forces of good.

Yet fantasy inspired by work such as Tolkien's can also move in the opposite direction, questioning current definitions of race, class, or gender. A prominent example is Junot Díaz's celebrated novel *The Brief Wondrous Life of Oscar Wao*. As various critics have remarked, Díaz does not simply write fantasy—rather, he uses fantasy culture as a sign system. In their introduction to *The Cambridge Companion to Fantasy Literature*, Farah Mendlesohn and Edward James observe that scholars often resort to describing fantasy in terms of a "grammar" or as an ongoing "conversation" (2). Díaz uses fantasy in a similar way, creating new forms of fiction which serve to describe the experience of migrating from the

Caribbean to the U.S. In an interview, Díaz has pointed out that his own immigrant experience included learning not only the English language, but also the languages of fantasy and science fiction. Díaz argues that it was these languages that enabled him to describe the experience of moving from the Dominican Republic to the United States: "I was thinking about how in the world to describe the extreme experience of being an immigrant in the United States, the extreme experience of coming from the Third World and suddenly appearing in New Jersey. [...] Every language that I was deploying, every language system, fell apart. [...] But science fiction, fantasy, and comic books are meant to do this kind of stupid stuff, they are meant to talk about these extreme, ludicrous transformations" (Díaz in Celayo 15).

Recently, Tim Lanzendörfer has argued that Díaz's use of fantasy, especially his intertextual references to Tolkien's works, goes even beyond this conception of fantasy as a language which describes the encounter of immigrant and dominant culture. In Lanzendörfer's reading, fantasy becomes "a valid interpretative tool, the only one approximating an adequate rendering of Dominican and Caribbean history" (135) as a marvelous reality which has become "almost completely forgotten in an increasingly secular Dominican diaspora" (127). While the novel is influenced both by Caribbean and Latin American traditions of marvelous realism and of neorealism (Lanzendörfer 130), Díaz's use of Western fantasy offers additional narrative strategies by pointing to the diasporic state of the protagonist Oscar and the narrator Yunior, emigrant Dominicans steeped in Euro/American fantasy and science fiction culture. Lanzendörfer argues that this diasporic perspective does not "seek explanation in an autochthonous Caribbean culture capable of explaining itself" (138). Rather, it is fantasy culture which allows the protagonist and the narrator to reconnect with the marvelous aspects of Caribbean history. Nevertheless, neither can Euro/American fantasy alone fully explain the Caribbean: "Dominican reality exceeds Western fantasy" (Lanzendörfer 139).

Thus, following the work of Jameson, we can attempt both: to place fantasy in its historical and political context and to examine how fantasy, as "traveling theory," can serve to explain and establish new historical and political contexts. Such an approach seems especially fruitful in contemporary discussions of identity markers such as race, class, gender, sexual orientation, age, national affiliation, or religion.

Another approach to exploring the political in fantasy culture is to examine fantasy's contribution to theorizing the political as a social process. In this context, we are highly indebted to Dirk Wiemann's essay in this volume for bringing into the debate the works of Chantal Mouffe and Jacques Rancière on the political. Basically, both theorists claim that what constitutes the genuinely political is a productive form of antagonism, what Mouffe refers to as "agonistic pluralism" ("Introduction" 4) and Rancière as "*dissensus*" (38). Precisely because "we are in fact always multiple and contradictory subjects, inhabitants of a diversity of communities [...], constructed by a variety of discourses, and precariously and temporarily sutured at the intersection of those subject positions" (Mouffe, "Radical Democracy" 20), conflict is constitutive and therefore irreducible. For this reason, the sort of "conflict-free" universalism envisioned as the end of the political trajectory in the traditional liberal project—a project that is based on the Enlightenment belief in the capacity of the individual to found itself in itself as a holistic subject—must at least be questioned. This is not to downright reject universalism, Mouffe argues, but rather to strip it of its hegemonic tendencies, to "particularize" it: "Radical democracy demands that we acknowledge difference—the particular, the multiple, the heterogeneous—in effect, everything that had been excluded by the concept of Man in the abstract" ("Radical Democracy" 13).

According to Rancière, "[p]olitics, before all else, is an intervention in the visible and the sayable" (37). By this, he means that genuine politics are capable of questioning a hegemonically instilled "order" of perception: only certain things are meant to be *seen* as "normal," while others are outside the regulative precinct of reality; they are "beyond," often also because there is not even a proper language to refer to them. Since successful fantasies, it could be argued, function as vehicles that transport or give expression to "intervention[s] in the visible and the sayable," they could thus at least potentially serve genuinely political ends. After all, as Edward James and Farah Mendlesohn claim, "fantasy is about the construction of the impossible" (1); everything, that is, which lies beyond the limits of what has been defined as "real." Salman Rushdie's *The Satanic Verses*, although and maybe because it does not belong to "genre fantasy" in Attebery's sense, is a case in point. When, in a crucial scene, one of a group of British immigration officers, without saying a word, points his finger at Saladin Chamcha, a man about whom he knows nothing but whom he deems, on account of various "indicators," amongst them outward appearance, to be an illegal immigrant (which, actually, is not the case), Chamcha begins to factually turn into a "monster": "Saladin Chamcha, following the line of Popeye's pointing finger, raised his hand to his forehead [...][:] there, at his temples, growing longer by the moment, and sharp enough to draw blood, were two new, goaty, unarguable horns" (Rushdie 141). It is part of Rushdie's fantasy that Chamcha's mutation into a goat-like, devilish monster is not imagined but can be witnessed by all who see him. By this, it traces and narratively disrupts the logics behind processes of meaning construction, especially when these logics serve the constitution of selves by the identificatory exclusion of others. As the manticore, another mutant, answers shocked Chamcha's "how do they do it?": "They describe us [...][.] That's all. They have the power of description, and we succumb to the pictures they construct" (Rushdie 168). Rushdie's novel, it could be argued, by revealing the fantastic nature of such processes of construction, offers dynamic counter-descriptions that are political precisely on account of their dis-sensual nature.

Hence, via fantasy, alterity can find expression by way of various themes that signify (post)modern dis-location. Complementing the "impossible" representation of fantastic creatures that are clearly perceivable, as in Saladin Chamcha's case, the frequently used theme of "invisibility" equally functions as a means to question a tendency in our culture that "equates the 'real' with the 'visible' and gives the eye dominance over other sense organs" (Jackson 45). To a large degree, in the creation of Western knowledge since the Enlightenment, empirical methods have been used to determine the structures of our world: "invisibility" as a theme is meant to question not so much the reliability of empirical data but rather the conceptual ground upon which empiricism itself is based. As Rosemary Jackson claims, "[t]hat which is not seen, or which threatens to be unseeable, can only have a subversive function in relation to an epistemological and metaphysical system which makes 'I see' synonymous with 'I understand'" (45). If, as Rancière suggests, "[t]he essence of politics is dissensus," and if "[d]issensus is not a confrontation between interests and opinions" but "the demonstration (*manifestation*) of a gap in the sensible itself" (38), then fantasy, maybe more than other genres, is equipped to make this gap tangible.

In its own way, then, the politics of fantasy may productively work against the reified "symbolic constitution of the social" which Rancière terms "the police" and whose "essence [...] lies in the partition of the sensible that is characterized by the absence of void and of supplement" (36). In fact, we might say that fantasy, due to its generic characteristics, is practically bound to represent void and supplementarity, that is, the dynamic and productive beyond of any "given" reality, precisely because it is founded on a double impossibility. As John Clute defines "fantasy" in *The Encyclopedia of Fantasy*: "When set in this world, [fantasy] tells a story which is impossible in the world as we perceive it; when set in an otherworld, that otherworld will be impossible, though stories set there may be possible in its terms" ("Fantasy" 338). Either way, "truth," as connected to "possibility," is always removed at least by one step. Admittedly, Clute begins his definition by claiming that "[a] fantasy text is a self-coherent narrative" (338), and "self-coherence," of course, might pose a problem of its own kind in that it subverts fantasy's own generic dynamics: after all, the possibility to tell an intelligible story, one that has a beginning, an ending and a clear teleology, always also harbors a claim to truthfulness.[2]

According to Chantal Mouffe, a politically informed democratic order is "based on a distinction between 'enemy' and 'adversary.' It requires that, within the context of the political community, the opponent should be considered not as an enemy to be destroyed, but as an adversary whose existence is legitimate and must be tolerated" (4). Of course, fantasy has not gotten rid of enemies. However, with the notable exception of most Hollywood fantasy blockbusters, many narratives have avoided to feature the utterly evil Sauron type as the protagonist's worst enemy. Indeed, in Ursula Le Guin's early *A Wizard of Earthsea* (1968), the dark-skinned hero Ged's severest opponent is also a Sauron-like shadow, but this time the monster is not precisely an evil Other, since it has originated from *within* the protagonist: "[Ged] sought for some protection, but there was none; the thing was not flesh, not alive, not spirit, unnamed, having no being but what he himself had given it [...]. All he knew of it was that it was drawn to him and would try to work its will through him, being his creature" (83). Similarly, in Philip Pullman's *The Amber Spyglass*, the third part of the *Northern Lights* trilogy, the dreaded Authority turns out to be neither omnipotent nor utterly evil, but "old [...] and terrified, crying like a baby and cowering in the lowest corner" (366). As many of the following essays will show, other, more recent, ventures are equally dedicated to erode all-too clear-cut divisions between enemy and hero, evil and good.

This erosion plays itself out predominantly in the politics implicit in the discourses of race, class, gender, sexual orientation, and religion. Many of the essays in this volume interrogate the construction of categories of identity within the tension between "subversive" and "conservative" versions of such categories. Most authors locate the works under discussion in the space in-between, highlighting the ambiguity of contemporary fantasy. This becomes especially pertinent because the essays collected here focus on narrative structures and thus combine the question of the political and the aesthetic. In consequence, the articles also begin to interrogate the fantastic elements of politics and the way in which the political can be understood via the language of fantasy. Thus they explore what Sladja Blažan, in her contribution to the volume, calls "the fantasy of politics."

Questions of identity serve as the volume's starting point. Stefanie Fricke's contribution examines the construction of identity in Suzanne Collins's *The Hunger Games* trilogy. Fricke traces the way in which the trilogy has been read as a dystopian comment on current social and political events (ranging from the dangers of media surveillance to the Iraq war or the Occupy movement) but argues that the trilogy also functions as a *bildungsroman* which examines the question of identity and "depicts in great detail how identity is shaped by factors such as social and racial inequality, the media, gender roles, politics and violence." Fricke hence argues that Katniss Everdeen can be read as a protagonist whose identity is not fixed, but is painfully and disturbingly fractured by severe trauma and the blurring of the lines between media representations of her persona and fragile conceptions of more "authentic" versions of selfhood.

The political implications of the construction and deconstruction of identity are taken up again in Andreas Blüml's insightful overview of how the discourses of gender and race implicit in computer role-playing games have evolved throughout the history of this young genre. In particular, he reflects on how the considerable widening of technical possibilities, especially since the arrival of Massively Multiplayer Online Role-Playing Games, on the one hand has enabled the creation of avatars whose appearance can deviate from that of the usual hyperbeautified and normally Caucasian characters, and whose sexual orientation might be either hetero- or homosexual when it comes to "romance options." On the other hand, many of such alternatives regarding character customization often stay on the surface, simply catering to market (and recipient) expectations.

Various contributions to the volume build on the (de)construction of identities to take a closer look at the political implications of fantasy's larger narrative structures and aesthetics. Beatrix Hesse begins her analysis of the film *The Nightmare Before Christmas* by examining the popularity of the movie in Goth subculture. She attributes this popularity to the tension between the work's conservative versus countercultural elements, arguing that the film itself dramatizes several shifts between mainstream and counterculture, shifts which critics have associated also with practices of members of the Goth subculture. Hesse locates the film's main tension in the negotiation between Halloween, associated with paganism, anarchy, and death, and Christmas, associated with Christianity, domestic space, and birth. However, as Hesse shows by building on the work of Stephen Nissenbaum, Christmas itself in its current form is a recent invention which has displaced the unruly and carnivalesque English traditions of celebrating Christmas which, to a contemporary audience, would more resemble the anarchy of Halloween. Thus, as Hesse shows, the film's enactment of a takeover of Christmas by Halloween can actually be read as the re-establishment of tradition. The film's eventual affirmation of the division between Christmas and Halloween, and between the identities and functions of Santa Claus and Jack Skellington, moreover, negates the revolutionary potential of the takeover of Christmas and confines the countercultural impulse to the realm of the film's aesthetics.

Christian Knirsch compares two U.S.-American vampire series and, by heeding the politics of aesthetics, relates them to Roland Barthes's conception of readerly and writerly texts. Whereas Stephenie Meyer's *Twilight*, both in its written and filmic versions, is highly conservative in its barely veiled endorsement of a white, patriarchal order, *True Blood*, the HBO adaptation of Charlaine Harris's Sookie Stackhouse novels (*The Southern Vampire Mysteries*), is much more open. As Knirsch argues, in this writerly text, "vampires function as an overarching symbol of 'the Other' in American society." Innovatively updating the genre traditions of the vampire gothic, the series depicts how processes of "othering" work on various discursive levels in today's U.S.-American society (race, class, gender, sexuality, religion).

Sebastian Domsch elaborates on Dave Sim's 300-volume graphic novel series *Cerebus*. While Sim initially created the character of the aardvark Cerebus in order to parody Robert E. Howard's hypermasculine Conan, the epic increasingly seemed to attain misogynist traits. As Domsch shows, though, a successful assessment of gender politics (or any other politics, for that matter) in fantasy texts like *Cerebus* must not only "simply" focus on content issues, but always also consider both the poetological nature of the narrative text itself, including its specific take on "referentiality," and the formative effects different reading strategies will have on its meaning. Domsch traces the narrative's movement from fantasy to realist modes and from realist to metafictional discourse. Due to the complicated extra- and intradiegetic genesis of *Cerebus* and Sim's play with different perspectives, the outcome of reading *Cerebus* will inevitably be ambiguous.

Rainer Emig deals with a text that recently has acquired nearly as much popularity as Tolkien's work: George R.R. Martin's epic *A Song of Ice and Fire*. Although the novels are still caught within the partly conservative logics of fantasy's generic shibboleths, Martin, not least through the formal employment of multi-focalization, succeeds in negotiating and extending traditional structural boundaries on many fronts, especially when it comes to the link between power and politics. In Martin's world, physical and military strength, just like blood, cannot guarantee power and authority anymore; money, political intrigues, sexual politics, religion, even the seasons, all of these aspects and more, unfold their own thorny political mechanisms and influence the plot—and the extradiegetic meanings it conveys—in various, dynamic ways.

Matthias Kemmer examines the politics of the open world single player role-playing game *Fallout 3* via three crucial dichotomies: the realist strategies used to effect player immersion versus the fantastic elements of the fictional universe; interactivity as either a disturbing strategy of training for violent action versus an experience of narrativity; and the contrast or relatedness between the symbols and structures internal to the game and those external to it. In the post-apocalyptic world of *Fallout 3*, both an action's ethical implications and the narrative structures, Kemmer shows, are to a large degree open-ended, allowing for a large number of conflicting positions. Kemmer's reading nevertheless carefully traces the limits of this open-endedness to the political undercurrents of the game, most crucially in the "biographer framing" that occurs after the player's final moral-dilemma decision.

In her reading of the *Harry Potter* books, Bärbel Höttges takes into account the heated debates about the religious orientation of the work. While representatives of the Christian right in the U.S. have claimed that the *Harry Potter* books support witchcraft and Satanism, others have argued that the narrative is inherently atheist, while a third group of critics read the books as advocating essentially Christian values. Höttges uses Wolfgang Iser's aesthetic response theory, which views texts as webs or networks in which the reader must bridge gaps and thus contributes significantly to a text's interpretation, and expands on this theory by arguing that readers' ideological orientation and their ability to negotiate text and context also play a crucial role in the interpretative process. Via a close reading of a key scene in *Harry Potter and the Deathly Hallows*, Höttges shows how J.K. Rowling's narrative can be read to support occult, atheist, and Christian values in turn. She claims that a reading which highlights the Christian underpinnings of the books must pay special attention to the way in which Christian beliefs are presented in new contexts that are not immediately recognizable since "Rowling and Harry have left *institutionalized* religion behind. Christianity clearly is still there [...] but the indicators that usually mark a religious perspective [...] are absent. Rowling, who has stated several times that she *is* a Christian, serves a Christian world view in a non–Christian context."

Christina Flotmann examines the function of political rhetoric in the *Star Wars* and *Harry Potter* series. Flotmann argues that both stories reflect the dichotomy of good and evil which she also identifies as a crucial structure in contemporary post–9/11 political rhetoric. In Flotmann's interpretation, the formulaic pattern of *Star Wars* and *Harry Potter* is questioned in several scenes and through various characters who either temporarily assume identities in-between categories or otherwise serve to reflect on the ambiguity of good and evil. Nevertheless, in both stories, the dichotomy is ultimately affirmed and stabilized, mirroring much of the political rhetoric produced in the aftermath of the attacks of September 11, 2001.

Dirk Vanderbeke considers the politics inherent in the depiction of fantastic cities by focusing on China Miéville's "weird fiction." Especially *The City and the City*, with its paradoxical setting of two overlaying cities—the inhabitants of which have to actively "unsee" the respective other side—obviously alludes to divided or segregated cities in the "real world" (pre-1989 Berlin, Jerusalem, Belfast). However, in this case, Miéville, by way of a politically motivated metapoetic gesture, does not so much support, but rather questions, the utopian tenets of (primarily postcolonial) theories that insist on the productivity of in-between spaces: there simply is no livable or alternative "contact zone" available between Besźel and Ul Qoma. Matters are different in *Perdido Street Station*, in which otherness, due to New Crobuzon's extreme heterogeneity, indeed assumes a dynamic and fruitful quality.

If these contributions point to contemporary political issues and positions as useful for the analysis of fantasy, Flotmann's and Vanderbeke's essays in particular also serve to introduce the question of how fantasy can in turn elucidate the political as a process. In this vein, Gerold Sedlmayr argues that Joe Abercrombie's *The First Law* trilogy subverts the traditions of the genres of the portal-quest and the immersive fantasy through its presentation of scarred and mutilated bodies. Sedlmayr reads Abercrombie's presentation of bodies against the backdrop both of the contemporary "sacralization of the body" (as theorized by Baudrillard) and its insertion into a capitalist logic. If bodies function as capital, Sedlmayr argues, the idea of quasi-sacral wholeness attributed to them is merely a ruse, since their value lies in their positioning. In this way, the body "is fantastic precisely because it purports to be whole and essential while in fact *it is not.*" In Abercrombie's work, mutilated bodies become the narrative norm. This can serve, in Sedlmayr's reading, to point to the function of the body not only in the realm of the fantasy world, but also in late capitalism. Such a reading is supported by the way in which magic, in Abercrombie, is both associated with money and described in terms which are highly reminiscent of (post)modern, Foucauldian definitions of power. Abercrombie's mutilated bodies thus do not serve to tell stories of heroic struggle and growth, but point to the way in which power structures and produces the protagonists throughout.

Sladja Blažan examines the relationship between fantasy and politics by highlighting fantasy's relationship with what is perceived as the "real world." Locating fantasy in the space that negotiates between imagined and actual worlds, Blažan argues that just as the reader of fantasy, while placed in the imagined world, retains the "real-world" categories of fact, evidence, reason, and truth, "the observer of world events also depends on fantasy, as only an imaginary external perspective onto the machinations of the world will make it understandable. In other words, in certain situations, indeed, only fantasy allows access to reality." Blažan interprets Reza Negarestani's *CYCLONOPEDIA* as enacting exactly this insight, creating an almost unreadable "convergence of fantasy with reality with the purpose of constructing a narrative in the service of addressing world politics." As Blažan shows, the narrative can serve to envision—but ultimately does not enact—the possibility of interrogating the political situation in the Middle East and the "war on terror" by positing oil as the narrator, thereby moving away from anthropocentric views and questioning the philosophical underpinnings of humanism in a way which Blažan relates to speculative realism. Negarestani's work finally cannot function as an example of this project because unlike the productive tension between imagined and actual worlds explicated above, *CYCLONOPEDIA* supplies no relation between materialist and human perspectives. Blažan's essay thus interrogates not just the politics of fantasy, but also asks us to consider further the "fantasy of politics."

Finally, Dirk Wiemann's article brings us back to Tolkien's work to discuss whether Tolkien's luring of "his reader with apparently non-essentialist, non-foundationalist and non-dichotomizing baits" can ultimately create a productive political agonism not simply despite, but paradoxically rather because of, the novel's tendency to rigorously confirm a metaphysically grounded Manichaeism. Tellingly, the example Wiemann chooses in order to test the limits of the politics of *The Lord of the Rings* is the narrative's employment of the *topos* of (in)visibility. Although the text chosen by Wiemann is the least contemporary, his reading of Tolkien via the theories of Chantal Mouffe and Jacques Rancière, similarly to the readings offered by Sedlmayr and Blažan, opens up and explores further alternatives to political readings that focus on the politics and aesthetics of identity markers. In this way, the placement of his essay serves both to close the circle and to open up new circuits, underscoring the dynamics of the entire volume.

Taken together, the works collected here exemplify the immense scope of relations between politics and contemporary fantasy. As the authors argue, examining these relations closely can both invigorate our discussion of fantasy and provide crucial impulses for our conceptions of politics.

Last but not least, we would like to thank Verena Adamik and Julia Becker for their painstaking proofreading of the manuscript and their many valuable and insightful suggestions.

Notes

1. In the words of Karen Armstrong: "Our modern alienation from myth is unprecedented. In the pre-modern world, mythology was indispensable. It not only helped people to make sense of their lives but also revealed regions of the human mind that would otherwise have remained inaccessible. It was an early form of psychology. The stories of gods or heroes descending into the underworld, threading through labyrinths and fighting with monsters, brought to light the mysterious workings of the psyche, showing people how to cope with their own interior crises" (11).

2. Yet, in its complex relationship to questions of "truth" and "coherence," fantasy may serve to question the social as a rational consensus and could thus open up exactly the agonistic spaces envisioned by Mouffe, who observes: "one of the main tenets of [...] liberalism is the rationalist belief in the availability of a universal consensus based on reason. No wonder that the political constitutes its blind spot. Liberalism has to negate antagonism since, by bringing to the force the inescapable moment of decision—in the strong sense of having to decide in an undecidable terrain—antagonism reveals the very limit of any rational consensus" (Mouffe, "Artistic Activism"). In a combination of both approaches to the political described in this essay, much contemporary fantasy is aware of the conservative tendencies of the genre and both writes against stereotypical representations and addresses new ways to theorize the political.

Works Cited

Armitt, Lucie. *Fantasy Fiction: An Introduction*. New York: Continuum, 2005. Print.
Armstrong, Karen. *A Short History of Myth*. Edinburgh: Canongate, 2006. Print.
Attebery, Brian. *Strategies of Fantasy*. Bloomington: Indiana University Press, 1992. Print.
Bould, Mark, and Sherryl Vint. "Political Readings." *The Cambridge Companion to Fantasy Literature*. Ed. Edward James and Farah Mendlesohn. Cambridge: Cambridge University Press, 2012. 102–12. Print.
Celayo, Armando, and David Shook. "In Darkness We Meet: A Conversation with Junot Díaz." *World Literature Today* 82.2 (2008): 13–17. Print.

Clute, John. "Fantasy." *The Encyclopedia of Fantasy*. Ed. John Clute and John Grant. London: Orbit, 1997. 337–39. Print.

———. "Taproot Texts." *The Encyclopedia of Fantasy*. Ed. John Clute and John Grant. London: Orbit, 1997. 921–22. Print.

Díaz, Junot. *The Brief Wondrous Life of Oscar Wao*. New York: Riverhead Books, 2007. Print.

Fimi, Dimitra. *Tolkien, Race and Cultural History: From Fairies to Hobbits*. Houndmills: Palgrave Macmillan, 2010. Print.

Jackson, Rosemary. *Fantasy: The Literature of Subversion*. London: Routledge, 1981. Print.

Jameson, Fredric. "Magical Narratives: On the Dialectical Use of Genre Criticism." *The Political Unconscious: Narrative as a Socially Symbolic Act* [1981]. London: Routledge, 2002. 89–136. Print.

Kim, Sue. "Beyond Black and White: Race and Postmodernism in *The Lord of the Rings* Films." *MFS Modern Fiction Studies* 50.4 (2004): 875–907. Print.

Lanzendörfer, Tim. "The Marvelous History of the Dominican Republic in Junot Díaz's *The Brief Wondrous Life of Oscar Wao*." *MELUS* 38.2 (2013): 127–42. Print.

Le Guin, Ursula. *The Earthsea Quartet*. London: Penguin, 1993. Print.

McLarty, Lianne. "Masculinity, Whiteness, and Social Class in *The Lord of the Rings*." *From Hobbits to Hollywood: Essays on Peter Jackson's* Lord of the Rings. Ed. Ernest Mathijs and Murray Pomerance. Amsterdam: Rodopi, 2006. 173–88. Print.

Mendlesohn, Farah, and Edward James. "Introduction." *The Cambridge Companion to Fantasy Literature*. Ed. Farah Mendlesohn and Edward James. Cambridge: Cambridge University Press, 2012. 1–4. Print.

Mouffe, Chantal. "Artistic Activism and Agonistic Spaces." *Art & Research* 1.2 (2007). Web. 19 Dec. 2013.

———. "Introduction: For an Agonistic Pluralism." *The Return of the Political* [1993]. London: Verso, 2005. 1–8. Print.

———. "Radical Democracy: Modern or Postmodern?" *The Return of the Political* [1993]. London: Verso, 2005. 9–22. Print.

Pullman, Philip. *The Amber Spyglass*. New York: Del Rey, 2000. Print.

Rancière, Jacques. "Ten Theses on Politics." *Dissensus: On Politics and Aesthetics*. Ed. and trans. Steven Corcoran. London: Continuum, 2010. 27–44. Print.

Rushdie, Salman. *The Satanic Verses* [1988]. London: Vintage, 1998. Print.

Todorov, Tzvetan. *The Fantastic: A Structural Approach to a Literary Genre*. French Original 1970. Trans. Richard Howard. Ithaca: Cornell University Press, 1975. Print.

Tolkien, John Ronald Reuel. "On Fairy-Stories." *The Monsters and the Critics: And Other Essays*. London: HarperCollins, 2006. 109–61. Print.

I. IDENTITY

"It's all a big show": Constructing Identity in Suzanne Collins's *The Hunger Games* Trilogy

STEFANIE FRICKE

It seems that the next successful movie franchise based on a young-adult fantasy book series is less about magic (*Harry Potter*) and love (*Twilight*), and more about children killing each other for the benefit of an eager TV audience. Irrespective of how comfortable one might feel about the premise of Suzanne Collins's dystopian *The Hunger Games* trilogy, there is no denying its appeal, not only to teenagers, but also to adult readers all over the world.[1]

The Hunger Games trilogy is set in a post-apocalyptic future in which the nations of North America have collapsed and a country called Panem has been established in their stead. Panem is a totalitarian state in which a central, highly technologized seat of power, the Capitol, controls 12 surrounding districts. The citizens of the Capitol, who depend for food, energy and consumer products on the districts, live a hedonistic life while the people in the districts are kept near starvation. Seventy-four years before the action of *The Hunger Games* sets in, the then 13 districts rebelled against the Capitol, but failed. As retribution, District 13 was destroyed and the "Hunger Games" were installed: every year each district has to select a girl and boy between the ages of 12 and 18—the so-called "tributes"—by lottery, who are then put together in an arena and have to fight to the death until only one victor is left. This is broadcast live on TV all over Panem, to entertain the citizens of the Capitol and cow the inhabitants of the districts.

The novels follow the first-person-narrative of Katniss Everdeen, a 16-year-old girl from District 12. In the first book, *The Hunger Games*[2] (2008), Katniss's little sister Prim is drawn to participate in the Hunger Games, and Katniss offers to take her place. The male tribute from District 12 is Peeta Mellark, who in an interview leading up to the games declares his love for Katniss. She had no idea of this and doubts his sincerity, but goes along since the romance gives them public support and hence an edge in the Games. They manage to survive until the very end, and when Katniss finally threatens to commit suicide together with Peeta by eating poisonous berries, the gamemakers cave in and declare both victors.

In *Catching Fire* (2009), the president of Panem and villain of the trilogy, Coriolanus Snow, informs Katniss that her successful threat of suicide was seen as an act of rebellion in many of the districts, which are now on the brink of a new revolt. As punishment she and Peeta, together with other former victors, are once again forced to participate in the Hunger Games. At the end of the novel, those still alive manage to break out of the arena and are picked up by a hovercraft from District 13, which has not been destroyed after all, but has been left alone by the Capitol because it possesses nuclear weapons.

In *Mockingjay* (2010), District 13 under the leadership of President Alma Coin has started a new rebellion against the Capitol. To boost the rebels' support in the districts, Katniss agrees to become the figurehead of the rebellion, the so-called "mockingjay."[3] When she participates in the final attack on the Capitol, Katniss has to watch as her sister Prim, who works as a paramedic, is killed by a firebomb. Later Katniss learns that the bombing was probably a ploy by District 13 to end the war quickly. Deeply traumatized, she then kills Alma Coin. At the end of the novel Katniss returns to District 12, where she slowly recovers and finally starts a relationship with Peeta.

According to the author Suzanne Collins, her story was in part inspired by European antiquity, i.e., by the myth of Theseus, in which every nine years seven boys and seven girls from Athens have to be sent to Crete to be devoured by the Minotaur until Theseus finally kills it. Further influences were the Roman gladiator games with their connection of violence, death and entertainment, and the story of the gladiator Spartacus, who broke out of the arena and started a rebellion. Another strong influence was Collins's father, who fought in Vietnam, later worked as a military specialist and took the family to battlefields during vacations because he wanted his children to understand the causes and effects of war (see Margolis, "The Last Battle"). But the story of *The Hunger Games* only came to her one night when she was watching TV:

> I was lying in bed, and I was channel surfing between reality TV programs and actual war coverage. On one channel, there's a group of young people competing for I don't even know; and on the next, there's a group of young people fighting in an actual war. I was really tired, and the lines between these stories started to blur in a very unsettling way. That's the moment when Katniss's story came to me [Collins in Margolis, "A Killer Story"].

A strong connection to present issues—even though the stories are mostly set in the future—is, of course, typical for the genre of dystopian fiction. This topicality is also often given as explanation for the astonishing success of the *Hunger Games* trilogy. The novels have been interpreted as a comment on the widening gap between rich and poor, the Occupy movement and the relations between the First and the Third World; on the dangers of media surveillance and on a U.S. public sating itself on fast food and reality TV while their civil liberties are eroded and young American soldiers die in Iraq and Afghanistan; on High school life; and on U.S. reality TV shows such as *Survivor* and *America's Next Top Model* (see Ebert; Miller).

The Hunger Games trilogy, however, is not only a dystopian tale, but also a *bildungsroman* which chronicles the coming-of-age of the heroine Katniss and her quest for her role in the world. As this essay will show, Collins depicts in great detail how identity is shaped by factors such as social and racial inequality, the media, gender roles, politics, and violence.

Hunger, Food and Consumption

When the readers meet Katniss for the first time, her self-perception and social role are defined by her need to keep her sister and mother safe and fed. When her father died some years ago, their family was close to starvation until Katniss took over as provider. She has been hunting in the woods ever since, feeding her mother and sister with game or trading it on the black market. This is a strenuous and dangerous pastime, but it also gives Katniss purpose and a sense of identity: "What would my life be like on a daily basis? Most of it has been consumed with the acquisition of food. Take that away and I'm not really sure what I am, what my identity is. The idea scares me some" (*HG* 378).

The woods not only provide Katniss with game and edible plants, but also with a space where she can be herself. As is typical for dystopian fiction, nature is set up as a contrast to and refuge from the tyrannical, highly technologized government: "The woods have always been our place of safety, our place beyond the reach of the Capitol, where we're free to say what we feel, be who we are" (*CF* 29). There are two versions of Katniss: one for District 12, a person who constantly controls her facial expressions and what she says for fear of spies and Capitol cameras, and the real Katniss, who can only exist in the woods (*HG* 7).[4]

All throughout the trilogy, food, hunger and severe poverty, their impact on society and their use as political means, are major themes. While the state is called "Panem," implying the promise of enough food for all its citizens, in reality all provisions are controlled by the Capitol, which uses them to rule the districts. The institution of the Hunger Games shows this perfidious system at its height: children can volunteer for more lots in the "lottery" to get extra rations of food, thereby helping their families survive at the price of raising their chances to be killed in the arena (*HG* 15–16). The ceremony in which the tributes are drawn is called "the reaping" (*HG* 3), a national holiday which is supposed to end in a celebration (*HG* 12). And as reward for winning the games, the victors and their families get food for the rest of their lives, while their District receives extra provisions for one year (*HG* 22, 378).

In such a system, food can also become a means of resistance.[5] To prevent citizens from feeding themselves, hunting in the woods is strictly forbidden. So from the very beginning Katniss defies the authorities, albeit less because of a conscious political choice than out of necessity. According to Collins,

> She is a girl who should never have existed. [...] Because of these lapses in security and the Capitol just thinking that 12 is not ever really going to be a threat because it's small and poor, they create an environment in which Katniss develops, in which she is created, this girl who slips under this fence, which isn't electrified, and learns to be a hunter. Not only that, she's a survivalist, and along with that goes a degree of independent thinking that is unusual in the districts [Collins in Margolis, "The Last Battle"].

Food—and in the broader sense consumption in general—is also a means for Katniss to define her own identity in contrast to the citizens of the Capitol. Katniss as narrator describes in great detail the sumptuous meals served to her once she is picked as tribute. She has known hunger all her life, and her veneration for food is contrasted with the behavior of the citizens of the Capitol, who have no scruples to throw food away and even make themselves vomit at feasts to have space for ever more elaborate dishes (*CF* 96–98).

For Katniss, the citizens of the Capitol seem alien, hardly human. Their behavior and reactions to the Games appall her (*HG* 429–30), and their high pitched accent, strange fashions and body enhancements look silly and freakish in her eyes (*HG* 74; *CF* 60). Even when Katniss starts to grow fond of the team which is responsible for her styling, she thinks of them more as "pets" than real people (*HG* 428–29; *CF* 297).

With their shallow and hedonistic lifestyle and their lust for violent entertainment, the citizens of the Capitol embody the concept of "Panem et Circenses," i.e., they condone the politics of President Snow as long as he provides them with food, consumer products and entertainment in the form of the Hunger Games (*MJ* 260–61). It is hardly surprising that *The Hunger Games* is often read as a critique of consumerism. Interestingly, however, once the books became bestsellers, and especially with the release of the movies, a great range of *Hunger Games* products—including jewelry, underwear, nail polish, action figures, and even a Katniss Barbie—were created to be bought by avid fans. You can even play the *Hunger Games* game on Facebook ("'Hunger Games' Merchandise"). While in the novels the readers take up a double position as spectators to the games and as someone who, through Katniss, are made to feel their cruelty, the merchandise strengthens their roles as voyeurs and consumers, thus placing them into the position of the inhabitants of the Capitol.

Race and Social Class

Katniss's identity—just as the society of Panem as a whole—is also defined by social class. Not only is there segregation between the Capitol and the districts, but also among the different districts (*HG* 115; *MJ* 97–98). Katniss's home, which lies in the Appalachian Mountains and is the coal-mining center of Panem, is the smallest district and—just like this region today—one of the poorest (*HG* 245). Within District 12, society is divided into the coal miners, who live in a poorer part of the district, and the merchant class, who is better off and suffers less from starvation (*HG* 4, 9). Another class is constituted by former victors of the Hunger Games, who are celebrities, live in a separate "Victor's Village" remote from the community, and are given money and food for the rest of their lives (*CF* 15).

The social segregation in District 12 also has a racial component in that the miners are described as having predominantly "[d]ark straight hair, olive skin, grey eyes" (*CF* 14), while the members of the more affluent merchant class have mostly light hair and blue eyes (*HG* 9). Katniss comes from a mixed family—her father was a miner while her mother belonged to the merchant class—but she herself looks like the miners, lives in their part of the District, and feels that she belongs to them (*HG* 9–10). Peeta, by contrast, comes from a merchant family (and looks like it), and sometimes Katniss feels that because of this he does not understand her like someone from her own class would (*HG* 360). Even with her mixed origins, Katniss does not transcend the social structure. It is only at the end of the novel, in an epilogue which—similar to the ending of *Harry Potter*—is set about 20 years after the end of the story, that class and race boundaries seem to have been blurred in Katniss and Peeta's two children, who have dark hair and blue eyes, and blond curls and grey eyes respectively (*MJ* 454).

The novels also hint at the connection between race and social inequality with regard to District 11, which is located in the south of Panem (*CF* 61). The population of this district seems largely to consist of people with dark skin color (*HG* 152; *CF* 257), and the descriptions the readers get about life there—for example that people are publicly whipped when they are found eating the crops (*HG* 245)—are reminiscent of slavery in the U.S. South before the Civil War.

The issue of race gets even more interesting when one looks at readers' reactions to the characters. When the cast for the movie version was made public, many fans were surprised that Rue (a small girl from District 11 whom Katniss befriends in the arena) would be portrayed by an African American actress, even though her description in the novel ("She has dark brown skin and eyes" [*HG* 55, also 120]) is quite clear. Reactions on online message boards and on Twitter were harsh and often racist. One commentator, for example, wrote: "Awkward moment when Rue is some black girl and not the little blonde innocent girl you picture," another "call me racist but when I found out Rue was black her death wasn't as sad" (quoted in Holmes). It seems that even if an author gives specific information on the appearance of a character, many readers will still perceive positive characters by default as white (see Holmes). It is also telling that the part of Katniss, who in the books is described as having dark hair and olive skin, went to Jennifer Lawrence, who—in real life—looks very blond Caucasian, and thus probably appeals to a wider audience.

Appearance Is Everything

Ironically, the casting of the movie version thus confirms one of the principles of the Hunger Games: appearance is everything. It is fairly obvious that *The Hunger Games* trilogy can be read as a sharp satire of reality television shows and the celebrity culture they are part of. The Games follow similar rules, and elements like the makeover of the contestants, the parading of dresses and the interviews are familiar from shows like *American Idol*.

For the tributes, their participation in the Hunger Games means that from the moment their name is drawn they come under media surveillance. They are turned into celebrities, the emotional focus of the whole nation, which also means that new identities are constructed for them. Interestingly, Collins shows that the tributes are not passive victims of this process, but actively participate in it. They have watched the Hunger Games for years and know very well that their public appearance is crucial to attract fans and sponsors who might help them by sending gifts into the arena. Thus, as soon as Katniss volunteers for her sister, she takes care not to cry in front of the cameras because she does not want to appear weak (*HG* 27–28). When she later sees Peeta, she immediately thinks that his behavior might also be part of a plan:

> Peeta Mellark, on the other hand, has obviously been crying, and interestingly enough, does not seem to be trying to cover it up. I immediately wonder if this will be his strategy in the Games. To appear weak and frightened, to reassure the other tributes that he is no competition at all, and then come out fighting [*HG* 49].

Later in the arena, Katniss calculates carefully what to say, when to wear a certain expression for the viewers or when to step into the light so that the cameras get a good shot of her (*HG* 198–200, 219–20).

As part of the tributes' new media identity the contestants are beautified according to the standards of the Capitol, which means removing all blemishes and scars, for the girls removing all body hair, and potentially even plastic surgery (*HG* 75, 430). Each tribute is assigned a stylist and a team of makeup artists who remodel them for the audience: "They erase my face with a layer of pale makeup and draw my features back out. Huge dark eyes, full red lips, lashes that throw off bits of light when I blink" (*HG* 145). Again, attractive tributes are more likely to attract support, so it is vital for them to look their best (*HG* 70). The tributes' bodies thus become mere commodities, to be changed, displayed and ultimately violated and destroyed according to the wishes of the Capitol.

While the spectators eagerly "consume" the tributes in their various states from glamorization to mutilation, real consumption of bodies is frowned upon, perhaps because it gets uncomfortably close to what the Games really are: "There are no rules in the arena, but cannibalism doesn't play well with the Capitol audience, so they tried to head it off" (*HG* 173). In the third novel, Katniss learns that the commodification and consumption of the tributes' bodies went on even after the Games, for President Snow forced the victors to prostitute themselves, using them for his political gain (*MJ* 198–99).

The tributes are not only beautified, but also dressed up in special costumes and then paraded in front of the viewers on a number of occasions. These clothes are a major part of the new media identity created for the tributes, and influence how they are perceived by the audience. Katniss's reactions to her outfits, designed by her stylist Cinna, are ambivalent. While Cinna becomes a real friend, and though Katniss cannot help taking delight in his beautiful creations (*HG* 146), more often than not she feels like a doll being dressed up for the viewers: "I feel like dough, being kneaded and reshaped again and again" (*CF* 201). For Katniss, who claims that she has never been interested in clothes and makeup (*CF* 107, 258),[6] this staging of her as a beautiful girl wearing stunning dresses makes her feel estranged from her real self, being pressed into a feminine role that is alien to her (*HG* 106). Even at home when her mother dressed her in one of her old dresses for the "reaping" and put up her hair, Katniss commented that she looked "nothing like myself" (*HG* 18). When Katniss took over her father's part as hunter to feed her family she also took on an active, aggressive and implicitly male role. She always had a stronger connection to her father than her mother (*CF* 388), and the piece of clothing she feels most comfortable in is her father's old hunting jacket (*MJ* 16). Katniss is contrasted with her mother and her sister, who conform more to typically female roles, and also with Peeta, who is less aggressive than she is and good at baking, decorating cakes and painting (*HG* 116–17; *CF* 47). When Peeta is injured during the Games, it is Katniss who rescues him, not the other way round, and in the end it is Peeta who desperately wants children, not Katniss (*MJ* 454).

After winning the games, Katniss removes her fancy clothes and makeup, and thus attempts to transform back into her old self:

> I excuse myself to change out of my dress and into a plain shirt and pants. As I slowly, thoroughly wash the make-up from my face and put my hair in its braid, I begin transforming back into myself. Katniss Everdeen. A girl who lives in the Seam. Hunts in the woods. Trades in the Hob. I stare in the mirror as I try to remember who I am and who I am not. By the time I join the others, the pressure of Peeta's arm around my shoulders feels alien [*HG* 450].

As Katniss finds out in the second novel, however, she can never go back to her old self. Her experiences in the Games have changed her too much, and try as she might, Katniss cannot get rid of the media image constructed of her and Peeta, and of the expectations of the viewers: "And every year they'll revisit the romance and broadcast the details of your private life, and you'll never, ever be able to do anything but live happily ever after with that boy" (*CF* 53). Winning the games has also isolated her from her old community, for Katniss now lives a privileged life in the Victor's Village. Moreover, since she and her family will be given food and money for the rest of her life, Katniss has lost her role of provider (*CF* 4–6) and consequently her sense of purpose.

Deeply uncertain about who she really is, Katniss finally tries to find a new identity and self-worth in her defiance of the Capitol, but cannot be sure of herself:

> The berries. I realize the answer to who I am lies in that handful of poisonous fruit. If I held them out to save Peeta because I knew I would be shunned if I came back without him, then I am despicable. If I held them out because I love him, I am still self-centred, although forgivable. But if I held them out to defy the Capitol, I am someone of worth. The trouble is, I don't know exactly what was going on inside me at that moment [*CF* 143].

Real or Not Real

All throughout the novels, Katniss struggles to find out what her true feelings and motives are and what kind of person this makes her. This quest for understanding herself ties in with a larger motif of "real or not real," of discerning what and who is real, true and truthful, that runs through the whole trilogy.

The Hunger Games are the prime example for this: their whole environment is manmade and controlled by the gamemakers, who also decide how to use the footage they get, what to air, what to cut and how to combine the pictures to tell an exciting story. When, after the first Games, Katniss has to watch a rerun of the highlights, she feels alienated from what she sees: "Something inside me shuts down and I'm too numb to feel anything. It's like watching complete strangers in another Hunger Games" (*HG* 441).

In the arena, everything has to be doubted, and this holds especially true for the tributes' motives and behavior. As described above, as soon as they are picked for the Games they play certain roles to maximize their chances for survival. Katniss's mentor Haymitch reminds her that it is not her real feelings and her real self that counts, but what she shows to and what is transmitted by the media: "Who cares? It's all a big show. It's all how you're perceived" (*HG* 164). During the time in the arena the tributes are under constant surveillance, which means that Katniss has to keep up appearances at all times. This is especially relevant with regard to her relationship with Peeta: because he proclaimed his undying love for her, they have to play the roles of lovers if they do not want to disappoint their fans (*HG* 316, 364–68). So Katniss pretends to be madly in love with Peeta, kissing him to make sure their viewers' heartstrings are pulled, while in reality her feelings about him are indecisive, and it gets ever harder for her to distinguish what is real and what is an act:

> I haven't even begun to separate out my feelings about Peeta. It's too complicated. What I did as part of the Games. As opposed to what I did out of anger at the Capitol. Or because of how it would be viewed back in District 12. Or simply because it was the only decent thing to do. Or what I did because I cared about him [*HG* 435].

In the third novel Katniss experiences how the Capitol and the rebels each try to fabricate and broadcast their version of reality in propaganda films. The war seems to be just as much about who can air what, who can stir the viewers' emotions and make them believe their story, as about actual fighting (*MJ* 125–26).

Katniss also finds again and again that people keep secrets from her and hide their real agendas. Moreover, in *Mockingjay* she cannot even trust herself because of the physical and psychological traumas she suffered: "The memories swirl as I try to sort out what is true and what is false. [...] [M]y thoughts still have a tendency to jumble together. Also, the drugs they use to control my pain and mood sometimes make me see things. I guess" (*MJ* 4). To find out what is true and what is not, Katniss uses "a technique one of the doctors suggested. I start with the simplest things I know to be true and work towards the more complicated. [...] *My name is Katniss Everdeen. I am seventeen years old. My home is District 12. I was in the Hunger Games*" (*MJ* 5). Reminding herself of the plainest facts that constitute her identity helps Katniss to anchor herself to reality.

When Peeta is held captive by the Capitol in the third novel, he is brainwashed until his memories of and feelings for Katniss are altered and he no longer loves, but fears and hates her (*MJ* 209–11): "The problem is, I can't tell what's real any more, and what's made up" (*MJ* 316). The one thing that Katniss learned to trust in—Peeta's love—seems to be lost to the torture and lies of the Capitol. Only very slowly and with the help of friends, with whom Peeta plays a game they call "Real or Not Real," does he manage to find out which of his memories can be trusted (*MJ* 316–18). At the end of the novel, he asks Katniss: "You love me. Real or not real?" and she answers "Real" (*MJ* 453). Whatever reality her feelings had before, she finally decides that she wants to be with Peeta.

Power and Impotence

In the third novel Katniss eventually agrees to take on the role as figurehead of the rebellion (*MJ* 36–37) and her public identity transforms again, this time into the title-giving "mockingjay."[7] She is told that she is essential to the rebellion (*CF* 466), and experiences this when she visits a hospital: "A new sensation begins to germinate inside me. But it takes until I am standing on a table, waving my final goodbyes to the hoarse chanting of my name, to define it. Power. I have a kind of power I never knew I possessed" (*MJ* 109). Katniss soon learns, however, that her real power is limited and that the rebel leaders do not want her to play an active role in the war, but just need her to act in propaganda spots: "I won't have to do it alone. They have a whole team of people to make me over, dress me, write my speeches, orchestrate my appearances—as if that doesn't sound horribly familiar—and all I have to do is play my part" (*MJ* 12).

Just like before, she cannot just be herself, but has to look good and wear the right clothes: "As a rebel, I thought I'd get to look more like myself. But it seems a televised rebel has her own standards to live up to" (*MJ* 71). As it turns out, with regard to her media identity, being the figurehead of the rebellion is not that different from being a tribute in the games, and the rebels under the leadership of District 13 use the media just like the Capitol does—it is even a runaway gamemaker who is in charge. Like the Capitol, the rebels also exploit tributes for their ends, for example when the wedding of two former victors is staged and broadcast (*MJ* 261–62), or when spots about dead tributes are produced "so we can target the individual districts with their dead" (*MJ* 140).

This also shows that Collins does not set up District 13 as a desirable alternative to the Capitol. District 13 turns out to be a militaristic, strictly controlled society, in which the day of every citizen is rigorously regularized (*MJ* 21–22, 34). Food is precious and eating more than one's share or even stealing food is considered a crime which the authorities punish severely (*MJ* 55–59). President Coin, who is probably responsible for the bombing that killed Prim and who proposes one last installment of the Hunger Games with the children of Capitol politicians (*MJ* 430–31), is cast in a hardly more positive light than President Snow.

Katniss resents Coin and District 13's authoritarian structures and—like back in District 12—only feels free and unobserved out in the woods (*MJ* 61–

63, 135). She is also furious when she realizes that Coin tries to use her for her political ends, just as Snow did: "It's an awful lot to take in, this elaborate plan in which I was a piece, just as I was meant to be a piece in the Hunger Games. Used without consent, without knowledge. At least in the Hunger Games, I knew I was being played with" (*CF* 464).

All throughout the novels Katniss fights being a pawn, but there is not much that she can ultimately do against it (*MJ* 70, 251). This is also due to the fact that with the exception of District 13 there seems to be no real alternative to the society she lives in. We never learn what happened to the world outside of Panem, and even the woods, which are set up as a positive counter space, ultimately seem to be under the surveillance of the Capitol (*CF* 28–29, 35). After Katniss has killed President Coin, her greatest fear is that the new powers will also exploit her: "What if they have more plans for me? A new way to remake, train, and use me?" (*MJ* 440).

Violence and Trauma

In the course of the novels Katniss's identity is not only changed by her exposure to the media and her political exploitation by others, but especially by the experience of violence. In the first novel, before the Games, Peeta tells Katniss that he hopes that they will not change him: "I want to die as myself. [...] I don't want them to change me in there. Turn me into some kind of monster that I'm not" (171). But in the third book he admits: "To murder innocent people? [...] It costs everything you are" (27). Katniss similarly finds that she cannot forget the people she killed (*MJ* 81). While Peeta and Katniss retain their basic moral goodness, Collins shows very drastically how Katniss is more and more traumatized by the violence she experiences and metes out.

All throughout the second and third novel and even in the Epilogue set more than 20 years later, Katniss suffers from posttraumatic stress disorder, which manifests itself in nightmares and depression (*CF* 66; *MJ* 455). When she learns in the second book that she has to go back into the arena, she has a nervous breakdown (*CF* 210–11), and for large parts of the third book she is under heavy medication (*MJ* 4–5, 212–13). Katniss also feels severe self-loathing and guilt because of all the people killed in retribution for her actions (*MJ* 6, 10). The victors of former Hunger Games suffer similarly, many of them trying to dull their memories with alcohol or drugs (*CF* 265, 281).

Considering the fact that these are novels marketed to teenagers from the age of 12 upwards, Collins describes a lot of drastic violence. The shocking nature of this serves to remind the readers that to watch people die is not something that should be entertaining. As Collins put it in an interview:

> But there is so much programming, and I worry that we're all getting a little desensitized to the images on our televisions. If you're watching a sitcom, that's fine. But if there's a real-life tragedy unfolding, you should not be thinking of yourself as an audience member. Because those are real people on the screen, and they're not going away when the commercials start to roll [Collins in Margolis, "A Killer Story"].

In the third novel one of the major themes is how far you can go in war and whether there should be moral scruples with regard to using certain weapons or tactics. Katniss, who in spite of everything that has happened still believes that certain lines should not be crossed, is contrasted with her friend Gale, who thinks that there should be no qualms when it comes to the Capitol (*MJ* 216–17, 258–59). It is the position represented by Gale—namely that it might be acceptable to kill children if it ends the war—which is probably responsible for the death of Prim, the event which brings about a final dramatic change in Katniss's identity.

The Girl on Fire

When Katniss sees Prim in the Capitol at the end of the third book, she is forcefully reminded of the beginning of her story when Prim's name was drawn and she volunteered in her place. But this time Katniss cannot save her, the bomb goes off before she reaches her sister and she sees Prim burn to death (*MJ* 412).

Katniss herself is caught by the fire from the blast and severely burned. All throughout the novels, fire has been an important motif connected to Katniss, who has been styled as the "Girl on Fire" because of her stylist's spectacular costumes for her (*CF* 27, 125). But at the end the metaphor turns into reality and Katniss burns for real: "[A ball of flame] caught me, ran its tongue up the back of my body and transformed me into something new. A creature as unquenchable as the sun" (*MJ* 407). Katniss survives, but is physically and psychologically scarred. She feels estranged from her burned body and describes herself as "a bizarre patchwork quilt of skin" (*MJ* 412), a "hideous creature, fired into my current form by the blast from the bombs" (424). She is a "fire-mutt" (407, 412), one of the gruesome genetically engineered mutations of the Capitol, whose doctors have—by saving her—reshaped her once again.

From the beginning, Katniss's self-perception was founded on the need to keep her sister alive and safe (*CF* 148), and consequently Prim's death causes Katniss to lose her main purpose in life. She feels stripped of the things that constituted her identity: "Gradually, I'm forced to accept who I am. A badly burned girl with no wings. With no fire. And no sister" (*MJ* 409).

Nevertheless, since Katniss's face was spared from the flames, as soon as she is put into her old costume for the execution of President Snow, people watching her on TV will hardly notice that she has changed: "I can't believe how normal they've made me look on the outside when inwardly I'm such a wasteland" (*MJ* 427). Her old media identity still works.

Conclusion

The message of *The Hunger Games* trilogy (if there is one) is ambivalent. On the one hand Suzanne Collins stresses how identity is performed and shaped and reshaped by external factors. On the other hand, however, and in spite of all the changes she goes through, Katniss seems to have a "true self" which is anchored in love, especially for her sister, and in a set of moral rules. This power of the individual, the "acts of goodness I've seen someone do" (*MJ* 455) that Katniss lists in her head to fight off depression, is contrasted with and presented as an alternative to the two political systems shown in the novel, which are both negative. At the end of the novel, the Hunger Games are over and a kind of democracy is installed (*MJ* 99, 441, 454). This new political system, however, remains rather vague. The readers do not get much information on it and Katniss does not have a real place in it, but lives a quiet life far away from the center of power.

With *The Hunger Games* trilogy Suzanne Collins has created a story which is surprisingly bleak, not only with regard to its premise, but also its conclusion. At the end Katniss is no victorious heroine reaping the reward for her courageous actions. Instead, she has lost nearly everything and everyone who was important to her and is deeply traumatized. Only very slowly does she manage to make a new life for herself. Collins shows no teenage superhero, but the development of a realistic girl who is often heroic, but also passive, jaded and angry, and who is forever painfully transformed by the choices she makes, and those others make for her.

Notes

1. In August 2012, Amazon announced that the three novels had outsold the seven *Harry Potter* books ("*Hunger Games* Surpasses *Harry Potter*"). According to Laura Miller, the success of *The Hunger Games* is part of a larger recent boom in dystopian fiction written for young adults.

2. Titles will be abbreviated in references: *HG* = *The Hunger Games*; *CF* = *Catching Fire*; *MJ* = *Mockingjay*.

3. A bird associated with the rebellion 70 years ago whose picture Katniss wears as a pin in her first Games and which then becomes a symbol for the new rebellion (*HG* 46; *CF* 112, 228).

4. Katniss's connection to nature is also strengthened by the fact that her name (just like the names of her sister Prim and of her friend Rue) is a plant name.

5. For example, when in the first novel the people of District 11 send Katniss bread into the arena and thus for the first time ever side with the tribute from another district (*HG* 288–89). In *Catching Fire* a loaf of bread with the picture of a mockingjay stamped on it is a symbol of the rebellion (163, 167). And, of course, there are the poisonous berries which Katniss threatens to eat, thereby forcing the Capitol to let her and Peeta live.

6. One could of course argue that the loving detail with which she describes her clothes undermines this claim.

7. Katniss's identity as "Mockingjay," which is stressed by the costumes Cinna designed for her (*CF* 298–304; *MJ* 51), ironically moves her closer to the Capitol which creates genetically manipulated animals with human genes, and whose citizens sometimes surgically alter their appearance to resemble animals (*HG* 404–6; *CF* 60; *MJ* 363, 372–74).

Works Cited

Collins, Suzanne. *Catching Fire*. London: Scholastic, 2009. Print.
_____. *The Hunger Games* [2008]. London: Scholastic, 2009. Print.
_____. *Mockingjay*. London: Scholastic, 2010. Print.
Ebert, Roger. "The Hunger Games." rogerebert.com. 20 Mar. 2012. Web. 27 Jan. 2013.
Holmes, Anna. "White Until Proven Black: Imagining Race in *Hunger Games*." *The New Yorker*. 30 Mar. 2012. Web. 27 Jan. 2013.
"*Hunger Games* Surpasses *Harry Potter*." *Publishers Weekly Online*. 17 Aug. 2012. Web. 27 Jan. 2013.
Margolis, Rick. "A Killer Story: An Interview with Suzanne Collins, Author of *The Hunger Games*." *School Library Journal*. 1 Sep. 2008. Web. 27 Jan. 2013.
_____. "The Last Battle: With *Mockingjay* on Its Way, Suzanne Collins Weighs In on Katniss and the Capitol." *School Library Journal*. 1 Aug. 2010. Web. 27 Jan. 2013.
Miller, Laura. "Fresh Hell: What's Behind the Boom in Dystopian Fiction for Young Readers?" *The New Yorker*. 14 June 2010. Web. 27 Jan. 2013.
"The Most Ridiculous *Hunger Games* Merchandise." *Zimbio*. Web. 27 Jan. 2013.

Gender and Racial Roles in Computer Role-Playing Games

Andreas Blüml

Computer games have come of age and are today respected—if not necessarily as a form of art—at least as a relevant part of the narrative corpus of modern storytelling. The ties between fantasy literature and this relatively new medium are very tight: the earliest computer games were "adventure" games set in futuristic or fantastical environments. With a strong market—more than 600 million units of computer games were sold in 2011 worldwide (see "Global Yearly Chart 2011"), with a total consumer spending of about $25 billion (see ESA 11)—their cultural and political relevance and impact cannot be underestimated and merits study.

I want to suggest that computer role-playing games—especially fantasy and science fiction CRPGs—make certain discussions of race and gender topics possible that could not be explored before this medium existed. Specifically, the analysis of the player character's race and gender choices allows comparing and analyzing racial and gender bias in a way not feasible in other, analog or non-interactive, media. In this paper I will try to first give a short introduction to the topic of computer role-playing games in general—how they developed, how they work, what makes them interesting—and then look at different relevant aspects: the depiction and meaning of sex, gender, and sexual orientation, the portrayal and function of race, as well as the interpretation of "class" in these games.

Compared to books and even movies, CRPGs are an extremely young medium. The first variants appeared during the "mainframe" era of the 1970s and early 1980s and were heavily influenced by pen-and-paper games like *Dungeons & Dragons*, fantasy literature in general, and the works of J.R.R. Tolkien in particular.

The earliest computer RPGs have been called "Roguelikes." The term stems from the first game in this vein, simply called *Rogue*, developed in 1980 by two students in Santa Cruz (see Wichman), which featured a pseudo-graphical interface made from text characters that depicted an underground "dungeon": *Rogue* was the first visual "dungeon crawler" with a very basic quest as a plot that, in one version of the game, is summarized as follows:

> You have just finished your years as a student at the local fighter's guild. After much practice and sweat you have finally completed your training and are ready to embark upon a perilous adventure. As a test of your skills, the local guildmasters have sent you into the Dungeons of Doom. Your task is to return with the Amulet of Yendor. Your reward for the completion of this task will be a full membership in the local guild. In addition, you are allowed to keep all the loot you bring back from the dungeons [Toy and Arnold].

Soon after, "real" graphics appeared on computer screens, which were adapted to be used in other Roguelikes, most notably the games *dnd* and *Moria*, both dungeon crawlers of the same type as *Rogue*, but with one important improvement: they allowed influencing the setup of the player's character or "avatar." That is to say, they were perhaps the first games to allow player character customization, a concept that is highly relevant when looking at the depiction of gender and race.

With the rise of the personal computer, computer RPGs left the mainframes of universities and invaded the floppy drives and hard disks of a much greater group of potential players. One of the staples of the genre is Richard Garriot's *Ultima* series. This series started around 1982 as a Roguelike with graphical elements and evolved into one of the most influential RPG series with nine installments in total, the most important ones being *Ultima VI: The False Prophet* and *Ultima VII: The Black Gate*. Both feature multi-character parties, complex character creation and a fully-fledged portal fantasy world displayed in an isometric art style.

Ultima paved the way for multiple high-profile CRPGs that appeared in the years to follow. The most important ones are the *Might and Magic* series (1986–2002; *Might and Magic X* appeared in 2014) in a pretty standard fantasy setting, *Fallout* (1997), imagining a post-apocalyptic science fiction vision of the USA, and *Baldur's Gate* (1998), again employing a fantasy setting. These games featured increasing detail regarding graphics and sound and put more and more focus on enabling the player to participate in a story with a complex plot and multiple sub-plots.

In modern gaming with its current 3D graphics, RPGs have caught up to movie quality with in-game cinematic scenes, music, spoken dialogue and complex, pre-scripted plots. Current examples are *Dragon Age*, a dark high fantasy game showing the world "Ferelden" overrun by evil demonic forces, and the

Mass Effect series of three science fiction games that tell of an epic struggle against the forces of certain synthetic super-beings.

Parallel to these single-player games, Massively Multiplayer Online Role-Playing Games—MMORPGs or simply MMOs—add something to the genre that was otherwise only possible in live action role-playing: the ability for several hundreds or even thousands of players to create characters in the same persistent virtual world, to interact with it and with each other. Games like *Ultima Online* (1997), based on the *Ultima* series, *Everquest* (1999), set in a fantasy world, *Star Wars Galaxies* (2003), featuring the science fiction world known from the movies, *World of Warcraft* (2004), the most successful fantasy MMO to date, or *Lord of the Rings Online* (2007), set in Middle-earth, are each played by several million people. *World of Warcraft* alone has more than ten million subscribers (see Ziebart). MMOs differ plot-wise from their single-player counterparts mainly by the fact that they can—per definition—not have any plot development that would bring about real change in the game world, given that the world itself is persistent and cannot alter significantly. New players can enter the game even years after its initial release and still experience the "early" content while veteran players have advanced their characters and plots very far but still play in the same game world.

In general, the process of creating a character in a CRPG or MMO is similar to that of traditional pen-and-paper games: after selecting a name for the character, the player has a limited amount of "skill points" to distribute between various statistics that will affect his or her abilities and skill in certain aspects of gameplay. For example, putting many points into the attribute "strength" will increase how much damage an attack does to an enemy. Regularly used attributes (or "stats") are strength, agility, dexterity and intelligence. These attributes define how a character fares in certain situations, like combat, crafting, stealth or conversations. Race selection, the choice to become, for example, a human, elf or dwarf, is also often part of character creation. In addition to race, the player can frequently also choose a "class." A class in an RPG sense entails the acquisition of a set of abilities; abilities such as the wielding of a bow, the power to do magic, the skill to move stealthily and the like. Typical classes are fighter, healer, wizard, hunter or thief, each with fitting abilities. Players are usually also asked to choose a gender for their character.

Two key concepts in CRPGs are "experience" and "leveling." A player usually starts out with a freshly created character at Level 1, which means that she is normally just experienced enough to fight very basic enemies without dying. By gaining "experience points" or "XP," the character progresses upwards in levels, increases her existing attributes and gets the chance to acquire additional skills. This may also lead to skill specialization later in the game—RPGs and most MMOs allow customizing higher-level characters in a semi-unique way by mixing and matching different skills inside the chosen class that are sometimes mutually exclusive. This concept of "leveling" is the driving force behind nearly all RPG systems.

In early games with very simple graphics or just text display, characters were extremely minimalistic, reduced to a letter on the screen or a few pixels. At the time of *Ultima VI* (1990), it became possible to display the characters' physical details in the game world in a more lifelike way, and games started to offer different character models and portraits to choose from. With recent games, it is usually possible to define multiple aspects of the appearance of the character—from height to weight, bone structure, complexion, hairstyle and so on—even making it possible to fashion appearances after real-life persons.

In the game *Mass Effect 3*, for instance, this process of character creation and depiction is implemented in the following way: after selecting the character's gender and first name, the preset names being John and Jane Shepard, the player can either choose the default appearance for the character or customize the appearance in multiple ways. The next steps are class and skill selections, followed by the definition of a psychological profile for the character. These choices define the protagonists' backstory and how other characters react to them.

I have mentioned that the selection of the character's gender is usually one of the first choices to be made by the player when creating a new character. While this may seem an obvious selection that is also driven by how the character customization process works, it also shows that this basic selection is among the most important decisions a player has to make. How then does gender (in-)equality function within the narrative logic of CRPGs?

Analyzing gender choice and the effects it has only became relevant once games allowed these selections. In early CRPGs character gender was either absent or undefined and without any relevance for the gameplay. While we might go so far as to say that this is—from a gender-equality point of view—possibly one of the best ways to treat the subject, it was in most cases not based on a decision by the creators of the games but merely either not thought about at all or ignored due to technical constraints. From *Ultima*, though, when technical features allowed gendered depiction, both in-game portrayal and advertising heavily featured the "white muscular male" as a hero. Significantly, in the last couple of years, this has changed and become more of an "equal opportunity" matter.

Ultima VI (1990) allows six default appearances for each gender, with five of the males of different ages being muscular and manly, one being somewhat more boyish. The female appearances are also diverse regarding their age, and five of the six are obviously supposed to look beautiful, with only one being slightly out of square with common (western) beauty ideals. *Dragon Age*, a much more recent RPG from 2009, has six male and six female default appearances each for human, elf and dwarf. Here, the male pre-sets are much more gaunt and haggard-looking than the female ones; they do explicitly not feature any extremely muscular character. Not only the female human and elf options, but even the dwarf options, correspond to current beauty ideals. None of the characters are over-sexualized or extreme regarding their looks or outfit.

With *Mass Effect 3*, the male avatar features a slightly care-worn face with a bit of stubble and a military haircut, giving him very masculine features with an explicitly western European/U.S.-American touch, similar to many generic heroes from action movies. The female counterpart has a much less weathered look and proportions close to the western beauty ideal. With freckles, red-brown hair and green eyes, she does not, however, fit the "damsel in distress" cliché but instead displays self-assurance and independence. The bodies of the default "Shepards" generally fit their faces, the male being a standard muscular hero, the female being well-proportioned, but not designed in an over-sexualized manner.

The fantasy MMO *TERA*, released in 2011 for an international market by a South Korean company, takes a completely different route and, instead of eschewing gender stereotypes, aggressively makes use of them. The game developers have created super-masculine male heroes, big-busted females that are only scantily clad (even when wearing heavy plate armor), and also anime-like child-women that were possibly designed to fill a special-interest gap in the target demographic. The programmers even went so far as to program special "jiggle physics" for the animation of the busts of the female avatars. In *TERA*, gender clichés are strongly reinforced and in most cases not questioned but rather increased and catered for in an extreme way without any hint of irony (see End_Break_Fomar).

Regarding sex choice and stereotypical gender roles it would appear that modern gaming is rather well-developed in some cases and very backwards in others: while the default appearances of and pre-sets for characters in many games are obviously influenced by the perceived target demographic, options to create "off-cliché" characters are usually available. Men are not necessarily burly, muscular and good-looking; the default pre-set is often not even typical hero material. The cliché that all female characters feature big busts and hardly wear any clothing also does not hold up in most of the games mentioned here. Just as with other media, game design is diversified and caters to different target audiences, allowing the complex depiction of characters and gender roles in some games and relying heavily on gender stereotypes in others. One notable example of game developers trying to compensate—or possibly overcompensate—in this regard is the depiction of the character Ellie in *Borderlands 2*, a science fiction action RPG, with which the creators tried to explicitly not fall into any of the stereotypical gender pitfalls and hence created a huge, heavy, techno-savvy wench-with-a-wrench as a companion character (see Wilde).

Due to technical difficulties in the earlier games and probably pressure to be politically correct, the basic abilities of characters in most RPGs generally do not differ in any really relevant way when it comes to gender: women are generally just as strong, agile or heavy-lifting as men, can wield the same weaponry and, likewise, do not excel in any special area. The influence of the character's sex on the plot development is apparent in other areas, though, and can be categorized with respect to three main areas: grammatical gender, rule adjustments and romantic options.

The most obvious influence is the change of the appellation and gender pronouns in the game dialogues. Non-player characters (NPCs) usually speak to the character directly, so their way of addressing him or her has to correspond, just like possible direct references to the character's gender in the dialogue. The amount of work necessary to achieve this cannot be underestimated: all lines of dialogue—in modern games these are usually pre-recorded—have to be either done in a gender-neutral way or created twice, once for each gender.

"Real" rule adjustments to the game based on the character's gender are usually rather rare, as is the direct influence on story or quest structure. One of the main reasons for this is probably the great amount of work that is necessary for the implementation of such elements, especially when it comes to their relatively slight effect. One case that might serve as a good example is from the modern fantasy RPG *Skyrim*. The documentation wiki for the game explains that

> Your character's sex has no effect on skills or abilities. However, NPCs will address you differently, and may treat you differently, depending upon your sex (Allure perk in Speech skill allows you to get 10 percent better prices with the opposite sex). Also, there is a quest that provides you with the added bonus of dealing more damage to the opposite sex ["Skyrim: Character Creation"].

The most prominent effect the main character's sex has is probably that on the possible romantic relationships available to him or her. In recent years, the plots for computer games have become increasingly complex and multi-layered; they contain multiple sub-plots running parallel to the main story, just like in novels or movies. One stock plot element is romance, the character's ability to have relationships or start affairs. For obvious reasons, this presents a challenge to the creators of the game: not all NPCs are available as romantic partners, but if they are, it has to be decided whether the player characters can only romance them if they are of the opposite gender or whether there are also homosexual options.

With queer rights still being one of the most important current political topics, it is hardly surprising that such decisions by the game makers are also hotly debated in the media, leading so far as to cause open protests from right-wing groups in the U.S. The decision-making processes regarding character relationships in the *Mass Effect* series may serve as good indicators as to how game developers address this issue, and how this has changed in recent years.

In the original 2007 *Mass Effect*, a male Shepard can have a heterosexual romance with a human female, or a xenophilic romance with the pseudo-female non-human "Liara." A female character can romance a male crewmate and—again—Liara, thereby allowing a pseudo-lesbian relationship but no male gay relationship. This pseudo-lesbian option, however, was enough to get the game banned in Singapore for a short period (see "Romance"). *Mass Effect 2* (2010) offers similar options: three heterosexual ones each for a male or female protagonist, as well as the option for both genders to start an affair with a human female—allowing a "real" lesbian affair—and again two pseudo-female alien options. The last installment of the series—published in 2012—provides eleven romance options in total, with the choice of hetero-, bi- and homosexual partners much more open than in the previous two games: a male Shepard can have relationships with four different women or an openly gay man, a female Shepard can have a relationship with a male alien or a lesbian partner. Both genders can in addition become romantically involved with four other characters of both genders. The inclusion of the openly gay option started what the media termed a "gay controversy" in the U.S. (see Brightman). Counting out the options it becomes obvious that the gay option is the anomaly, while the lesbian or pseudo-lesbian option is actually the norm for female characters.

Only indirectly related but still relevant as an index of the rising gender awareness on the developer's side is the fact that *Mass Effect 3* was the first game in the series to actually offer an official definition of what the female protagonist should look like—that is, a normative pre-set appearance created by the game artists—and include this version as one of the two possible covers for the game's DVD. Hence, the game box, in one of its versions, featured a strong female hero on the cover, something rather unusual in computer games.

A quite interesting aspect of the sex/gender discussion is introduced into the *Mass Effect* universe by including the mono-sexed alien race of the "Asari," the pseudo-females mentioned above. Although the blue-skinned Asari are a race with only one sex, they are depicted with distinctly female characteristics. When asked about her gender identity, an Asari responds that she is "not precisely a woman." On the one hand, looking at the issue from the standard Euro-American perspective on gender roles, the Asaris' sex and female appearance is put into contrast to the role they play in the galactic society: they provide some of the fiercest fighters and operatives, very able scientists and important artists. On the other hand, this emancipatory thrust is mitigated by the fact that the Asari, even if mono-sexed, are still depicted in a culturally multi-gendered way. An Asari needs a partner (not necessarily another Asari) to reproduce, with one becoming the father and the other the mother, as is explained when Shepard talks to one of his Asari partner's parents, an older Asari by the name of Matriarch Aethyta:

> AETHYTA: "She never met her father and—well—that was me."
> SHEPARD: "You mean you were her other mother, right?"
> AETHYTA: "No, I didn't pop her out. No. She's never even met me."
> SHEPARD: "Sorry, if you'd be human, you'd both be called the mother. Regardless of which one gave birth."
> AETHYTA: "Well, I'm not human, am I? Anthropocentric bag o' dicks..." [*Mass Effect 3*, Citadel Cutscene].

The juxtaposition of gender role, gender identity and sex is thus played out in a very direct and impactful way, even furthered by the fact that the "bag o' dicks" player character can be both male and female. Shepard then goes on to tell his partner about the conversation with the words: "That Matriarch over there? [...] She's your father" (*Mass Effect 3*, Citadel Cutscene).

To return from in-game technicalities and rules to a more general question regarding player character gender choice: what is the influence of the player's gender on the choice of character gender? What little reliable data there is shows that about 60 percent of all U.S. players of videogames are male, most of them in the age group around 37, with the upper limit of player age rising steadily in the last couple of years—this last point might explain the increasing depth in the plotlines and layouts of modern RPGs (see ESA 3–12).

Players choosing their character's gender in accordance with their own is the less interesting case—more rewarding are the reasons for people to "cross-gender" their characters. Again, there is not enough quantitative data available (see Yee, "Gender-Bending"), but an analysis of forum posts and relevant articles leads to three main reasons why male players choose female characters: aesthetics, multiplayer benefits, and role-playing. The first two are relevant on a meta-gaming level, whereas the last directly relates to the intratextual level.

The first, aesthetics, is a bit of a euphemism. It can really be captured in one telling quote: "If I have to stare at my avatar's ass for hours, I at least want it to look shapely!," which may be rather chauvinistic, but regarding the fact that the view is usually from behind the character and most of the game creators are men and take pains to make the female character models pretty—this is sometimes called the "Lara Croft Syndrome"—it is easily explained (see Yee, "Gender-Bending"). Yet to interpret this camera mode as inherently sexist is too simplifying: third-person over-the-shoulder perspective is generally the best choice for action RPGs and offers a better overview of the surroundings than the often alternative possible first person view.

The second reason—multiplayer benefits—is very interesting from a social point of view: there is a generally acknowledged consensus that female characters in MMOs do get significantly more help from other players than male characters. Commentators remark that it is somewhat funny to realize that the numbers reveal a huge percentage of these receiving female avatars to actually be men who exploit this very effect (see Yee, "Gender-Bending"). There is an old joke that MMORPG really stands for "Mostly Men Online Role-playing as Girls." This aspect shows that—whatever the intended design decisions of the game creators may have been—the real social interaction of the players is still heavily influenced by the real and perceived structure of the player base. To oversimplify grossly, the cliché of the male nerd too shy to make real-world contact with girls is not completely wrong.

The last reason is the most obvious: a role-playing game offers the unique chance to "try out" the other sex, so players accept this option and cross-gender their character. While it cannot be proven in numbers, I am certain that the amount of gender-bending in main characters—meaning the first character a player creates in a single player game or the one played most in an MMO—is significantly lower than the amount in subsequent alternative characters: once a player has tried out playing a character of their own gender, why not try the game again with a different character of the opposite gender?

Related to this role-playing effect is the fact that changing the gender away from the established stereotype for a certain role heightens the experience. As one female author puts it:

> The most important [reason for choosing female] was simply that the epic proportion of the games would make a female lead character much more awesome in my mind, as silly as that might sound, simply because the "male superhero soldier guy rescues the universe and is bad-ass while doing it" is so tired now [...] [quoted in Chambers].

While we are looking at a player's selection of options with respect to gender, it might be worthwhile to have a quick glance at "gendered classes," meaning character classes that are played more regularly by players of a specific gender.

Available data shows quite clearly that the "gendering" you would expect when a game offers "healing and support" classes on the one hand and "fighting and attacking" classes on the other does actually occur: In the MMO *World of Warcraft*, women indeed prefer playing Priests and druids—support classes—while men prefer rogues and warriors, which are more all-out attack classes (see Yee, "WoW").

Of course gender stereotyping happens in modern RPGs, yet not more blatantly than in other media but rather, and quite interestingly, in a more "open" manner due to the protagonist's inherently "open" gender. The fact that players can actively choose their character's gender opens up multiple options and possibilities, allowing stereotyped gender roles to be broken or at least indirectly subverted. The RPG gaming situation allows a form of gender interpretation and interaction that is easier to achieve than in non-interactive fiction or in games whose plot is more linear or which have a scripted narrative. Still, the analysis of "romance" options has shown that, while homoerotic interactions are possible, the bias towards lesbian relationships might be interpreted not as an improvement in this regard at all, but rather as a veiled way to introduce semi-pornographic lesbian content for the intended male target demographic. The gender situation has gone from a no-topic during the "unisex pixel on screen" days through a phase of white muscular male Anglo-Saxon to a rather realistic or possibly post-realistic depiction of (fantastic) reality.

When talking about race in RPGs the usual distinction is not between lighter and darker skinned humans, but between "proper" races: humans, dwarves, elves, orcs, trolls and various aliens. Regarding these races, the most obvious question is: are racial choices a stand-in for ethnic clichés and prejudices? In other words, does race work as a metaphor for ability? It is important to mention that character races in games are generally really species in a biological sense, while race in a real-world context is used to denote phenotypic characteristics in humans only. The term "race" is however what is generally accepted wording in RPGs, which is quite telling in itself. So the answer is clear: racial choices are really "ability" choices in a very general way. From a gaming perspective, the race of a character is the second most important indicator of their abilities (after class) and generally influences the skills and attributes of a character in a very important way. This shows a very deeply ingrained racism in CRPGs, which is, however, mitigated by the mentioned implied distinction between race and species.

Interestingly enough, within the races of the game world, it is usually possible to differentiate the characters by way of human-like racial phenotypes, making it possible to create black hobbits, Asian dwarves or Caucasian elves. As such, race in the RPG sense is layered with the semantics of race in a real-world sense, but these race distinctions have no influence on gameplay, alleviating the inherent real-world racism inherent to the basic structure.

Having established that racial stereotyping for player characters is at the base of the gameplay mechanics of modern RPGs, what remains to be considered is the impact the racial stereotyping of non-player-characters and enemies has within the fantasy setting. With species/races playing such an important part in these worlds, the inherent racism of the setup becomes very apparent in the common juxtaposition of enemy camps: the "Free Peoples" of elves, dwarves, men and hobbits against the orcish hordes of Mordor in *Lord of the Rings Online*, the alliance of men and friendly aliens against the hive-mind-controlled "Collectors" in *Mass Effect*, or the Grey Wardens against the Darkspawn in *Dragon Age*.

The main enemy in all games covered here are of a different species than the player character, with many physical features differentiating the "other" from the player. The most common design choice for depicting the enemies is the use of darker skin colors, often black or dark brown, or, alternatively, the employment of very pale skins, sometimes of the greenish-yellow type. This method of "othering" is obvious, and although simple direct equations, like "Orcs are Blacks" or "Aliens are Asian," are of course too bland, the underlying clichés inherent in western culture can easily be discerned in these design choices. Therefore, to repeat, "racism" is an element inherent to the structure of many of the games, using a clear-cut definition of a different species as a means to separate good from evil. Again, however, the fact that these design choices are also rooted in gameplay functionality (enemies have to be discernible quickly) must not be overlooked. Also, this hard delineation can be subverted to achieve effects similar to those discussed above regarding gender: over-simplified racism opens up options to counteract this very racism.

Regarding the connection between race and gender, it is telling that enemy characters—orcs in *LotRO*, Darkspawn in *Dragon Age*, Collectors in *Mass Effect*—are nearly always defined as asexual, yet tending to the male end of the spectrum. Middle-earth's orcs are all definitely male or at least not discernible as female and the only obviously female enemy in *Mass Effect 3* is an over-sexualized zombie version of the pseudo-female Asari. When enemies are female, their design mostly recurs to traditional roles of evil women, as for example witches in *Dragon Age* or the witch-like Asari Banshee.

Tolkien's apparent dislike of allegory has often been mentioned. Irrespective of that, the potential allegorical features of fantasy literature and fantasy or sci-fi role-playing games are hardly questionable. Nevertheless, fantasy worlds allow for a form of escapism into a more desirable or at least "different" world, often with clearer rules and sharper distinctions between good and evil. Given this setting, the ability of a player to create and define a customized character in these fantastical environments offers narrative and analytic possibilities that were not available before the emergence of this medium. The character traits race, gender, and class are given meaningful gameplay functions. At the same time, these labels are used in a more specific way than the general terms indicate when taken as social or biological definitions.

Works Cited

Brightman, James. "EA Defends Itself Against Thousands of Anti-Gay Letters." *Gamesindustry International*. 4 Apr. 2012. Web. 10 Dec. 2012.

Chambers, Becky. "For They Are Weary of Space Marines: Why Some Men Are Playing Women, and Why Game Developers Should Take Note." *The Mary Sue*. 16 Jan. 2012. Web. 10 Dec. 2012.

End_Break_Fomar. "Tera's Elin Censorship Photos Released!" MMOSite.com. 1 Sep. 2011. Web. 10 Dec. 2012.

ESA—Entertainment Software Association. *2011 Sales, Demographic and Usage Data: Essential Facts about the Computer and Video Game Industry*. 2011. Web. 10 Dec. 2012.

"Global Yearly Chart 2011." *VGChartz*. Ed. Chris Arnone. Web. 7 Dec. 2012.

Mass Effect 3. PC, EA/Bioware, 2012.

"Romance." *Mass Effect Wiki*. N.d. Web. 10 Dec. 2012.

"Skyrim: Character Creation." *The Unofficial ELDER SCROLLS Pages.* N.d. Web. 10 Dec. 2012.

Toy, Michael C., and Kenneth C. R. C. Arnold. "A Guide to the Dungeons of Doom." Computer Systems Research Group. University of California, Berkeley. N.d. Web. 9 Dec. 2012.

Wichman, Glenn R. "A Brief History of 'Rogue.'" wichman.org. 1997. Web. 9 Dec. 2012.

Wilde, Tyler. "Meet Borderlands 2's Ellie: The 'Opposite of How Most Females Tend to Be Represented in Games.'" *PC Gamer*. 16 July 2012. Web. 10 Dec. 2012.

Yee, Nick. "The Demographics of Gender-Bending." *The Daedalus Project: The Psychology of MMORPGS*. 3 Sep. 2003. Web. 10 Dec. 2012.

_____. "WoW Character Class Demographics." *The Daedalus Project: The Psychology of MMORPGS*. 28 Jul. 2005. Web. 10 Dec. 2012.

Ziebart, Alex. "World of Warcraft Subscriber Numbers Remain over 10 Million." *WoW Insider*. 7 Nov. 2012. Web. 12 Dec. 2012.

II. THE POLITICS OF FANTASY

Conservative and Countercultural Elements in *Tim Burton's The Nightmare Before Christmas*

BEATRIX HESSE

Introduction

The starting point of this paper was the purchase of a *The Nightmare Before Christmas* mobile phone cover. The production company Touchstone, which is part of the Walt Disney Corporation—or, more precisely, the owners of the franchise—had produced abundant merchandising articles to accompany the release of the film, including T-shirts, collectible figures, coffee mugs, shoulder bags, calendars and board-games. These products were sold, however, in a shop that seemed to cater exclusively to the needs of a specific subculture, alongside T-shirts featuring countercultural icons like Bob Marley, articles of clothing designed for members of Goth subculture, and the paraphernalia of drug abuse. *The Nightmare Before Christmas* hence seemed to have become an icon of a particular sub- or counterculture, the subculture generally referred to as "Gothic" or "Goth." The webpage www.gothicsubculture.com (Smith) identifies it as one of a handful of cult films of Gothic subculture. Three more films by Tim Burton are also listed, but more importantly, a number of aspects of Gothic design are noted that are particular to *The Nightmare Before Christmas* merchandise:

- Spider webs, spiders—spider web design on tights, shirt, jewelry
- Skulls, skeletons—in jewelry, on tights or clothing
[...]
- Coffins—most often a coffin shaped box (the cross between a lunch box and purse) or jewelry holder

[Smith, under the heading "What Is Gothic?" > "Common Culture" > "Misc. things Goths tend to like"].

The similarities between this list and characteristic features of *The Nightmare Before Christmas* merchandise are intriguing, prompting the question of whether it was the film that influenced Goth style of clothing and accessorizing or whether the designers of either the film or the merchandising articles were inspired by the preferences of Goth subculture and maybe deliberately targeted this population group as potential customers.

Goth subculture is distinct from other subcultural groups since it is not a specific "youth culture," as Dunja Brill has pointed out:

> Gothic boasts an unusually high proportion of adults with steady professions; especially in science and academia, art and design, social work or computer programming. Many older Goths lead a fairly normal life with a well-paid job, their own car and flat, and a steady relationship or even family. This makes for typical scene biographies where an increasing separation between subcultural and everyday life is practised. In Schmidt and Neumann-Braun's [...] words, most Goths "notoriously manoeuvre between adjustment and deviation" vis-à-vis common social pressures to square their extraordinary subcultural practices and preferences with a socially well-integrated everyday life [86–87].

As Brill claims, Goth subculture is a part-time cultural identity, necessitating constant negotiation between the norms and values of the counterculture and adjustment to the mainstream. The fondness of Goths for the film *The Nightmare Before Christmas* may therefore partly be explained by the fact that the film itself dramatizes this process of negotiation and seems to promote the possibility of taking part in counterculture on a part-time basis, as a holiday from the mainstream.

What Is Counterculture?

The use of the term "counterculture" in this context is of course debatable. What kind of a countercultural impulse is it that spends itself in the purchase of mass-produced merchandise—and mass-produced by the Walt Disney Corporation at that? In his article "Does Counter-culture Exist" of 1983, Umberto Eco famously attacked the use of this term, at least insofar as it was applied to "hippies" and "drug culture," subcultures Eco identifies as parasitic and dependent, since they "can survive only as a tolerated alternative within a much larger cultural model [...] which allow[s] them to languish on the periphery of their model of repressive tolerance" (123). It is perhaps unnecessary to point out that the only representative of an "authentic" counterculture from Eco's point of view is the "intellectual as critical spokesman of the great cultural transformations" (127).

I will be using "counterculture" in a less restricted sense, following the argument of John Desmond, Pierre McDonagh, and Stephanie O'Donohoe in their article "Counter-Culture and Consumer-Society." The authors contest the distinction between counterculture and subculture established by Dessaur, et. al., according to which counter-culture is a term referring to "a coherent system of norms and values that not only differ from those of the dominant system (where this and nothing else is the case we speak of subcultures) but also comprise at least one norm or value that calls for commitment to cultural change, that is to a transformation of the dominant system of norms and values" (quoted in Desmond, McDonagh, and O'Donohoe 245). Instead, Desmond, McDonagh, and O'Donohoe distinguish between revolutionary and aesthetic countercultures:

> Several authors [...] have discussed movements in culture and counter-culture which are characteristic of two broad tributaries, the apocalyptic or revolutionary, and the aesthetic, or gnostic. These represent different space/time responses to living with the otherwise intolerable reality of the crushing power of the mainstream. Revolutionaries are motivated by the principle of Becoming, the promise of transcendence in the time to come, and invest all their will and effort in fighting the mainstream in furtherance of this vision. In contrast the aesthetic response to force is to privilege Being, or space over time, in searching for timeless and immutable values [248].

Hence, while revolutionary counterculture realizes itself in the dimension of time by aiming at a complete political transformation of the entire society, aesthetic counterculture realizes itself in the dimension of space, creating alternative spaces in which ideals and norms apply that are different from those of the cultural mainstream. I will return to the distinction between revolutionary and aesthetic counterculture towards the end. For the present purpose it may suffice to state that the working definition of "counterculture" to be applied in my paper is the one provided by *The Blackwell Dictionary of Twentieth-Century Social Thought*: "[a] minority culture marked by a set of values, norms and behaviour patterns which directly contradict those of the dominant society" (Outwaite and Bottmore 116).

The Nightmare Before Christmas as a Disney Film

The most striking aspect of *The Nightmare Before Christmas* as an icon of counterculture clearly is that the film was produced by Touchstone pictures, which is part of the Walt Disney Corporation, a company generally associated with conservative, even reactionary, political values. The association of Disney with reactionary politics is partly due to the politics of its founder, who was an

FBI informant—as Marc Eliot's biography reveals—and believed that the strike among his studio workers in 1941 was due to a Communist conspiracy. More important than the individual convictions of Walt Disney, however, is the underlying ideology of the products of the Disney company. In their volume *From Mouse to Mermaid: The Politics of Film, Gender, and Culture*, Elizabeth Bell, Lynda Haas and Laura Sells have collected articles that address the political issues in Disney's films that usually remain hidden under the pretense of "innocence": "Disney's trademarked innocence operates on a systematic sanitization of violence, sexuality, and political struggle concomitant with an erasure or repression of difference" (7). The anthology addresses questions of pedagogy, gender and identity construction. Since Disney films are aimed at children, they frequently revolve around a coming-of-age narrative, which usually ends with the integration of an outsider into mainstream society. Disney's version of *Pinocchio* is a particularly pertinent case in point. As Bell, Haas, and Sells point out in summing up Claudia Card's article, "[t]he consequences of 'becoming a real boy' are elided by the generic 'good child,' or to use Foucault's idiom, a docile body, prepared for the Disney ideology of consumption" (9).

As I will argue in the following, the influence of Disney is still much in evidence in *The Nightmare Before Christmas*. In my following analysis I will show that the film actually contains both a conservative, mainstream strain (that we may associate with the conventional Disney product) and a subversive, countercultural, anarchic strain that is more commonly associated with the works of Tim Burton.

The Nightmare Before Christmas as a Tim Burton Film

The name "Tim Burton" in the film's title, however, functions more or less as a brand name, for while Burton composed the initial poem from which the plot of the film is derived and designed the main characters, the film was actually directed by Henry Selick.

At this point, a brief digression on "authorship" in the medium of film seems called for. The notion of the filmmaker as an "author" (or rather "auteur") was first propagated by the French film critics of the *nouvelle vague* in their attempt to elevate film to an art form worthy of serious study and criticism. And while, interestingly, the concept of "authorship" has become increasingly contested in the field of literary criticism (from where it was first derived), it is a category still of major relevance in film studies. *The Nightmare Before Christmas* itself is a case in point: in order to find critical studies of the film at all, one has to consult monographs on the oeuvre of Tim Burton, although he did not even direct the film. Scholars of Tim Burton are eager to integrate the film into Burton's oeuvre: Dorota J. Wiœniewska for instance claims that "[a]lthough Burton had relatively little to do with the production phase of the film, most of the elements that make the movie a 'Tim Burton film' are well in place" (150).

Moreover, the example of *The Nightmare Before Christmas* demonstrates that the notion of authorship is even more questionable in the case of film than in the case of literature, since the finished product is always the result of the collaborative effort of various creative contributors. Regarding *The Nightmare Before Christmas*, the diverging influences of the creative team around Henry Selick and Tim Burton on the one hand and the Disney executives on the other hand are particularly noticeable. Both Selick and Burton were Disney dropouts, and in interviews they regularly commented on the distance between their aesthetic vision and that of the Disney executives (see French 35–36).

Tim Burton's seminal poem "The Nightmare Before Christmas" was an obvious parody of the well-known Christmas poem "Account of a Visit from St. Nicholas" attributed to Clement Clarke Moore. Burton imitates the original's basic meter of anapestic tetrameter and the scheme of rhyming couplets and, even more conspicuously, includes direct verbal echoes. "Account of a Visit from St. Nicholas" begins:

> 'Twas the night before Christmas, when all thro' the house
> Not a creature was stirring, not even a mouse.
> The stockings were hung by the chimney with care,
> In hopes that St Nicholas soon would be there
> ["Account of a Visit from St. Nicholas" ll. 1–6].

Burton parodies this famous opening in his stanza 14:

> 'Twas the nightmare before Christmas, and all though the house,
> Not a creature was peaceful, not even a mouse.
> The stockings all hung by the chimney with care,
> When opened that morning would cause quite a scare!
> [Burton ll. 93–98].

It is hence immediately obvious that the main aim of "The Nightmare Before Christmas" is to satirically attack and undermine a classical poem that presents the foundational fantasy of the cult of Santa Claus. Both poems present a fantastic narrative and are structured similarly. They begin by setting the scene in the first stanza, conveying contrasting moods of a cozy winter night spent indoors and a chilly autumn night outdoors, respectively. The second stanza introduces the respective focalizers, a benign patriarch in the original poem and an elegantly dressed skeleton with a midlife crisis in Burton. In the third stanza, a mildly frightening event occurs, announcing the main fantastic action described in the following stanzas. In "Account of a Visit from St. Nicholas," however, the fantastic creature—Santa Claus—intrudes into the humdrum everyday world of the beholder, while in Burton, the poem's protagonist passes a portal into the fantastic world. By this time, Jack Skellington has become so familiar to the reader that the fact that he himself is a fantastic creature no longer registers. Selick was to pursue a similar policy in the film version: we, the audience, are passing through one portal—the iron gates of the cemetery—, enter Halloweenland and are introduced to Jack Skellington. Having become familiar with him through his extensive aria—a device that, like the soliloquy, is likely to encourage audience identification—we follow Jack through a second portal into Christmastown, a fantasy world with which we are more familiar than Jack, but which is becoming defamiliarized by Jack's surprised response to it.

The remaining stanzas of "Account of a Visit from St. Nicholas" are devoted to an ever more detailed description of Santa Claus, who enters through the chimney and may now be portrayed in close-up. The plot structure of Burton's poem is more complex, involving various transfers between Christmastown and Halloweenland and basically presenting the entire plot of Selick's later film. (However, the villain character of Oogie Boogie and the love subplot revolving around Sally are as yet absent.) The almost verbatim quotation from the original poem quoted above introduces the climax of Burton's poem, which gleefully plays havoc with the traditionally peaceful festival of Christmas. As Christmas is becoming increasingly deconstructed by Halloweenfolk, the parodic stance of the poem is simultaneously becoming increasingly noticeable. Burton's poem, however, ends on a conciliatory note: "Back home, Jack was sad, but then, like a dream, / Santa brought Christmas to the land of Halloween" (Burton ll. 152–53).

A Brief Plot Synopsis of the Film *The Nightmare Before Christmas*

Tim Burton's The Nightmare Before Christmas is a stop-motion puppet musical first released in 1993. Its basic plot idea is that public holidays such as Christmas, Easter or Halloween do not simply "exist" or "occur" but are deliberately produced by highly specialized professionals in segregated small towns called "Christmastown," "Halloweentown," etc. While Christmastown is (unsurprisingly) run by Santa Claus, Halloweentown is presided over by the Pumpkin King Jack Skellington, a skeleton gifted with the graceful movements of Fred Astaire. At the beginning of the film, Jack is going through a midlife crisis—although he is highly successful in his profession, Halloween can no longer content him. One night by accident he discovers Christmastown and is at once very much taken by this other festival which is so very different from Halloween. After returning home, Jack announces to the inhabitants of Halloweentown that this year, they will be taking over Christmas as well, and lectures them on the essentials. However, it becomes immediately obvious that both Jack and his collaborators fail to grasp the entirely different aesthetics and emotional dynamics of Christmas. Sally, a ragdoll in love with Jack, tries to reason with him but to no avail: Jack has Santa Claus (whose name he persistently mispronounces as "Sandy Claws") kidnapped by three mischievous youngsters and proceeds to take the part of Santa himself, flying through the sky in a sleigh drawn by skeleton reindeer and delivering Christmas presents made in Halloweentown that frighten the recipients out of their wits. Alerted by worried parents, the police intervene and shoot Jack's sleigh down with a missile. He survives undamaged (he already *is* dead, after all) but in the meantime, another crisis has occurred: the three mischievous youngsters Lock, Shock and Barrel have delivered Santa Claus into the hands of Oogie Boogie, the arch villain of the film, and Sally has also been captured while attempting to save Santa Claus. Jack has to come to the rescue; he kills Oogie Boogie and frees Sally and Santa, who still has time to perform his task properly and make sure that the children have a happy Christmas after all. Jack and Sally live happily ever after.

The Politics of *The Nightmare Before Christmas*— The Racist Charge and the Sexist Charge

Two main aspects of the film have come under attack from the proponents of political correctness: the character of Oogie Boogie has been criticized on grounds of racism, and the love interest revolving around Sally has been attacked from a feminist viewpoint. Since I consider these political aspects of minor importance for the film as a whole (and, particularly, for its politics), I will address them first.

The character of Oogie Boogie has been considered a racist caricature because Oogie has a recognizably "black" voice. The producers of the film have countered this accusation by declaring that the singer himself, Ken Page, did not consider the part problematic (see Felperin 28). Obviously, however, this does not constitute a valid defense, for if racism is omnipresent, a black person may be just as much imbued with racist ideology as a white one. Even though Oogie Boogie may sound like a black man, his outward appearance is more reminiscent of a member of the Ku Klux Klan, since he is entirely covered by a green bag with slits for his eyes and a pointed hood at the top of his head. Oogie Boogie appears at his most horrifying and repulsive, however, at the instant his real identity is finally disclosed: Jack unravels the bag that covered the monster, and out drop worms, spiders and insects that die in a boiling cauldron below— nothing else remains. The character of Oogie Boogie hence becomes a striking illustration of the deconstruction of a coherent identity in postmodern culture. I do not intend to suggest, however, that *The Nightmare Before Christmas* offers avant-garde postmodern anthropological philosophy, because the disintegration of identity is obviously not considered the common human condition but a particular punishment appropriate for a particularly unpleasant individual. However, Oogie Boogie is not the only character in the film permanently threatened with physical disintegration. Several other characters are also afflicted, albeit to a minor extent: the "Clown with the tear-away face," as his name suggests, can tear off his face—which reveals that there is nothing behind; Sally can detach her limbs from her body at will, while these maintain their ability to move independently. Instead of becoming entirely unraveled like Oogie Boogie, however, these two supporting characters still retain their "identity" in some sense.

The character of Sally may attract charges of sexism on account of her design: she has, as Selick has observed, a "voluptuous" figure (French 46), huge eyes and long hair, but tiny hands and feet—she is therefore sexually appealing but limited in her abilities of action and movement. She literally cannot stand "on her own two feet" (French 46), as a designer pointed out to Tim Burton, who insisted on this design for Sally: the ankles simply would not support the weight of the puppet. In her basic measurements, Sally hence resembles the design of the popular Mattel Barbie doll that has itself come under attack for providing unhealthy body images for young girls. Criticism has largely focused on Barbie's lack of body fat and the ratio of her bust, waist and hip measurements which is approximately 12 to 6 to 11 (see Dittmar, Halliwell, and Ive). The symbolic significance of extremely small hands and feet suggesting lack of initiative and independence to my knowledge has not yet been discussed.

However, while the design for Sally is clearly sexist, it is meant to be, because in terms of plot she is the female equivalent of Frankenstein's monster, a creature sewn together from various bits and pieces and artificially animated by Dr. Finklestein, a wheelchair-ridden mad scientist. Since he has made her according to his personal taste, it is not surprising that she looks like the ultimate sex object. Another point of criticism concerning the Sally-character is the love sub-plot around Jack and Sally, which provides a traditional happy ending consisting of a stable heterosexual union. Worse still, in the course of the plot, Sally takes up the position of the "damsel in distress" that needs to be saved by heroic male action. In this respect, Sally's behavior accords well with traditional models of gender performance. What is more subversive, however, is Sally's relationship to Dr. Finklestein, particularly if we compare *The Nightmare Before Christmas* to another famous American film musical on the Frankenstein theme, George Cukor's *My Fair Lady* (1963). For the musical version, Alan Jay Lerner had added a traditional happy ending to George Bernard Shaw's *Pygmalion*, in direct opposition to Shaw's specifications in the afterword to the play, in which he rejects all suggestions that Eliza might want to marry Higgins after all: "Galatea never does quite like Pygmalion: his relation to her is too godlike to be altogether agreeable" (119). While the Hollywood Eliza Doolittle was expected to fall in love with the mad scientist who created her, Sally repeatedly poisons Dr. Finklestein with deadly nightshade—until he learns from his mistake and creates Sally 2, his new monster-mate, in his own image.

The Politics of Holidays: Christmas versus Halloween

After considering these issues of race and gender, which are of minor importance for the film as a whole, I will now devote the remainder of this paper to the central plot device of *The Nightmare Before Christmas* that we might call "The Deconstruction of Christmas by Halloween." Even though Jack's attempts to study Christmas scientifically provide little result (they merely destroy what they seek to illuminate), let us not be deterred but consider the politics of holidays.

If we compare the way Christmas is celebrated today in American culture (and Western cultures strongly influenced by it) to the celebration of Halloween, Christmas at once emerges as the festival more closely aligned with mainstream cultural values. In fact, an opposition between the two types of feast is highly instructive.

Fig. 1: Christmas versus Halloween

Christmas	Halloween
Birth	Death
Christian	Pagan
Consumption	Performance
Mass Production	Individuality
Domestic	Public
Patriarchy	Anarchy

The first opposition is that between birth and death. The central event around which Christmas celebrations revolve—as even in our secularized age most people still realize—is a birth, while Halloween acknowledges the omnipresence of death, the presence of death as a part of life.

The second aspect is the opposition between Christian and pagan. Historically, of course, both Christmas and Halloween were pagan feasts that were superseded by Christian holidays in the process of Christianization, much in the manner of Jack's attempt to hijack Christmas. But while the Christian significance of Christmas is still relatively well-known, the religious meaning of Halloween is familiar to hardly anyone—it is a feast day dedicated to all Christian martyrs. The

U.S. folk historian Jack Kugelmass has argued that it is precisely the perceived paganism that contributes to the present popularity of Halloween, which thus becomes part of a New Age alternative religion: "Halloween's increasing popularity as an American adult festival may partly speak to a decline in modernism's rationalist paradigm and the resulting possibility of religious enchantment, given the emerging popularity of New Age religious beliefs and practices such as channeling and psychic readings" (24). Besides, studies of Halloween—like for instance the volumes by Nicholas Rogers and Jack Santino—tend to stress the pre–Christian heritage of the festival. Rogers locates the source of Halloween in the Celtic feast of Samhain, a day on which the gates to the otherworld (that is, the world of the spirits, not the world of the dead) were believed to be wide open. A traditional element of Samhain that has survived into present-day Halloween was the playing of practical jokes and the donning of disguise. Likewise, Mexican participants in the festival of the *Dia de los muertos* (on 1 November) tend to stress not only the difference between the day of the dead and (American) Halloween, but also its pre–Christian heritage. This identification of Halloween as "pagan" has led church functionaries to protest against the celebration of this holiday.

Celebrating Christmas—Celebrating Halloween

The following four aspects in my table are more closely concerned with the cultural practices connected to the two festivals. At Christmas, children are given presents by their parents in their family homes as a reward for good behavior. At Halloween, children disguise themselves as scary characters, they roam the streets at night, knock at doors, demand candy and threaten mischief with the slogan "Trick or Treat!" When Jack lectures the inhabitants of Halloweentown on Christmas, the giving of presents emerges as the central aspect. While Christmas thus centers on consumption (a central value in a consumer society), Halloween centers on performance—you dress up to frighten others.

Consumerism in a capitalist society is of course closely linked to mass production, and this is an aspect particularly highlighted in *The Nightmare Before Christmas*. In Christmastown, identical presents are mass-produced in highly automated production processes—Santa's elves are working at sewing machines and assembly lines and, moreover, they themselves look absolutely identical and mass-produced—an effect easily accomplished in stop motion; you simply use the same mold for different puppets. The inhabitants of Halloweentown, by contrast, not only look highly individual, they also produce highly individual presents, for instance by turning road-kill into fur caps. It would be tempting to read this in the context of "Do-It-Yourself" counterculture—if it did not turn out on delivery that these home-made presents are not appreciated.

The following opposition between the domestic and the public setting of the two holidays is of particular interest. Adding a historical perspective, Tad Tuleja observes: "Victor Turner and Jack Santino have discussed Halloween usefully as an exploration of liminality, and most of the destruction visited on nineteenth-century householders by Halloween pranksters may be seen as an attack on domestic borders. The majority of popular pranks were 'threshold tricks' that assaulted, if only temporarily, ordered space" (87). *The Nightmare Before Christmas* finds an intriguing visual image for the attempt of policing the boundary between domestic and public sphere: after the news has been broadcast that a dangerous impostor has taken over the part of Santa Claus, concerned parents light fires in the grate to prevent him from coming down the chimney. (Entering a house through the chimney may in itself constitute a curious form of liminality.)

The final opposition in my table is "patriarchy" versus "anarchy." We have already briefly touched on the aspect of patriarchy in the context of the character of Sally. However, as tends to be forgotten, "patriarchy" operates along two dividing lines—not only the gender division but also the line between the generations. The spirit of Christmas is embodied in the benign patriarchal figure of Santa Claus—tellingly alternatively dubbed "*Father* Christmas"—and, as pointed out before, he is doling out presents on the basis of desert. The pivotal scene of the kidnapping of Santa Claus (from 0:43:32) gives a striking illustration of the different codes of behavior operating at Christmas and at Halloween: at first we see Santa sitting in his armchair, going through his list of children and neatly categorizing them as "naughty" and "nice." There is a knock at the door, and Lock, Shock and Barrel challenge Santa with "Trick or Treat!" Before he has time to answer, he is put in a bag and carried away, still trying to reason with his kidnappers: "Don't do this, naughty children don't get any presents!" (0:46:17). Before they push him down a pipe that will conduct him into Oogie Boogie's den, Santa issues one last appeal to the youngsters' moral sense: "Haven't you ever heard of peace on earth and goodwill to all men?" (0:45:34), to which the answer is a gleeful "Nooo!" in unison. As the formula "Trick or Treat!" reveals, at Halloween, presents are not given as a reward for obedience but acquired by means of intimidation. Incidentally, the practice of "trick or treat" is a fairly recent tradition—it was first introduced in the 1930s and had become widespread by the 1950s.

A Brief History of Christmas

This brings us to a further interesting point: the historical development of public holidays and the cultural practices associated with them. For Christmas, like Halloween, underwent significant historical changes, as Stephen Nissenbaum has sketched in his monograph *The Battle for Christmas*. According to Nissenbaum, Christmas in its present form was established between 1810 and 1830 by a small group of wealthy conservative New York bourgeois families, including Clement Clarke Moore. Nissenbaum sums up the central points of his study in an interview with Berit Haugen Keyes:

> What you can see happening between 1810 and 1830, is the invention of a tradition. A new kind of Christmas is created, complete with its own mythical figure—Santa Claus. It takes place in the house, and does not involve opening the doors if you are rich. On the one hand this is a new development, because it excludes the outside world. On the other hand, by centering the holiday on children, in a structural way it replicated old patterns: people in authority still give gifts to their inferiors; not along the lines of class but within the family [Nissenbaum quoted in Keyes].

As Nissenbaum points out, the traditional "merry old English" Christmas involved "behavior that most of us would find offensive and even shocking today—rowdy public displays of excessive eating and drinking, the mockery of established authority, aggressive begging (often involving the threat of doing harm), and even the invasion of wealthy homes" (Nissenbaum 5). This reversal of established moral codes and hierarchies conforms to Mikhail Bakhtin's description of the carnivalesque, and the reversal of social ranks was particularly in evidence in the election of a "Lord of Misrule." As far as "aggressive begging" is concerned, Nissenbaum particularly refers to the practice of "wassailing":

> The poor—most often bands of boys and young men—claimed the right to march to the houses of the well-to-do, enter their halls, and receive gifts of food, drink, and sometimes money as well. [...] The Lord of the Manor let the peasants in and feasted them. In return, the peasants offered something of true value in a paternalistic society—their *goodwill*. [...] The exchange of gifts for goodwill often included the performance of songs, that articulated the structure of the exchange. [...] The wassail usually possessed an aggressive edge—often an explicit threat—concerning the unpleasant consequences to follow if the beggars' demands were not met [9–10, italics in the original].

Wassailing thus bears marked similarities to present-day "trick-or-treating," and it may be argued that Jack Skellington's attempt to take over Christmas merely restores the festival to its original shape. Jack, the apparently anarchic character, thus paradoxically turns out to be more "traditional" than the supposedly conservative character of Santa Claus.

Conclusion

To sum up, in its confrontation between Christmas and Halloween, *The Nightmare Before Christmas* dramatizes the conflict between a conservative mainstream culture and a subversive counterculture. Moreover, we are encouraged to sympathize with the representatives of the Halloween counterculture: Jack is the hero of the film, not Santa Claus, and we watch Christmas from the perspective of Halloweentown rather than the other way round. This, however, does not make *The Nightmare Before Christmas* a genuinely subversive and anarchic film. Jack's initial attempt to take over Christmas would have been an act of "revolutionary" counterculture in the sense established by Desmond, McDonagh and O'Donohue. The ending of the film, however, in which Halloween is once more produced in Halloweentown and Christmas in Christmastown, partly takes back the initial anarchic impulse. The ending propagates a neat segregation of the diverse cultures in their respective spaces, and this turns Halloweentown into a merely "aesthetic" counterculture. It may be just this emphasis on aesthetics and style, along with the suggestion that one may be a member of a counterculture on a part-time basis, that makes *The Nightmare Before Christmas* so attractive to members of Goth subculture.

Works Cited

"Account of a Visit from St. Nicholas." Facsimile of first publication. Variations 2823–1844. InterMedia Enterprises, 2003. Web. 20 Dec. 2013.

Bell, Elizabeth, Lynda Haas, and Laura Sells. "Introduction: Walt's in the Movies." *From Mouse to Mermaid: The Politics of Film, Gender, and Culture*. Eds. Elizabeth Bell, Lynda Haas, and Laura Sells. Bloomington: Indiana University Press, 1995. 1–17. Print.

Brill, Dunja. *Subversion or Stereotype? The Gothic Subculture as a Case Study of Gendered Identities and Representations*. Giessen: Ulme-Mini, 2006. Print.

Burton, Tim. "Nightmare Before Christmas Original Poem." *The Tim Burton Collective*. Web. 20 Dec. 2013.

Desmond, John, Pierre McDonagh, and Stephanie O'Donohoe. "Counter-Culture and Consumer Society." *Consumption, Markets, Culture* 4.3 (2001): 241–80. Print.

Dessaur, C.I., A. Naess, and E. Reimer. *Science between Culture and Counter-Culture*. Nijmegen: Dekker & van de Vegt, 1975. Print.

Dittmar, Helga, Emma Halliwell, and Suzanne Ive. "Does Barbie Make Girls Want to Be Thin? The Effect of Experimental Exposure to Images of Dolls on the Body Image of 5- to 8-Year-Old Girls." *Developmental Psychology* 42.2 (2006): 283–92. Print.

Eco, Umberto. "Does Counter-culture Exist?" Trans. Jenny Condie. *Apocalypse Postponed*. Ed. Robert Lumley. Bloomington: Indiana University Press, 1994. 115–28. Print.

Eliot, Marc. *Walt Disney: Hollywood's Dark Prince*. New York: Birch Lane Press, 1993. Print.

Felperin, Leslie. "Animated Dreams." *Sight and Sound* 4.12 (1994): 26–29. Print.

French, Lawrence. "*Tim Burton's The Nightmare Before Christmas*: The Making of a Stop-Motion Fantasy Film Masterpiece." *Cinefantastique* 24.5 (1993): 32–47. Print.

Keyes, Berit Haugen. "Christmas Reborn: The Creation of a Consumer Christmas: Professor Steven Nissenbaum in Interview." *Three Monkeys Online: A Curious Alternative Magazine* 2004. Web. 28 Nov. 2013.

Kugelmass, Jack. *Masked Culture: The Greenwich Village Halloween Parade*. New York: Columbia University Press, 1994. Print.

Nissenbaum, Stephen. *The Battle for Christmas*. New York: Knopf, 1996. Print.

Outhwaite, William, and Tom Bottomore, eds. *The Blackwell Dictionary of Twentieth-Century Social Thought.* Oxford: Blackwell, 1993. Print.
Rogers, Nicholas. *Halloween: From Pagan Ritual to Party Night.* Oxford: Oxford University Press, 2002. Print.
Santino, Jack. *Halloween and Other Festivals of Death and Life.* Knoxville: University of Tennessee Press, 1994. Print.
Shaw, George Bernard. *Pygmalion.* London: Penguin, 2003. Print.
Smith, Alicia Porter. *A Study of Gothic Subculture: An Inside Look for Outsiders.* gothicsubculture.com. Web. 11 Feb. 2013.
Tim Burton's The Nightmare Before Christmas. Dir. Henry Selick. Screenplay by Caroline Thompson. Touchstone Pictures, 1993. Film. 2 DVD Collector's Edition. Walt Disney Studios Home Entertainment.
Tuleja, Tad. "Trick or Treat: Pre-Texts and Contexts." *Halloween and Other Festivals of Death and Life.* Ed. Jack Santino. Knoxville: University of Tennessee Press, 1994. 82–102. Print.
Wiœniewska, Dorota J. "Strangers in the Strange Land: The Gothic Mode in Tim Burton's Films." *American Studies* 20 (2003): 143–156. Print.

Subversive or Conservative? Vampires and Ideology in the *Twilight* Series and *True Blood*

CHRISTIAN KNIRSCH

At first glance, popular cultural texts are primarily infested with emotions and the affective. As Lawrence Grossberg points out, however, the affective always needs some form of legitimation through the ideological (234). Thus, popular culture is also a field of implicit ideological debate (216). Of course, this also applies to fantasy film and literature, which are an integral part of contemporary popular culture. Usually, popular cultural texts are described as being expressive of "the cultural character [and political stance, C.K.] of the working class," as Raiford Guins and Omayra Zaragoza Cruz state (8). Cultural texts from the fantasy genre and subgenres, though, have traditionally been characterized as anything but working class. On the contrary, the current master narrative in cultural studies characterizes fantastic literature in general and fantasy literature in particular as deeply conservative when it comes to the depiction of gender roles and relations, metaphysical hierarchies within the great chain of being, and social class relations.[1] According to Craig Carter, J.R.R. Tolkien's epos *The Lord of the Rings* is a prime example of the conservatism of cultural fantasy texts, "theologically [as well as] politically, culturally, and ethically." As Carter ultimately argues, both the novels and Peter Jackson's film adaptations "embod[y] an Augustinian conservative worldview" that violates basic principles of liberal democracy. The apparently not all too subtle conservatism of both novel and movies certainly did not damage their financial success, though: the films of the trilogy became the highest-grossing movies not only in the first decade of the twenty-first century, but in the whole history of film.[2]

In even more recent years, two popular cultural fantasy texts from the subgenre of the vampire gothic, Stephenie Meyer's *Twilight* and its sequels, and Charlaine Harris's Sookie Stackhouse novels, as well as the respective movie and television adaptations, have enjoyed enormous popular success, too, both in the U.S. and abroad. However, the audiences who are responsible for this huge success on the heterogeneous market of popular culture could not be more different: While Anna Silver refers to "a large community of *girls and women* who have made the *Twilight* series among the best-selling *young adult* novels of all time" (121, emphasis added),[3] the *True Blood* viewership of up to 6.3 million per episode in season 1 in the U.S. alone is far more diverse, as Joseph Adalian relates: on average, forty-eight percent of the viewers are male.[4] One of the major reasons for the more heterogeneous viewership of *True Blood* in contrast to *Twilight* is its formal aesthetical setup: while *True Blood* is a prime example of a writerly text in the definition of Roland Barthes and a producerly text in John Fiske's definition, *Twilight* is more of a readerly text in the Barthesian sense. This formal aesthetical difference is also indicative of a difference in the social and political implications which, in combination with the genre aspects, accounts for the rather different viewership of these two sets of popular cultural texts.

After a brief definition of the interdependent concepts of readerly, writerly, and producerly texts, I will first assess the *Twilight* novel series as an example of a readerly text with a special focus on its presentation of gender and race. The main part of this article then deals with *True Blood*'s paradoxical capacity as both a writerly and a producerly cultural text at the same time. In a final twist, I will point out several major differences between Charlaine Harris's Sookie Stackhouse novels and the TV series *True Blood*, most of which are decisive in terms of the overall political assessment of the respective text.

In *S/Z*, Roland Barthes distinguishes between writerly and readerly texts. While largely passive in the reception of readerly texts, which are both linear and closed, the reader plays a more active role in the constitution of the meaning of a writerly text, which is an "absolutely plural text" anyway (4). The reader becomes part of the text, he or she is even "a producer of the text" (4). In John Fiske's definition, the producerly text is "the popular [version of this] writerly text" (*Understanding* 103). Consequently, Fiske defines the producerly text's interpretative "openness" and general "accessibility" as its key elements (*Understanding* 104). The major difference between Barthes's writerly and Fiske's producerly text is that the former refers to "*serious*," avant-garde literature and is "never closed, based as it is on the infinity of language" (Barthes 6). Due to these meta-reflexive, avant-garde elements, both formally and aesthetically, it does not appeal to the masses. The easy accessibility combined with the general openness of the latter, on the contrary, implies the potential appeal of a text to a multitude of different readers from different social and intellectual backgrounds.[5] In the end, the decisive factor for the popularity of a text is its relevance to different social groups; its "points of pertinence," as Fiske calls them (*Understanding* 133), with "everyday life" need to be "multiple" and "transient" (129).

Obviously, *Twilight* lacks both the openness and the multiplicity of its points of pertinence—but it is nevertheless very popular in the sense of financially successful. From a formal aesthetical perspective, however, with its linear and coherent structure, the ideologically consistent implicit and explicit comments on social and political issues, as well as its lack of narrative gaps, *Twilight* is a classic example of a readerly text. The political and social ideology predominant in the texts is overwhelmingly conservative. So far, academic research has mainly focused on the depiction of gender roles in the series. The common conclusion of these studies is that the "the novels' gender ideology is ultimately and unapologetically patriarchal," as Anna Silver relates (122). In the depiction of the growing relationship between Bella and Edward, for example, it hails the ideal of "old-fashioned courtship, in which only kisses are exchanged before the wedding" (127). The rules of the relationship are mainly defined by Edward, who generally plays the more active part in the relationship, as opposed to Bella, who remains largely passive. Although Edward appears like "a relic [of the past] and [a] model of Edwardian, if not Victorian, masculinity," his "arguments in favor of chastity are quite similar to [contemporary] Mormon concepts of sexuality and sin" (128). In a similar vein, extramarital sexuality is heavily punished in the novel.[6] Silver also considers *Twilight* "a monologic representation of the virtuous family and woman" (123). It perpetuates the myth "of the self-sacrificial, selfless mother, who is willing to die for the good of her [...] child, and the [myth of the] warrior-mother who successfully protects the integrity and survival of her family" (123). The language employed in both the romance and the domestic plot "is more patrimonial than romantic" (125). Moreover, Silver argues that the idealized depiction of the Cullens represents "a throwback to the mythic family of an imagined past" (127).

Due to this pronounced focus on gender, the representations of other social and political categories such as race have so far largely been ignored. Yet race does matter in *Twilight*, too, even though the list of *dramatis personae* almost exclusively consists of whites. One of the few exceptions is Laurent, a vampire of African-American origin. He betrays his co-members of a vegetarian coven in Alaska by secretly feeding on humans and tries to kill Bella upon his return to Forks, home of the Cullens.[7] In the end, he is killed by a pack of werewolves who come to Bella's rescue. The werewolves represent another example of non-white characters in the series: in their human form, they are Native Americans belonging to the tribe of the Quileute. Although they save Bella's life, they are not portrayed favorably throughout. As a matter of fact, Jacob, an adolescent member of the tribe and a werewolf himself, is Edward's rival in the attempt to win the love of Bella.[8] Significantly though, Bella chooses the Anglo-American

Edward over the Native American Jacob, thus embracing Edwardian or even Victorian family and gender values at the expense of Native American ideals centered on nature.[9] Similarly, the Volturi represent the feudal European past. They are considered "the closest thing our world has to a royal family" in the vampire community (*New* 17) and globally enforce the law that the existence of vampires must remain "a secret" (379).[10] They cling to their power and fight any other coven they consider a threat to their status as the kings and queens of the vampire world. Thus, in *New Moon*, they travel to Forks under the pretense of defending the Cullens against Victoria's army of newborn vampires as a retribution for Victoria's violation of Volturi law; their true intention, however, is to help Victoria destroy the Cullens since they consider them a threat to their global rule. Therefore, *Twilight*'s setup of characters betrays a clear racial bias in favor of white, Anglo-American, and Protestant identities which underlines the conservative worldview prevalent on many levels in the novel.

As opposed to *Twilight*, *True Blood* is more of a writerly text. After all, in *True Blood*, there are far more references to different cultural texts, both highbrow and low-brow, as well as meta-comments on the medium. Thus, "*True Blood* offers a fresh spin on the vampire genre that opens a rich vein of new philosophical queries," as George A. Dunn and Rebecca Housel state.[11] Indeed, *True Blood* contains many variations on the traditional vampire myth based on contemporary cultural texts.[12] In *True Blood*, crucifixes, for example, do not fend off vampires; this traditional stance is meta-reflexively unmasked as mere folklore when Bill says that "we [vampires] can stand before a cross [...] just as readily as any other creature of God" (S1E05, 0:21:01); in *True Blood*, silver does the job, as can be seen in the example of an anti-vampire version of pepper spray, water infatuated with silver (S3E11).[13] Therefore, an anti-vampire suicide bomber from the radically Christian Fellowship of the Sun drapes himself with silver necklaces and chains when he blows himself up during a vampire gathering (S2E08).[14] Furthermore, the vampires' sex drive is described as wild and animalistic; a characteristic that is enriched with several allusions to sado-masochism.[15] Thus, the sexuality that is latent in most vampire stories is out there in the open.[16] Moreover, possessing the fountain of youth, which Juan Ponce de León hoped to find in the U.S., the vampires' ultimate desire is to walk in bright sunshine. Thus, Vampires, too, pursue their own version of the American dream, i.e., the dream to be what one is not, as one could put it. Moreover, as Ariadne Blayde points out, "*True Blood* introduces the idea that human beings can exploit vampires as well"; actually, due to the effects of their blood which is sold as a drug called V, "vampires become a valuable commodity for human beings" (37). In addition, the series, as well as the novels it is based on, belong to a well-established cultural genre called the vampire gothic. Therefore, potential hypotexts include not only its immediate source novels, but a wide range of literary and filmic sources. In the end, as Rachel Carroll observes, such "a popular revival of a cult genre must address two audiences simultaneously: the expert and the unknowing" (3).[17]

Consequently, *True Blood* extrapolates on the image of the vampire as a symbol of the Other which was established in the original gothic texts such as Bram Stoker's *Dracula* or John Polidori's "The Vampyre" and transfers it to contemporary America. Even though most minorities in the U.S. are each represented individually, on a symbolic level, vampires function as an overarching symbol of "the Other" in American society. Significantly, vampires refer to themselves as Vampire-Americans, i.e., hyphenated Americans in general, but the most obvious minorities represented by vampires are African Americans and homosexuals. A poster held up during a demonstration by radical Christians in front of Fangtasia, a club where vampires and humans meet, reads "God Hates Fangs" (S4E02).[18] This is of course an allusion to the infamous slogan by the Westboro Baptist Church, "God hates fags." Vampires who belong to both groups alluded to on the sign are Talbot and Russell, homosexual vampires who have been together for 700 years—which sometimes rather feels "like 7 million years," as Russell relates (S3E06).[19] With remarks like that, this long-lasting homosexual relationship between two ancient vampires is implicitly likened to ordinary relationships among humans and thus normalized and integrated into the quotidian. Additionally, it is repeatedly suggested that homosexuality is latent even in heterosexuals, for example when Eric's vampire daughter Pam throws lascivious glances at Sookie, who wears a white t-shirt that gets soaked with blood and becomes transparent, an effect that is known from wet t-shirt contests that are currently very popular in American clubs.[20] The most prominent example of homosexuality, though, is Lafayette, who is openly homosexual and flirts with this image. Lafayette is in several homosexual relationships throughout the three seasons this article deals with and even works as a part-time prostitute for homosexuals; significantly, one of his best customers is the Republican congressman of the state of Louisiana, David Duke Finch, which betrays the hypocrisy of large parts of Southern conservatives in the series.[21] As a matter of fact, Lafayette is not only homosexual, but also African-American. Nicole Rabin suggests that Bon Temps symbolizes an American pastoral that "includes Caucasian and African-American characters of varying social classes, both heterosexual and homosexual. All the characters are friends despite their racial, class, and sexual differences." Joseph J. Foy even goes a step further, likens the Bon Temps community to the early settlers, and declares Bon Temps a *pars pro toto* for the nation: "The United States was formed largely out of groups of people as diverse as this collection of Bon Temps residents, all of whom agreed to establish a government that didn't impose a uniform way of life upon its citizens" and "allows citizens to pursue their own happiness" (54). Yet, is this really the case in *True Blood*? After all, some inhabitants of Bon Temps *do* want to force their way of life on others: the followers of the Fellowship of the Sun, for example. Moreover, while it is true that they live together, life is not always peaceful, as the sheer number of dead bodies shows that keep piling up from episode to episode—and life in Bon Temps is certainly not without racial and sexual prejudice.

An at least latent racial tension is obvious throughout the series. On the plot level, there are the frequent racist remarks by Arlene and others; for example, Arlene addresses two African-American customers with the words "you people." She also introduces race as a relevant category into a discussion about the moral responsibilities of Tara's ex-boyfriend Eggs and Arlene's ex-husband René: "Why [is Eggs not responsible]? Because of slavery?" When Tara accuses her of racism, Arlene follows a common pattern and argues that race does not matter to her at all but is only used as an excuse by the respective minority: "I hate when they make everything about race" (S3E01, 0:06:40).[22] Equally, there are many historical and rhetorical allusions that put an emphasis on the analogous situations of African-Americans and vampires—after all, *True Blood* is set in the South. Significantly, Vampire Bill was a plantation owner in his human life and fought for the confederacy in the civil war (S1E03)[23]; in the narrative present, the Ku Klux Klan sets up a burning cross in Sookie's yard because she's in a relationship with a vampire (S3E10).[24] The stereotype of the vampire rapist (S1E03)[25] is mentioned, as is an act of public lynching (S1E05), and the Vampire Rights activists consider the "separate but equal" status quo an important first step in the emancipation process of vampires (S1E03).[26] Finally, the so-called "Vampire Rights Amendment" is passed, and in the state of Vermont intermarriage is legalized (S3E09).[27]

On the plot level, a clear focus of the series lies on the relationship between vampires and humans. From a reception perspective, the sympathy levels are constantly shifting—sometimes, the viewer is tempted to support the vampiric cause; at others, he or she is repelled by the vampires' ferocity. When it comes to the respective representatives, there are several positive and negative examples. While some vampires consider themselves vegetarians, i.e., they do not feed on human blood but drink a chemical substitute instead, the eponymous TruBlood,[28] and try to coexist peacefully with humans, others keep the traditional lifestyle of vampires and are thus clearly a threat to the human community.[29]

This ambivalence is already apparent in the very first scene of the series when a young couple in party mood enters the service shop of a gas station at night and asks for "TruBlood." The TV in the background shows a political debate about the desirability of human-vampire co-existence starring Nan Flanagan, the spokesperson of the American Vampire League and the Authority, the highest body in international vampire politics.[30] The cashier has long black hair, he is clad in black, wears an upside-down cross on his chest, and speaks with an Eastern European accent. In short, he looks like a stereotypical vampire, which only dawns on the teenagers when he hisses that *"we* [vampires, C.K.] don't breathe" (S1E01, 0:01:32). Another customer, in contrast, looks like a typical Southerner with his military overall and a cap displaying the flag of the confederacy. When the attendant unmasks his true identity as a vampire imposter who played a trick on the teenagers, the supposed Southerner interferes and states that he "didn't think this was funny" (S1E01, 0:02:00). When he is addressed with the words "fuck you, Billybob," he himself reveals his true identity as a vampire (S1E01, 0:02:25). In the course of this very short scene, there are various shifts between fear, thrill, and relief that quickly succeed each other in the teenagers' interpretation of their encounter with a supposed and a real vampire. Remarkably, in *True Blood*, the vampire threat does not come from the outside, as it usually does, but from the inside.[31]

The sympathy of the viewer does not only shift between pro- and anti-vampire stances, but also between the individual characters; in the end, no-one is entirely good and hardly anyone is entirely bad, at least none of the main characters are. Sookie is undoubtedly the hero of the series, but she, too, acts inconsiderately at times, especially in her relationship with Bill. As a matter of fact, Sookie is very unsure of her role as a young woman in a relationship—after all, it is her first. This leads to several examples of contradictory behavior, as Lillian E. Craton remarks. At one point, "[s]he's upset that Bill has offered to pay her shopping tab at the strip mall he owns, in her mind placing her in the degrading role of 'kept woman' and turning her sexuality into a commodity"; shortly after, "she resents Bill's making a large financial gift to the Bellefleur family while she has to struggle to pay her own bill, as though she wanted Bill to help her out, too" (*Dead* 116). According to Lillian E. Crator, this is indicative of the series' status as "a critique and a celebration of contemporary feminism" (121). Bill, in turn, is depicted as Sookie's loving and caring partner who tries to protect her from all evil; later, however, it is revealed that he made Sookie fall in love with him because he was ordered to seduce her by his vampire queen.[32] Jason, Sookie's brother, holds up traditional family values and helps free the city from Maryann, a Dionysian semi-goddess.[33] The rhetoric he uses is ambivalent, though: first, he relishes the chance to fight in "the war I've been training for" (S2E10, 0:11:40) and defend "my town" (S2E11, 0:20:23). Second, he vaguely refers to "the Bible or the Constitution" to justify this war as a just war (S2E11, 0:09:57). Third, Jason feels free to do anything that serves the cause, irrespective of the circumstances. Again, this is backed up by a reference to the Bible: "Then 'we' are the law. […]. This is Armageddon" (S2E11, 0:09:25). With the words "Hasta la vista, baby," he enters the fight together with Terry, who actually fought in Iraq (S2E12, 0:12:24)—finally, Jason accidentally shoots Tara's boyfriend Eggs, which may well be called collateral damage. Equally, he kidnaps a vampire for his blood and sells it as V. Later, Jason joins the Fellowship of the Sun and trains to become an anti-vampire terrorist. Sookie's boss, Sam, who is always nice and understanding, confesses that he is a double murderer who killed his accomplice and her boyfriend after they wanted to cheat him out of his share of a bank robbery (S3E10). René is introduced as Arlene's loving partner and a caring step-father but turns out to be a rapist and a multiple murderer. Fittingly, Jason remarks that nobody is "what they're supposed to be" which, on a meta-level, is a self-reflexive comment on the series' characters (S3E11, 0:39:40).

This oscillation between affirmation and opposition is typical of the representation of the supernatural in *True Blood* in general. According to E.J. Clery, there are three different modes of the supernatural: "the real supernatural" (18), "the spectacular supernatural" (25),[34] and "the explained supernatural" (106), all of which can be found in the series. The most prominent example of the real supernatural is of course the sheer existence of vampires, werewolves, and all sorts of supernatural beings. Real divine interference seems to be at play when Jason asks for a "sign" whether he should join the Fellowship of the Sun despite its exorbitant membership fees and Sookie leaves him her share of an inheritance (S2E01, 0:22:52).[35] The return of Sookie's dead grandma as a ghost suggested by mysterious sounds in her kitchen and a shaking picture can be seen as an example of the explained supernatural—the supposed ghost is Jason (S1E07). Lastly, the continued and unshakeable belief of the members of the Fellowship of the Sun in divine signs and parallels between the bible and real life is often depicted in the mode of the spectacular supernatural. Sometimes, the different modes or states of the supernatural succeed each other as a particular scene develops, mostly spanning several episodes. Arlene, for example, tries to undertake a Wicca-abortion: therefore, she drinks herbal tea in a circle of burning torches which seems rather spectacular at first. Nevertheless, it seems to work: Arlene starts bleeding from her womb and seems destined to lose her baby which would make the abortion an example of the real supernatural; miraculously though, the baby survives, which, in turn, seems to confirm earlier hints at its devilish parentage. After all, it is René's child. This suspicion is finally confirmed by Jesus, a brujo, i.e., the Latin American version of a shaman (S3E12). His second sight is a similar case in point: at first, his visions seem to be drug-induced hallucinations; yet, strangely enough, Lafayette seems to share these visions which create some comic or parodic effects. As it turns out though, Jesus really has the ability to mentally travel in time and he can even take people along—at least if they fulfill certain spiritual criteria, like Lafayette, who, in season four, is revealed to be a medium. In his mental trips, he can see both the past and the future, which makes the supposed drug hallucinations an example of the real supernatural. Likewise, the representation of the exorcism of Tara's mother comes full circle when it comes to the different modes of the supernatural: from spectacular supernatural in the original depiction with the crone-stone chant, to the real supernatural when the chant seems to work, to the explained supernatural when Tara finds out that Miss Jeannette drugged her mother in order to create the desired effect. Ironically, later on, Tara herself calls upon Jeannette to perform another exorcism on herself—even though she technically knows better. In this case, individual belief seems to be the decisive factor for the evaluation of the supernatural.

Not only in this example, but throughout the series, the evaluation of the different belief systems mentioned—both real and fictitious—is constantly shifting between affirmation and opposition or even ridicule. An important part of this overall evaluation is the moral evaluation of different agents representing the respective belief system, and since Christianity is the main focus of *True Blood*, I will now assess several Christian representatives of the series. The local priest, for example, seems to be very devout and supportive but starts an extramarital relationship with Tara's divorced mother who, in turn, overcomes her addiction to alcohol through her belief in voodoo rites based on Christian exorcist practices (S1E10). After her transformation, her belief in Christian values and principles is very firm. As a consequence, though, she repudiates her daughter who is in jail for driving under the influence: "You can't come home. I'm not gonna let you" (S1E11, 0:33:30)—and this although Tara has never given up on her through all the years of alcoholism.[36] What is more, Jason finally joins the so-called soldiers of the sun and is involved in the preparations for a terror attack with a suicide bomber who is sent to a Vampire meeting (S2E08); of course, the suicide bomber is a clear reference to Islamist terror.[37] Interestingly enough, Russell, one of the proponents of Vampire supremacy, commits horrendous acts of violence and terror, too, and is consequently called a "Vampire terrorist" (S3E10, 0:12:37). Thus, the same reference is used for both radical Vampires and radical Christians. Finally, there is a slightly parodic note when Jesus talks about his origins and tells Lafayette that he does not have a father, which is obviously a reference to the biblical virgin birth (S3E06).[38]

To conclude, "the world envisioned by Ball and Harris," as Dunn and Housel put it (3), not differentiating between the novels and the TV series, combines both writerly elements, such as the self-conscious play with different genre conventions, and producerly elements, such as interpretative openness, transience, and multiplicity of points of pertinence that are relevant to different social and intellectual milieus, which explains the popular as well as the critical success of the series. Yet, does "the [one] world envisioned by Ball and Harris" really exist? Of course, *True Blood* is the TV adaptation of Charlaine Harris's Sookie Stackhouse novels. Yet, as is often the case when it comes to TV adaptations of contemporary popular novels, *True Blood*, according to Sarah Cardwell, is not very faithful to its immediate source texts, but "correspond[s] quite easily to existing television genres" (176).[39]

With regard to the Sookie Stackhouse novels,[40] this is especially true for the overall social and political stance of the novels. As opposed to the series, in the novels, the overwhelming majority of characters is white. The few African-American characters do not have a voice at all; even Tara, supposedly Sookie's best friend, is barely involved in any dialogue. Tara's homosexual brother, Lafayette, one of the main characters in the series, hardly utters a single word in volume 1 and is killed right at the beginning of volume 2. Both African-American characters, which are round and dynamic in the TV series, are at best flat and static in the novels. Lafayette's homosexual partner, Jesus, does not even exist in the novel. Accordingly, the entire homosexuality sub-plot of the series is not present in the novel. What is more, many of the few non-white characters are villains. Longshadow, a Native American vampire, secretly steals from Eric. In an internal tribunal, Sookie questions several human employees of Fangtasia: "'Which one from here?' I asked suddenly, and then I had the name" (*Dead* 204). Longshadow tries to kill Sookie before she can reveal his identity, but Bill interferes and kills him first. Chow is introduced as "the first Asian vampire I'd seen." The first thing Sookie notices about him are the "intricate tattoos that I'd heard members of the Yakuza favored. Whether Chow had been a gangster when he was human or not, he certainly was sinister now" (*Living* 41). Finally, the novels celebrate traditional community values of the American South, such as hospitality and solidarity, when Jason goes missing and a search party of volunteers gathers at his house: "Catfish told me he'd gotten together as many men as he could, and Kevin Pryor had agreed to be the coordinator, though off-duty. Maxine Fortenberry and her churchwomen were bringing out coffee and doughnuts from the Bon Temps Bakery. I began crying, because this was just overwhelming" (195). Sookie sums it up: "people like to help in our small town" (196). This sense of community, however, only includes the white citizens of Bon Temps and leaves out those of mixed racial ancestry.

Hence, as opposed to the idyll of the WASP community in Forks, Bon Temps is far from the American pastoral Nicole Rabin and Joseph J. Foy want it to be—both in the TV series and in the novels. On the contrary, racial, sexual, and ideological tensions between the different characters are omnipresent. Since most characters are—at least to some degree—representative of a certain (sub-) culture, the evaluation of these characters within the series is ideologically significant. Yet, unlike in *Twilight*, there is not one single character that is either continually "good" or "bad." Thus, the evaluation of the characters and the respective (sub)cultures is far from consistent and, accordingly, the levels of identification between the characters and the audience vary constantly, too. Through the symbolic ideological significance of these characters, several boundaries are consciously blurred. Traditional hierarchical models of class, race, and gender are undermined in *True Blood*, while they are left largely intact in *Twilight*. Therefore, *True Blood*'s points of pertinence with representatives from different social backgrounds are far more pronounced, which accounts for the far more heterogeneous viewership of the series, while *Twilight* mainly relies on characters and storylines that are derived from romances which traditionally attract an overwhelmingly female audience.

Notes

1. In his benchmark *The Fantastic*, Tzvetan Todorov defines "the concept of the fantastic" as "that hesitation experienced by a person who knows only the laws of nature, confronting an apparently supernatural event" (25). As such, it is a structural element characteristic of cultural texts from a wide variety of literary and filmic genres. In Farah Mendlesohn's definition, "fantasy," in contrast, is "defined by the way in which the fantastic enters the text and the rhetorical voices which are required to construct the different types of [supernatural] worlds which emerge" (2). Quintessentially then, fantasy literature is all about the construction of alternative worlds peopled by supernatural beings.

2. At $1,119,929,521, *The Return of the King* ranks 6th in the list of the highest-grossing films of all times, *The Two Towers* ranks 21st with $926,047,111, and *The Fellowship of the Ring* 31st with $871,530,324 (see "Worldwide Grosses"). In these sales figures, the revenues from the original theatrical exhibition are considered, the multiple re-releases of the films are not taken into account.

3. Even though there are no official sales figures available, *Wikipedia* lists the *Twilight* series among the best-selling book series of all times, with each individual volume selling more than 10 million copies (see "List of Best-Selling Films"). This makes *Twilight* the third best-selling novel series of all time in copies sold per volume.

4. Even 12.4 million watched the second season on average (see Seidman).

5. Fiske also labels popular culture a culture of the oppressed, a "bottom-up"-culture (*Understanding* 20); nevertheless, popular texts—due to their openness—always include the possibility to "decode it dominantly" (44), i.e., as an advocate of the dominant ideology.

6. Rosalie, for example, is gang-raped by her newly rich fiancé and his upper-class friends: "They seemed to enjoy that—the sound of my pain... [...]. They left me in the street, still laughing as they stumbled away. They thought I was dead" (*Eclipse*, 143). Carlisle Cullen, the head of the Cullen family, a clan of vampires that settled down in Forks, Washington State, finds her in the street and brings her over. Jasper, in turn, has only recently become a vegetarian so that "the scent of human blood was much harder for him to resist than the others—he hadn't been trying as long"—and thus he has to be kept back by Emmett when Bella bleeds so that he does not violate her (*Twilight* 446).

7. Bella relates that Laurent simply could not live as a vegetarian—it was against his nature: "he'd had no compunctions, at the time, against making a meal of me. Of course, he must have changed, because he'd gone to Alaska to live with the other civilized coven there, the other family that refused to drink human blood for ethical reasons" (*New* 208). As it turns out, such a change is not possible, and Laurent follows his natural instincts rather than obeying to the rules of the so-called civilized vampire world that looks down upon drinking human blood in order to satisfy one's appetites as uncivilized.

8. Jacob is the candidate Bella's father Charlie prefers. Jacob, a werewolf, is the son of Billy, one of Charlie's closest friends, and, as a boy, "used to go fishing with us during summer" (*Twilight* 6).

9. On a symbolic level, this may well be considered a synecdoche for the ideological orientation of the novel.

10. When a vampire threatens to reveal the secret, "the Volturi step in before it can compro-

mise them, or the rest of us" (*New* 379). In the past, they killed all humans who had come to know of the existence of vampires and, prophylactically, "the immortal children," i.e., humans that were turned when they were still kids, as children cannot keep secrets very well (*Breaking* 34). This is a rather conservative take on the relationship between humans and vampires which constitutes one of the major differences in comparison with *True Blood*: In *True Blood* as well as in the respective Sookie Stackhouse novels by Charlaine Harris, the vampire community has "c[o]me out of the coffin (as they laughingly put it)" (*Dead* 1), i.e., vampires have made their existence public. The human reactions to this have varied from country to country: "The vampires in the predominantly Islamic nations had fared the worst. [...] Some nations—France, Italy, and Germany were the most notable—refused to accept vampires as equal citizens. Many—like Bosnia, Argentina, and most of the African nations—denied any status to the vampires and declared them fair game for any bounty hunter. But America, England, Mexico, Canada, Japan, Switzerland, and the Scandinavian countries adopted a more tolerant attitude" (*Club* 6). Notably, the countries belonging to "Old Europe," Africa, Southern America, and, of course, Islamic countries, are portrayed in a not too favorable light whereas the North American countries are described as liberal.

11. George A. Dunn and Rebecca Housel's *True Blood and Philosophy* comprises essays on the vampire assimilation into the human quotidian, the legal dimension of the social contract between vampires and humans, the nature of vampire life, the feminist dimension of the series, and the respective commodification of humans and vampires.

12. In this article, I refer to cultural texts in the Fiskian sense of "cultural commodities or texts" (2) as defined in his benchmark *Reading the Popular*.

13. Since this article is mainly concerned with the TV series *True Blood*, the respective quotes from the Sookie Stackhouse novels are only provided as footnotes wherever they exist; after all, *True Blood* is a rather loose adaptation of the original novels. Both these variants on traditional elements from cultural texts belonging to the genre of the vampire gothic are not part of the novel series by Charlaine Harris.

14. In the novels, the Fellowship does not send a suicide bomber but a group of snipers who shoot at the vampires and retreat again. Sookie, however, senses the danger and warns the vampires, who immediately throw themselves on the ground so that, "when the Fellowship opened fire, it was the humans that died" (*Living* 210). The use of suicide bombers in the TV series alludes to similar acts of terrorism committed by Muslim extremists. Interestingly enough, in *True Blood*, it is not an anonymous foreign terror group that employs this strategy in order to kill American soldiers who, thus the perception in certain conservative circles in the U.S., only try to liberate a particular foreign country and spread democracy, but the self-proclaimed defenders of everything that is Christian and American in the homeland.

15. These tendencies are obvious both in the novels and in the TV series. The torture of Bill is much more explicit in the screen adaptation, but it is also alluded to in the novels. Moreover, some fangbangers, i.e., groupies who adore vampires and want to have sex with them, often show sado-masochistic tendencies. Dawn, for example, "like[s] pain" (*Dead* 107) and Ginger calls Eric her "master" (*Dead* 203).

16. The literary strategy of bringing repressed fears to the surface is a trait that is typical of the Southern gothic. In William Faulkner's *As I Lay Dying*, for example, a dead body is driven all over Alabama in broad daylight.

17. In *Adaptation in Contemporary Culture*, Rachel Carroll argues that the fidelity question with regard to movie adaptations of novels is an illegitimate question since any adaptation is always an interpretation in the first place, and "textual infidelity" is therefore inevitable (1).

18. Again, this reference is not taken from the novels, which shows that the analogy of vampires and homosexuals that is very prominent in the TV series is only latent in the novels.

19. In *Club Dead*, Talbot is merely introduced as Russell's "special friend" (160), "a man in love, and furthermore, [...] addicted to vampiric sex" (163). The various homosexual encounters between Russell, Talbot, and a number of other characters are not mentioned in the novels at all.

20. In *Dead Reckoning*, "Vic's Redneck Roadhouse" is introduced as a competitor of "Merlotte's" that organizes "[p]opular crap" such as "wet T-shirt contests, beer pong tournaments, and a promotion called 'Bring in a Bubba Night'" (5).

21. Lafayette is only a minor character in the novels, which is another indicator for the relatively low significance they assign to homosexuality. As a matter of fact, Lafayette hardly utters a single sentence and dies at the very beginning of *Living Dead in Dallas*. Homosexual activities are only mentioned as a natural part of the vampires' sex lives, but hardly any human character is a homosexual. Even the homosexual relationships between vampires are in most cases likened to the homosexual or even pedophile practices in ancient Rome. After all, most of the relationships mentioned in the novels are between maker and child. Eric's maker Ocella, for example, entertains homosexual relationships with both his children. Tellingly, Ocella himself is Roman and, "[i]n Ocella's time, [...] men of a certain station were free to indulge themselves with very little guilt or question" (*Family* 257).

22. This dialogue, too, is not included in the novels. Just like homosexuality, racism and civil rights are not too much in the focus of the novels. Here, Arlene is introduced as a good friend of Sookie's and only later becomes a member of the Fellowship of the Sun. Sookie comments on this change: "My weak-minded ex-friend had fallen hook, line, and sinker for the pseudo religion that the FotS propagated" (*From* 111).

23. In the novels, Bill was turned *after* the Civil War, not as a first lieutenant returning from the battle fields and seeking shelter at Lorena's remote mansion. In *Dead in the Family*, Bill's sister Judith relates that "Lorena saw Bill and his family through the windows of their house. [...] She fell in love. [...] [S]he waited until he came out in the middle of the night to find out why the dog wouldn't stop barking" (266).

24. In the novels, the Ku Klux Klan is not mentioned at all and there is no burning cross in Sookie's yard.

25. The vampire rapist is a reference to "the black rapist," a recurring image in American culture that features in various novels. In Ralph Ellison's *Invisible Man*, for example, Sybil gives this image yet another facet when she uses the nameless protagonist "to satisfy her masochistic desires inspired by [this] stereotype," as I have argued elsewhere (Knirsch 207).

26. As mentioned above, this dimension is almost entirely excluded from the novels.

27. Vermont was not only the first state to introduce so-called civil unions for partners of the same sex, but also one of only ten states that have never enacted anti-miscegenation laws which prohibited racial intermarriage, primarily between former African-American slaves and white Americans, in large parts of the U.S. well into the 20th century.

28. In the novels, "TrueBlood" is only introduced in *Club Dead* as "the front-runner among competing blood replacements" (15). Moreover, it is spelled differently. In the TV series, it is the only brand of artificial human blood.

29. The vampire way of life traditionally leads to "Unfortunate Incidents," "the vampire euphemism for the bloody slaying of a human" (*Dead* 5).

30. Nan Flanagan does not feature as a character in the novels. Accordingly, vampire politics are not very prominent in them, especially when it comes to the public relations efforts of the different vampire bodies.

31. Tellingly, vampires even have to be invited before they can enter a house inhabited by humans. Of course, this also applies to the role model for the vampires in most cultural texts today, Count Dracula. Yet, Count Dracula's "roots are in Eastern Europe—Slavic, Catholic, peasant, and superstitious," as Kathleen L. Spencer points out (318). Thus, Dracula represents the cultural Other whereas Billybob is a stereotypical representative of the South.

32. In both the novels and the TV series, Bill is ordered to get in touch with Sookie and secure her supernatural powers for the vampiric cause. "She ordered me to return to my human home, to put myself in your way, to seduce you if I had to... [...] She wanted your gift harnessed for her own use" (*Definitely*, 184; S3E12).

33. Maryann is introduced as a helpful social worker, but turns out to be a semi-goddess who practices Bacchian rites and even sacrifices humans to her God. Both in the novels and in the TV series, a maenad hypnotizes Eggs who, in a state of trance, kills several people without even knowing it. In the novels, the maenad, Callisto, escapes in the end. In *True Blood*, Sam disguises himself as "the horned God" who has descended to Earth to honor his disciple and thus tricks Maryann into self-sacrifice (S2E12).

34. The spectacular supernatural refers to a mode of gothic fiction that describes the supernatural phenomena it depicts in a very spectacular, exaggerated manner—nevertheless, in the logic of these gothic texts themselves, there is "not even a shade of hesitation regarding the truth status of the phenomenon" (Clery 25).

35. Both in the novels and the series, Bill kills Sookie's great-uncle, a "funny uncle [...] who molests his... the children in the family" (*Dead* 158). In the novel, Sookie gives her inheritance to "the local mental health center, earmarking it for the treatment of children who were victims of molestation and rape" (169). In the series, she gives it to Jason who uses it to pay for his membership fees at the Fellowship.

36. Lettie Mae's argumentation is inspired by the Christian belief in unshakeable faith as one of the fundamental values of Christianity: "The good Lord tested our faith by taking Miss Jeanette away from us. I stayed true. I wish I could say the same about you" (S2E01, 0:14:06). Like the explicit references to slavery and the civil rights movement, this latent criticism of ordinary Christianity is not quite as strong in the novels. Only in *Dead in the Family*, the church in Bon Temps is mentioned for the first time. Sookie goes to church in order to display her new "earrings" (277), while Sam goes to mass for micropolitical reasons after the shifters revealed their existence to the world and certain conservative circles repelled them (278).

37. See endnote 14.

38. He eventually explains that his mother was raped and that that's why he considers himself fatherless, but the initial allusion still stands.

39. In this particular case, one might even argue that HBO series form a genre unto themselves.

40. In this article, the focus is on volumes 1 to 10.

WORKS CITED

Adalian, Josef. "More Boys Watch *Girls* than Girls." *Vulture*. 14 June 2012. Web. 4 Oct. 2012.
Barthes, Roland. *S/Z*. Trans. Richard Miller. New York: Hill and Wang, 1974. Print.
Blayde, Ariadne, and George A. Dunn. "Pets, Cattle, and Higher Life Forms in *True Blood*." *True Blood and Philosophy*. Eds. George A. Dunn and Rebecca Housel. New York: Routledge, 2010. 33–48. Print.
Cardwell, Sarah. "Literature on the Small Screen: Television Adaptations." *Film and Literature: An Introduction and Reader*. 2nd ed. Ed. Timothy Corrigan. London: Routledge, 2012. 168–78. Print.
Carroll, Rachel. "Introduction: Textual Infidelities." *Adaptation in Contemporary Culture: Textual Infidelities*. London: Continuum, 2009. 1–7. Print.
Carter, Craig. "The Conservative Worldview of *The Lord of the Rings*." *The Politics of the Cross Resurrected*. 15 Mar. 2010. Web. 11 Sept. 2012.
Clery, E.J. *The Rise of Supernatural Fiction, 1762–1800*. Cambridge: Cambridge University Press, 1995. Print.
Craton, Lillian E., and Kathryn E. Jonell. "'I Am Sookie, Hear Me Roar!': Sookie Stackhouse and Feminist Ambivalence." *True Blood and Philosophy*. Eds. George A. Dunn and Rebecca Housel. New York: Routledge, 2010. 109–21. Print.
Dunn, George A., and Rebecca Housel. "Introduction: 'If a Tree Falls in the Woods, It's Still a Tree—Ain't It?'" *True Blood and Philosophy*. Eds. George A. Dunn and Rebecca Housel. New York: Routledge, 2010. 1–4. Print.
Fiske, John. *Reading the Popular*. Boston: Unwin Hyman, 1989. Print.
_____. *Understanding Popular Culture*. Boston: Unwin Hyman, 1989. Print.
Foy, Joseph J. "Signed in Blood: Rights and the Vampire-Human Social Contract." *True Blood and Philosophy*. Eds. George A. Dunn and Rebecca Housel. New York: Routledge, 2010. 51–64. Print.

Grossberg, Lawrence. "Zur Verortung der Populärkultur." Trans. Bettina Suppelt. *Cultural Studies: Grundlagentexte zur Einführung*. Eds. Roger Bromley, Udo Göttlich, and Carsten Winter. Lüneburg: Zu Klampen, 1999. 215–36. Print.

Guins, Raiford and Omayra Zaragoza Cruz. "Introduction." *Popular Culture: A Reader*. Ed. Raiford Guins and Omayra Zaragoza Cruz. London: Sage, 2005. 1–18. Print.

Harris, Charlaine. *Club Dead*. A Sookie Stackhouse Novel. Vol. 3. New York: Ace, 2003. Print.

_____. *Dead in the Family* A Sookie Stackhouse Novel. Vol. 10. New York: Ace, 2010. Print.

_____. *Dead Reckoning*. A Sookie Stackhouse Novel. Vol. 11. New York: Ace, 2011. Print.

_____. *Dead Until Dark*. A Sookie Stackhouse Novel. Vol. 1. New York: Ace, 2001. Print.

_____. *Definitely Dead*. A Sookie Stackhouse Novel. Vol. 6. New York: Ace, 2006. Print.

_____. *From Dead to Worse*. A Sookie Stackhouse Novel. Vol. 4. New York: Ace, 2004. Print.

_____. *Living Dead in Dallas*. A Sookie Stackhouse Novel. Vol. 2. New York: Ace, 2002. Print.

Knirsch, Christian. "Piercing the Veil: Visuality and Epistemology in American Modernist Fiction." *Folia Linguistica et Literaria* 5 (2012): 199–212. Print.

"List of Best-Selling Films." *Wikipedia*. 4 Oct. 2012. Web. 4 Oct. 2012.

Mendlesohn, Farah, and Edward James. "Introduction." *The Cambridge Companion to Fantasy Literature*. Eds. Edward James and Farah Mendlesohn. Cambridge: Cambridge University Press, 2012. 1–4. Print.

Meyer, Stephenie. *Breaking Dawn*. Twilight Series. Vol. 4. London: Atom, 2008. Print.

_____. *Eclipse*. Twilight Series. Vol. 3. London: Atom, 2008. Print.

_____. *New Moon*. Twilight Series. Vol. 2. London: Atom, 2007. Print.

_____. *Twilight*. Twilight Series. Vol. 1. London: Atom, 2007. Print.

Rabin, Nicole. "*True Blood*: The Vampire as a Multi-Racial Critique on Post-Race Ideology." *Journal of Dracula Studies* 12 (2010): n. pag. Print.

Seidman, Robert. "True Blood Averages 12.4 Million per Episode across Platforms in Second Season." *TV by the Numbers*. 19 Sept. 2009. Web. 30 Jan. 2013.

Silver, Anna. "Twilight is Not Good for Maidens: Gender, Sexuality, and the Family in Stephenie Meyer's *Twilight* Series." *Studies in the Novel* 42.1–2 (2010): 121–38. Print.

Spencer, Kathleen L. "Purity and Danger: Dracula, the Urban Gothic, and the Late Victorian Degeneracy Crisis." 1992. *Gothic: Critical Concepts in Literary and Cultural Studies*. Vol. 3: *Nineteenth-Century Gothic: At Home with the Vampire*. Eds. Fred Botting and Dale Townshend. London: Routledge, 2004. 304–30. Print.

Todorov, Tzvetan. *The Fantastic: A Structural Approach to a Literary Genre*. Trans. Richard Howard. Ithaca, NY: Cornell University Press, 1974. Print.

True Blood. The Complete First Season. Dir. Alan Ball. HBO, 2009. DVD.

True Blood. The Complete Second Season. Dir. Alan Ball. HBO, 2010. DVD.

True Blood. The Complete Third Season. Dir. Alan Ball. HBO, 2011. DVD.

Twilight. Dir. Catherine Hardwicke. Perf. Kristen Stewart, Robert Pattinson. Summit, 2008. Film.

The Twilight Saga: Breaking Dawn—Part 1. Dir. Bill Condon. Perf. Kristen Stewart, Robert Pattinson. Summit, 2011. Film.

The Twilight Saga: Breaking Dawn—Part 2. Dir. Bill Condon. Perf. Kristen Stewart, Robert Pattinson. Summit, 2012. Film.

The Twilight Saga: Eclipse. Dir. David Slade. Perf. Kristen Stewart, Robert Pattinson. Summit, 2010. Film.

"Worldwide Grosses." *Box Office Mojo*. 14 Jan. 2013. Web. 17 Jan. 2013.

From Hyper-Male Aardvarks to the Female Void: Gender Politics in *Cerebus*

Sebastian Domsch

This paper looks at gender politics in the graphic novel *Cerebus* over the course of its long run in relation to the traditions of fantastic storytelling out of which it developed.[1] Dave Sim's mammoth graphic novel series *Cerebus*, published serially between 1977 and 2004, offers one of the most complex and fascinating creations of a fantastic world. The world of *Cerebus* contains a complicated political geography complete with its own party factions, religious sects, theological debates and mythology. The complexity of this world is all the more astounding since it developed out of little more than a satiric spoof of sword-and-sorcery tales like *Conan* or *Red Sonja*. In order to better understand the significance of *Cerebus* as a graphic novel and as a piece of fantastic world-building, we will briefly look into the medial conditions of its origins, its peculiar development throughout the course of its creation, and finally the story that it is telling.

Cerebus initially grew out of two kinds of discontent: the first was a discontent with the stereotyped fantasy narratives of the so-called sword-and-sorcery genre that were most prominent in Marvel's series of comic books *Conan the Barbarian*, based on Robert E. Howard's character from the 1930s. The second was dissatisfaction with the dominance, the virtual monopoly, of the two major publishing houses for comics, DC and Marvel, in the American comics market. Inspired by the counter-culture, the late 1960s and early 1970s saw the rise of independent or "underground comix" that were published by tiny and short-lived publishers, or even self-published. Robert Crumb famously sold the issues of his first comics magazine out of a carriage that he walked up and down

Haight-Ashbury. Very far away from this center of underground comix, in the Canadian town of Kitchener, Ontario, the young and completely unknown artist Dave Sim decided in 1977 to self-publish a series of comic books containing a parody of *Conan* comics. The central joke was to be that instead of a hyper-masculine 7-foot mountain of muscle, the role of the invincible mercenary warrior would be filled by a 5-foot aardvark with grey fur that smelled evil when it got wet. The aardvark was called Cerebus.

Judging from the extremely high number of very short-lived independent comic books, it would already have been considered a success if a book like *Cerebus* had made it beyond issue 3. But Sim kept the issues coming with great regularity, while constantly improving his art as well as the scope of his satire and narrative, until it became the longest comics series created by an individual artist. Already in issue 12, Sim wrote in an editorial that he hoped to write 156 issues; in issue 19, after he moved from bi-monthly to monthly publication, this number was expanded to 300. Such a length was completely unprecedented in independent publishing, but Sim, joined by Gerhard as background artist from issue 65 onwards, managed to fulfill his promise in 2004 after more than 6,000 pages.

The peculiar nature of *Cerebus* in its entirety has a lot to do with the conditions of its creation. The two main aspects in this regard are the fact that Sim used the format of the serialized comic book *and* that he managed, as a single and independent creator, to maintain this series for such a long time while working towards a definitive end. Choosing to self-publish, Sim had no alternative to using the format that had for the longest time created the artistic stalemate he was so disappointed with in the first place. But it was this compromise that turned out to be the condition for his artistic success. The serialization of comics, when used by a profit-oriented company employing multiple authors, none of whom owned their own copyrights, had for decades limited the artistic growth of comics. But in the hands of an individual self-publishing artist, this very serialization became the mode of publishing that made the "Cerebus effect" possible. This effect describes the phenomenon that a serially published artwork vastly transcends its original ambition, reaching a complexity and depth that could not have been expected from its beginning.[2]

As to what happens in *Cerebus*, one can obviously give only the briefest of overviews of the many and intricate plotlines, or rather of the different types of plot. In the first 25 issues, Cerebus the character as well as *Cerebus* the publication fulfill the stereotype of barbarian mercenary stories in a sword-and-sorcery setting, with the main character constantly looking for riches but never getting anywhere. Every issue is a self-contained story in which Cerebus acquires something (mostly gold) and then inevitably loses it. The issues 25–50 introduce the first continuous long story arc: Cerebus comes to a wealthy city-state and gets involved in its politics. The narrative becomes a political satire, as Cerebus incongruously is elected as prime minister, finally launching a war and losing everything again. Issues 52–111 contain the even longer story arc "Church & State," in which Cerebus becomes pope and starts a reign of terror. The narrative again takes on a bigger scope as it turns out that Cerebus is also inextricably tied to his world's mythology. He makes an "ascension" and talks to the god-like character of the "Judge" about his significance in the universe. The Judge also makes a prophecy that Cerebus will finally die "alone, unmourned, and unloved" (issue 111, page 12, and echoed throughout the series). Most readers consider this to be the high point of achievement for the series.

After this cosmological widening of the scope, the story collapses to the microcosm of the personal, concentrating for a while on two other characters, before widening again in the "Mothers and Daughters" story arc (50 issues). The world is now ruled by a sect of "Cirinists" (militant feminists) and the story recounts a power struggle that is as much political as it is mythological, with the mythology being largely related to gender aspects. There is a second "ascension," and the narrative turns increasingly metafictional. The story collapses again (20 issues take place in a single barroom), then shows Cerebus as he tries to go home, and finally, many years later, as an old man. Theology becomes ever more important, as Cerebus dictates an elaborate and highly idiosyncratic exegesis of the Torah, which is included verbatim in the comic. In the end, he dies just as prophesied.

But this ever-growing world that Dave Sim created in 300 issues is not only a fascinating and complex example of fantastic storytelling, it is also experienced by most readers as highly problematic, particularly because of its theory of gender relations, a topic that has been addressed only rarely in *Cerebus* scholarship so far (see Mayeux 175). Indeed, as one reader writes: "Until Sim can confess that he is the working definition of a misogynist, I will never buy another comic written or illustrated by Dave Sim or acknowledge Dave Sim in any way ever again" (Champion). Especially the second half of the series is marked by the predominance of what critics regularly see as the author's own misogyny, most notoriously in the essays he attached to issues 186 and 265. Indeed, the story itself uses its fantastic framework to embody the struggle between the "creative male light" and the "emotional female void" as fixed elements of its storyworld. The following paragraphs will give an overview of the gender aspects in *Cerebus*, from its conception as a parody of hyper-masculinity to its gender politics proper.

The origin of the series in a critical comment on the hyper-male tradition of both the sword-and-sorcery genre and the visual modes of fantasy comics has to be noted first. The blueprint for *Cerebus*' initial parody is the hyper-masculine world of the fictional character Conan, originally created by writer Robert E. Howard in 1932, and particularly in its manifestation as the comic series *Conan the Barbarian* that started its very successful run in 1970. In all of its adaptations, the figure of Conan has become the exemplary case of a hyper-masculine body, the epitome of a masculinity that is grounded on physical strength and violence. As has already been mentioned, the constant substitution of this towering, bulgingly muscular body with the small, furry body of a grumpy aardvark provided the main parodic thrust of the early issues. Cerebus talks and acts like an invincible barbarian warrior, but—so the visual presentation of the comic constantly reminds us—he does not look the part at all.

This gender-focused parody is widened further with the introduction, already in issue 3, of the character Red Sophia, a parody of the Red Sonja character from the *Conan* comics. This original character would be certainly worth its own paper when it comes to gender politics, mixing the physical traits of a hyper-feminine *and* hyper-masculine body with a backstory of both rape and a Brünhild-like story regarding the connection between her abilities as a warrior and virginity. After being raped, Sonja is mystically granted her superior powers as warrior, provided she does not have sex with a man, unless he beats her in combat. *Cerebus'* Red Sophia is modeled in all respects very closely on Red Sonja, and is used again as a riff on incongruence: Cerebus fights with her and defeats her, but then he constantly rejects her sexual advances, apparently oblivious to the erotic "charms" of this character that have made her the archetype of this kind of male fantasy within fantasy. Indeed, *Cerebus* directly makes fun of the ridiculousness of dressing (or rather undressing) this female warrior in nothing but underwear made from chain mail.

Like with most other characters, as *Cerebus* changes in tone, her use for parody is also extended. When in issue 57, Cerebus wakes up with a hangover only to find out that he is now married to Red Sophia, the character also becomes more rounded and the humor is shifted towards poking fun at normal marital relationships. Still later, the straightforward parodic treatment of gender through the little grey aardvark is further complicated when, in issue 179, it is revealed that Cerebus is a hermaphrodite. By that point, the narrative has long since moved far away from being dependent on a single parodic foil, exploring aspects of gender in multiple ways, and using Cerebus as an unstable, shifting signifier in the games that the narrative plays with questions of gender.[3]

In the world of *Cerebus*, gender *is* indeed politics—since all the religious sects in the storyworld who compete for political power base their faith on questions of gender. In fact, the two main factions, the Cirinists and the Kevilists, are easily recognizable as satiric versions of historical waves of feminism. The Cirinists started out as knitting circles and soon turned into a paramilitary organization, growing increasingly militant and fascist in their views and methods, finally installing a forced matriarchy that seems to derive straight out of an anti-feminist's paranoia. While the women, who completely conceal their bodies and faces behind chador-like robes, work, men are allowed to linger and drink in taverns, where violence is accepted. Any kind of domestic violence, on the other hand, is punishable by a swift execution through a specially trained force of female assassins. The Kevillists mirror the Cirinists' philosophy, but would prefer power in the hands of daughters instead of mothers. Among their self-proclaimed aims are state-owned prostitution, pharmaceutically-assisted miscarriages, ownership of men, guaranteed minimum incomes for women over the age of fifteen and the inalienable right to self-determination within those parameters.

Even more fundamentally, the main theology of *Cerebus*' storyworld—as it is explained by Sim and incorporated into the narrative—involves the interaction between two principles, the "light" and the "void," that are tied to gender, though interestingly enough, the attribution varies from the beginning of the series to its end. In issue 110, the Judge describes the "void" as male and the "light" as female (issue 110, pages 9 and 15) while later this is reversed, when "Victor Davis" talks about "The Male Light and the Female Void: Seminal Energy and Omnivorous Parasite" (issue 186, page 12). In this later reading, "female" is further identified with emotion, "male" with reason and thought. These ideas are most notoriously propounded in a prose narrative that Sim attached to issue 186 of Cerebus, in which his persona Victor Davis speaks, saying things like: "Behind this [...] lies the Greater Void, the Omnivorous Engine which drives every [...] institutionalized waste of human time and energy, which drives, in point of fact, our entire degraded society. The wife and kids" (issue 186, page 11).

As has been seen earlier, *Cerebus* is clearly a fantastic narrative, but at the same time it as clearly implies that it wants to be read in reference to the actual world, as a reflection of questions pertaining to the actual world, in our case with reference to gender relations. That such a thing is no contradiction is obviously one of the basic assumptions underlying this whole volume, but a closer look will show how Dave Sim navigates the boundaries between the fantastic and the referential narrative modes in unique ways that mean that his own politics of the fantastic remain a problem with regard to finding the appropriate readerly strategy. When it comes to these boundaries, there are two interrelated movements discernible in his work, especially over the long course of its creation. The first is one that moves from the fantastic towards the realistic, and the other from the realistic to the metafictional. Both movements have in common a parodic intent, which in the first case leads to the inclusion of outward references, and in the second to a heightening of self-referentiality.

From the outset, *Cerebus* was both a work of fantasy and a parody of fantasy. Generally speaking, parody further removes the text from a reference to reality—and therefore realistic modes of presentation and reference—because it increases a text's self-referentiality. This was certainly true for the earlier issues of *Cerebus*, where the humor would only fully work for those readers who were aware of the parodied material. And this is still the basis for the work's later and highly metafictional engagement with its own medial status through the inclusion of "Ersatz" comics, called "reads," into the fictional world of *Cerebus*. But the satirical intent of parody also allowed Sim to seamlessly enlarge his humor to real-world concerns, to sneak his way back towards realism. This can be seen in a number of developments.

One of these is a shift in the targets of parody, from characters and stereotypes of sword-and-sorcery comics and books as well as superhero comics to parodies of authors and other real-life figures, such as Ernest Hemingway and Margaret Thatcher. Another development was the shift in subject matter and narrative organization from picaresque adventure to political intrigue, mythological-theological struggle, and finally the interiority of realist psychological narrative. While the earlier form mimicked and parodied the type of repetitive and largely inconsequential stories that came out of endless serialization, the move towards the fictional world-building of high fantasy in combination with satirical reference to the real world (as opposed to exclusively emphasizing the alterity of the fantastic fictional world) lent itself to a more referential engagement with reality.

This was accompanied and helped by changes in the more technical aspects of Sim's narration, such as the gradual lengthening of the story arches, first beyond a single issue, then across a run of 25 and 50 issues, and finally in the attempt to bind all of the proposed 300 issues into one coherent frame. Also noteworthy is a shift in the temporal contextualization of the narrative, from the early pre-historic (and therefore a-historic) setting reminiscent of the *Conan* storyworld to the later creation of a historical and political landscape, and even changes in the visual conception of the comic, such as the growing importance of backgrounds (notably with the introduction of Gerhard as background artist). Through the often elaborate backgrounds, Cerebus and his story became much more concretely localized.

But while *Cerebus* connects its storyworld and narrative mode in numerous ways to the actual world, establishing indirect, metaphorical, as well as direct references that lead from the fantastic world to the actual world, there is also a narrative counter trend that highlights not the referential but the artificial, self-referential qualities of the artwork. It is for example important to note that the different opinions offered in *Cerebus* are not given through a single, unified and authoritative voice, but through a number of voices conflicted over narrative levels as well as time. We will now look at the way in which these voices develop, and how they might be seen to relate to fantastic storytelling and world-building. For a better understanding of what happens when we read a text like *Cerebus*, we might want to look at the different kinds of discourses that it uses, and the claims that their respective statements make and which we could differentiate into factual discourse, fictional discourse, religious discourse, and fantastic discourse.

In factual discourse, statements refer to existents in the real or actual world and attempt to do so in a "truthful" way. Of course, in factual discourse statements can also be deceitful, misleading or serve any number of purposes, but the assumption here is that we are dealing with the intention of truthfully making a statement. Ideally, the speaker is aware of the limitations to the truth claims of his statement, such as the impossibility to know something for certain or the unbridgeable gap between sign and referent. In fictional discourse, statements refer to existents in a fictional world, that is, they are based on an agreement to temporarily accept something as true, or to pretend that something is true, even though it is not. This also means that there is no limitation to the truth claim of a statement, precisely because it does not refer to anything outside itself, but only to itself. In contrast to this, what I call here religious discourse is one that basically claims that its statements are absolutely true *while* referring to the actual world. That is, they claim to directly express a truth about the actual world.

Now, fantastic discourse is of course part of fictional discourse, and it can indeed be seen as the epitome of make-believe, of willfully creating the impossible, or at least the very highly improbable. This gives the creator of a fantastic world an absolute control over his creation that transcends the self-imposed limits of the "realist" creator. But not only is the creator not bound by reference to actual-world analogy or even probability, he can also include—as part of his fictional statements—statements about the storyworld that can cross over into religious discourse (often implicitly acknowledged in declarations such as "the world of × has its own mythology"). This makes for statements with an interesting referential status. Consider the famous "Fear is the path to the dark side," made by the wise character of Yoda in the second *Star Wars* movie. Does this relate only to the fictional and fantastic world, where the "dark side" is an actual reality? Is it a referential metaphor to the actual world, where fear exists, but the "dark side" is merely a concept, maybe another term for "ethically unacceptable attitude?" Or does it imply that the reality claimed (fictionally) for the "dark side" as an actually existing force has to be seen as a direct statement about the actual world, in the sense that we should accept that the "dark side" exists just as tangibly in our actual world?

Cerebus is interesting in this regard, because it constantly negotiates this line between (fictional) fantasy and (truth-claiming) theology in compelling, if problematic, ways. Through its beginning as a fantasy parody, it clearly partakes of and in fantastic discourse; it contains a completely fictional landscape that includes non-real elements like wizardry. As it gains in complexity, it increases both its realist references and its fantastic mode by widening the scope of its (fictional) mythology. It introduces theology as an intradiegetic discourse (characters within the fiction debating fictional theologies)—but these are at the same time recognizable as real-world social debates about feminism. And it embodies at least some of the theology as an extradiegetically guaranteed fact for the storyworld, in that something like the ascension does really happen, and the Judge does exist. Towards the end of the series, even the actual formation of the universe is depicted.

At the same time, the narrative turns increasingly metafictional, including self-parody, self-reflexivity, and a proliferation of "authorial voices." Thus, the storyworld has its own version of comics, called "reads," which become the focus of a sub-plot, or rather sub-section of the comic. Issue 175 introduces an author of such "reads," Victor Reid (note the homonym), as well as his (highly misogynist) alter ego Rotsieve. Rotsieve was allegedly inspired by Sim's experience of himself when drunk. Paradoxically, Reid does not appear in the comic itself (though he is part of *Cerebus*'s storyworld), but in a prose narrative that Sim published in serial parts alongside the comic narrative, until issue 180. The comic's narrative in issue 181 then depicts a climactic moment in the world of Cerebus, a battle to the death with his main enemy, but in the middle of fierce and bloody fighting, the "camera" seems to zoom out of the panel and finally the page, turning it into a piece of paper on a drawing board, in front of which a person is recognizable only in silhouette. After that comes another series of prose texts that start with the words "Viktor Davis turned away from his drawing board" (issue 181, page 19). In a classic metaleptic break, Sim (whose first and middle names are David Victor) introduces yet another author persona. It is in the voice of this persona that Sim acknowledges that "[i]t wouldn't be that big of a stretch to categorize my writing as Hate Literature against women" (issue 186, page 21), so that here we have a fictional character who is and is not Dave Sim talking about how readers might and probably will (mis)construe what *Cerebus* is. And to further complicate matters, the comic also includes a character called "Dave," drawn to look like Dave Sim, who later talks to Cerebus in his head and wields a god-like power over his world.

But while the structure of the comic, with the author dissolving into a series of more or less distorted mirror-images, seems to imply the loss of authorial authority, the real author Dave Sim becomes ever more vocal with his (controversial) opinions and starts to blur the boundaries between author and narrator from without. All through its serialized run, individual issues were framed with editorial comments, letters to the author as well as the author's answers to these letters. These paratexts (in contrast for example to the Victor Reid narrative which happens within *Cerebus*' storyworld) are clearly presented to be read as direct expressions of the biographical subject Dave Sim, who in addition had long since become a famous—and increasingly notorious—public persona not only through his success, but through his vocal role as public activist for independent comics and creator's rights. Reading *Cerebus* while it appeared in serial form, it was impossible not to be aware that Sim was not simply a storyteller, but also someone who had a political agenda and therefore a political message. The problem of how to distinguish between the two "Sims" becomes most apparent when regarding the essays that Sim started to attach to his comic books. Concerned with Islam, Canadian politics and anti-feminism, these essays (or rather, protracted rants) on the one hand clearly seem to belong to the referential texts such as the editorials and the answers to letters. However, their outlandish nature and the playful structuring of voices makes such an attribution at least ambivalent.

And finally, beginning in December 1996, the author himself publicly turns to religion, in that he declares to have given up atheism and adopted his own idiosyncratic mix of all monotheistic religions, a creed that includes fasting, celibacy, and prayer. Consequently, he therefore starts to regard his discourse as theological in the sense that it speaks directly of truths about the world. This is the moment when Sim's own "dark force" (the existence of the male light and the female void) seems to turn from either a fictional construct or a metaphor to an alleged reality. But then, in keeping with its paradoxical nature, the move towards theology is reflected in the narrative as well. The collection "Latter Days" contains a number of sections (published over the course of almost a year) of exegesis of the Torah made by an aged Cerebus, called "Chasing YHWH." Though most readers tend to skip these overly long prose passages, Sim has stressed their importance for an understanding of *Cerebus* (see Sim, *Collected Letters* 4–6, and, for more, Komora). The last of the collections, "The Last Day," starts with Cerebus dreaming about a cosmology, an origin story of the world, with a series of bible-like text paragraphs together with rather abstract illustrations. This depiction is further annotated through footnotes made by an unnamed voice speaking in the first person. Now, who is making these serious comments about a religious account of the creation of the world that a character in a fantastic story dreams about? And whose world does the cosmology refer to?

Thus, Sim increasingly turns from the lightly playful, anything-goes mode of fantasy ("It's all made up, folks!") towards an expressive mode that claims to speak absolute truth, while at the same time fragmenting the narrative position of authority of his masterpiece-in-the-making in a postmodern polyphony, and continuing to undercut everything he does with the irony he employs for its actual telling. But what are we as readers to do with fantasy turned dogma?

There are different possible reading strategies for *Cerebus*, especially when considering the second half of the series. The seemingly easiest strategy we might call "naïve fantastic" (innocent fantastic would probably have less of a negative ring to it). Such a reading takes the fiction-agreement between author and reader and allows it to be applicable to aspects of the storyworld that are usually seen as bound to an actual-world-reference (such as the nature of men and women). But according to the rules of fantastic storytelling, the author creates worlds that can be different from ours in *every* respect, thus, what we get when we read *Cerebus* is simply "the world of *Cerebus*" in which all things that the narrative voice (or voices) claims as true are indeed true, even though we might not accept them as true in our world. The attitude would take a form similar to this: "This is a world in which all women *are* emotional and *do* kill off the creative spirit in males." Arguably, Sim managed to stretch his reader's willingness for this type of reading to the breaking point.

The next strategy in line we might call "naïve postmodern": according to this reading, it is *all* tongue-in-cheek; Sim is playing a big old game with us, making fun of his own opinions just as much as he is making fun of that of his opponents. Such a reading can point to the metafictional elements of the comic, but it must either ignore Sim's desperate attempts to break out of the role of authorial personas and to convince people of the rightness of his own positions, or see them as part of the elaborate play.

With somewhat more differentiation, one could try to arrive at a critical reading of the text, and again this can be divided into a "fantastic" and "postmodern" or ironic variant. The critical fantastic reading would posit that though a fantastic world, the world of *Cerebus* still reflects opinions about the actual world, and these opinions can and must be evaluated according to ethical and critical criteria. This attitude might lead a reader to the conclusion that Sim is a hateful right-wing misogynist, that his work reflects this and that therefore it is condemnable on moral grounds and should not be read.

The final reading strategy that is here suggested takes on a "critical postmodern" attitude: according to this reading, the work performs both the impossibility *and* the inevitability of reading a piece of art as expressive of things adhering to the real world. Such a reading claims that it is impossible to draw a clear line between statements made by the author and statements made by or through his artwork. Furthermore, in both cases, statements are not necessarily coherent throughout the whole artwork, but can and will be contradictory, especially considering the long gestation period of a work like *Cerebus* (without the possibility of retroactive editing of earlier parts). But at the same time, it is at least difficult and even counter-intuitive to ignore Sim-the-author's authorial intrusions into his artwork, especially through the serial reception, just as it is impossible to ignore the opinions, particularly about gender politics, expressed in numerous ways in *Cerebus*. Thus, we are aware of actual-world reference, but equally aware that this reference will never be unambiguous. This is a reading that acknowledges the existence of the author's intentions, but refuses to be restricted to them in the understanding of the artwork.

That we can maintain such a relativistic attitude towards "the meaning of *Cerebus*" while Sim-the-author with increasing frenzy points to himself and screams out at us "Listen to me! I know the truth and I will tell you!" lies in the very nature and structure of this truly epic narrative undertaking. *Cerebus* might just be the prime example for the impossibility of seeing an artwork as a single object with a unified meaning. Through its long run, readers were able to watch the growth of an artist's mind as well as its turn into possible madness, to experience shifts in narrative mode and style as well as constant reinterpretations of the narrative through the narrative itself. In addition to that, *Cerebus* is also a prime example for the fact that an artwork can often be more clever, complex, and sophisticated than its artist. As a fictional narrative, *Cerebus* is always more ambiguous than some of its author's direct pronouncements. The parodistic and comic nature of the narrative always undercuts the (assumed) seriousness of its contents. As we saw, it started as a parody, but, as Sim grew serious in his storytelling, the subversive nature of the parody still remained, and it not only worked outwards (with its satiric targets from "feminists" to politics and the comics industry), but also inwards, towards itself, undercutting its own seriousness. Yet this undercutting is highly at odds with the narrative mode of high fantasy that the project settled into quickly after the more picaresque and episodic beginning. This is the final twist in the conflict between (inconsequential) playfulness and (referential) seriousness: the mode *Cerebus* uses for its fictional world-building is one that is perceived by most of its readers to combine absolute seriousness with absolute fictionality.

Every fictional narrative leads to the creation of a storyworld in the minds of the readers. The narrative mode of realism implies that it is "about" reality, that it in some way references reality (as in the art-as-mirror-to-nature theories). (Serious) coherence is therefore valued above (playful) incoherence and is guaranteed by constantly checking against the actual world through probability. Most postmodern theories shatter this realism claim on the most fundamental level, in that they argue that a direct and unambiguous reference to truth and reality is not possible. Much of postmodern fiction gave in to this insight and consciously presented itself as fiction, self-referentially highlighted its own fictionality and celebrated its own incoherence as inevitable. One might think that fantasy, as a fundamentally non-realist genre, is closely aligned to this development. Since the author of a fantastic world is by definition not bound in any way by the probabilities of the actual world, virtually everything is possible, not only the existence of dragons, but also the simultaneous existence and nonexistence of dragons. But, on the contrary, high fantasy, especially in the last two or three decades, has developed what we might call its own "higher order realism": its fictional nature is unquestionable, because it contains "impossible" things, yet, once accepted as fiction, the tacit assumption is that all expressions about the storyworld (the narratives proper) represent "the reality" of this fictional storyworld. The storyworld is not only taken as real exclusively for the sake of the narrative ("I will believe in the existence of Sherlock Holmes as long as this story about him lasts") but as being real *independently* of its narrative realizations ("Middle-earth/Spider-Man (fictionally) exists and I am reading one of the possible stories about it/him"). But this means that the author (or, with the proliferation of syndicated storyworld franchises, increasingly authors) is felt by readers to be bound by reference to this independently existing concept of the storyworld. This attitude manifests itself in several different ways, such as the care that is given to the creation and elaboration of fantastic storyworlds by the creators through multiple medial platforms, often involving the heavy use of paratexts (maps, chronologies etc.), and the attention paid to "continuity" by creators and recipients alike.[4] "Continuity" here refers exactly to this coherence with regard to the storyworld across a series of narratives set in this storyworld, such as the individual episode of a TV series like *Star Trek* or a comic book like *Superman*. Thus, it would be regarded as "against continuity" and a breach of the "higher realism" contract if a character that died in one episode were suddenly alive in the next one.

Because of the circumstances of its creation, production, and distribution, the world of *Cerebus* underwent a number of significant changes as the author changed his ideas about what *Cerebus* actually was, as well as changing his own philosophy and finally religion. This makes it highly probable that *Cerebus* in its totality presents a very incoherent storyworld. But the "higher realism" rules of fantastic story-world-building sketched above dictate that we "retro-fit" the earlier versions of *Cerebus'* world to accommodate these changes, in order to ensure continuity. Thus, *Cerebus* forces us to decide between fantasy's (pleasurable) claim to create an absolutely coherent (if non-realist) world and a more academic approach to fictional narrative that sees it as created and therefore potentially incoherent.

It seems that a "coherent" reading of *Cerebus* should lead any sane and halfway liberal person to abandon this storyworld as ridiculous, hateful, and genuinely unpleasant. Indeed, the Judge's prophecy rang true in a rather metaleptic way, since the so long and eagerly awaited finale of this, the most monumental single accomplishment in comics, was in the end greeted by a rather muted and subdued enthusiasm. Just like its main character, *Cerebus* had lived through a period of great fame, only to die alone, unmourned and unloved. An "incoherent" reading, on the other hand, not only enables us to appreciate and learn from Sim's artistic achievements in the evolution both of comics and fantastic storytelling, but to productively reflect on the inconsistencies of the project of fantastic world-building in general. In *Cerebus*, the guilty escapist pleasure that lies in taking a non-realist world seriously flies back into the face of the reader. This does not mean that there is no pleasure to be had, only that it comes with a mental parental advisory sticker.

Notes

1. The term "fantastic" is here used to designate a general mode of writing that will be differentiated further later in the text, but that is to be distinguished from the narrower concept of "fantasy." The latter describes a specific genre that partakes in fantastic discourse.
2. For more on the "Cerebus Effect," see Domsch, "Growing Complexity."
3. For more on Cerebus' transgression of gender, see Grace.
4. A related manifestation is the proliferation of fan fiction. The appeal of fan fiction lies mainly in its "illicit" play with and appropriation of established storyworlds, with an implicit assumption about the importance of continuity. For more on the different attitudes towards storyworlds, see Domsch, "Monsters against Empire" 106–108.

Works Cited

Champion, Edward. "Dave Sim: The Stalin of Comics." *Reluctant Habits: A Cultural Forum in Ever-Shifting Standing*. 27 May 2008. Web. 26 May 2013.
Domsch, Sebastian. "Growing Complexity or: The Cerebus Effect." *Cerebus the Barbarian Messiah: Essays on the Epic Graphic Satire of Dave Sim and Gerhard*. Ed. Eric Hoffman. Jefferson, NC: McFarland, 2012. 65–77. Print.
_____. "Monsters Against Empire: The Politics and Poetics of Neo-Victorian Metafiction in *The League of Extraordinary Gentlemen*." *Neo-Victorian Gothic: Horror, Violence and Degeneration in the Re-Imagined Nineteenth Century*. Ed. Marie-Luise Kohlke and Christian Gutleben. Amsterdam: Rodopi, 2012. 97–122. Print.
Grace, Dominick. "Testing the Limits of Genre/Gender." *Cerebus the Barbarian Messiah: Essays on the Epic Graphic Satire of Dave Sim and Gerhard*. Ed. Eric Hoffman. Jefferson, NC: McFarland, 2012. 163–74. Print.
Komora, Edward M. "YHWH's Story, or, How to Laugh While Reading 'Chasing YHWH' and Still Have Enough Stamina for *The Last Day*." *Cerebus the Barbarian Messiah: Essays on the Epic Graphic Satire of Dave Sim and Gerhard*. Ed. Eric Hoffman. Jefferson, NC: McFarland, 2012. 199–216. Print.
Mayeux, Isaac J. "Anti-Feminist Aardvark? Gender, Subjectivity and Authorship." *Cerebus the Barbarian Messiah: Essays on the Epic Graphic Satire of Dave Sim and Gerhard*. Ed. Eric Hoffman. Jefferson, NC: McFarland, 2012. 175–89. Print.
Sim, Dave. *Cerebus*. Issues 1–64. Kitchener, Ontario: Aardvark-Vanaheim, December-January 1977–1978 to July 1984. Print.
_____. *Collected Letters*. Kitchener, Ontario: Aardvark-Vanaheim, 2005. Print.
_____, and Gerhard. *Cerebus*. Issues 65–300. Kitchener, Ontario: Aardvark-Vanaheim, August 1984 to March 2004. Print.
_____, and _____. *Reads*. Kitchener, Ontario: Aardvark-Vanaheim, 1995. Print.

Fantasy as Politics: George R.R. Martin's *A Song of Ice and Fire*

RAINER EMIG

Introduction: Fantasy's Orientation Towards the Past—And Its Political Effects

Not all fantasy texts are set in the past. The *Harry Potter* series, the *Artemis Fowl* novels, or Jonathan Stroud's Bartimaeus sequence use parallel worlds situated in the present for their plots. Nonetheless, a vast amount of fantasy literature chooses as its settings not only the past, but a very specific past, namely a usually clichéd version of the European Middle Ages. This is, of course, blatantly true for the two master texts of contemporary fantasy, J.R.R. Tolkien's *The Lord of the Rings* and C.S. Lewis's Narnia novels. Yet even newer texts, such as Ursula Le Guin's *Earthwind* saga, not to mention the plethora of popular sword-and-sorcery texts, films, and computer games, take recourse to mock-medieval settings. The present essay will inquire if this choice of a past setting determines the politics of fantasy in a predictable way, the cliché being that an orientation towards the past inevitably means a conservative or indeed reactionary concept of politics. Politics, it has to be admitted, have hitherto been neglected in fantasy scholarship.[1] George R.R. Martin's vastly successful *A Song of Ice and Fire* is both a highly political fantasy—and one that is set in several fictional versions of the Western and Mediterranean past, partly a Dark Age, in parts a mock-medieval and in others a mock–Renaissance one. The present chapter will ask how the recourse to an immersive fantasy that presents an enclosed alternative world squares with Martin's strategy of multiplying and diversifying plots and leading characters as well as their perspectives on power. In short: can fantasy be closed and open, singular and multiple in terms of forms and, consequently, in terms of politics?

The argument will proceed in two steps. First it will look at the origins of and reasons for medieval settings in fantastic texts and at the political structures that these introduce into the novels. In a second step it will examine Martin's epic fantasy (1996–2011, five volumes to date), a worldwide bestseller also because of the success of its TV version *A Game of Thrones*, and analyze the ways in which it depicts power and politics. Finally it will assess in its conclusion whether a postmodern relativizing of power and politics, as potentially exposed in Martin's epic, can enter a productive alliance with mock-medieval settings.

The origin of modern fantasy lies in the late–Victorian period. Among its immediate generic ancestors are the historical novel and gothic romances. Both point the orientation of fantasy towards the past. Fantastic plots that aimed in the opposite direction, the future, were quickly subsumed under the equally new genre of science fiction.[2] Utopias and dystopias, further benevolent fairies at the cradle of modern fantasy, determine the switch between the status quo known to the readers and the entry into a different reality on which Tzvetan Todorov famously bases his first and still rather crude structural definition of the fantastic. The supernatural enters fantasy through a line of tradition leading through the gothic towards ultimately medieval romances, and even the historical novel, famously begun by Sir Walter Scott with a reconciliatory version of the Anglo-Scottish past in *Waverley* (1814), quickly discovered the potential of the Middle Ages in novels like *Ivanhoe* (1819).

The frequent accusations of escapism leveled at fantasy as much as at its precursors of romance, gothic fiction, and historical fiction, are however only partly justified. Already medieval romances negotiated political concepts, gender roles, and religious issues, among others. Gothic fiction clearly deals with class, nation, gender and family models of the eighteenth and nineteenth centuries by placing them at a safe cultural and historical distance. The historical novel was also evidently an attempt to provide a safely remote setting for current political debates. Modern fantasy, this becomes clear, can therefore never be simply escapist. Even when it evidently wishes to look away from modern trends and tendencies, most importantly industrialization, class struggle, or the increasing emancipation of women, it shows its concern for these issues by the very effort that goes into denying them. This has become evident in recent investigations on Tolkien and Lewis in connection with the two World Wars or race, for instance.

Yet it remains equally evident that idealized past settings, especially of the mock-medieval kind, bring with them certain effects on the text's view of history, politics and culture that the present essay will, for reasons of brevity, subsume under the heading "politics." This is most evident in Tolkien, in whose *The Lord of the Rings* four Ages of the world are narrated, spanning many thousand years. Yet at the end of the Third Age, the world is still feudal and patriarchal in terms of politics, and agrarian in terms of economy. Neither an Enlightenment nor bourgeois revolutions have occurred, much less a socialist rebellion of the underclass, and what happens to those who want to introduce industrial measures into a world that seems stuck in a stagnant time can be glimpsed in the fate of the magician Saruman, who ends up a deposed refugee in a reality that clearly has no place for him. Similar assessments can be made concerning Lewis's Narnia novels, in which again time shifts encompassing hundreds of years happen. Yet at the end of them, the country is still ruled by male kings (the only female contender to power is labeled a witch from the start), and technology also remains unchanged.

The appeal of much fantasy lies exactly in this supposed "timelessness," which is, in fact, the very opposite of an existence out of time; ahistoricism rather than superhistoricism, to use Nietzsche's terminology. What is often lovingly created is a replica of some features rightly or wrongly associated with the European Middle Ages. Feudalism as the dominant political structure is *de rigueur*, which also determines that among the main protagonists one has to find an appropriate number of kings and princes, and their liegemen as much as their opponents. Patriarchy is also a staple, despite the fact that there are usually a few female characters that resist the pattern and often occupy the position of outsiders or evildoers. Technology is also generally medieval, with any device that goes beyond the scope of medieval science and engineering being relegated to the realm of magic. This does not leave much scope for a modern view of politics, culture, and economy, one must grudgingly concede.

The Political Framework of *A Song of Ice and Fire*

This, in fact, is also true when one examines the set-up of George R.R. Martin's *A Song of Ice and Fire*. In common with high or immersive fantasy (see Mendlesohn 59–113) of the *Lord of the Rings* ilk, its basic structural principle is the map. It shows the continent of Westeros separated from a larger continent called Essos by the Narrow Sea, while to the South a further, largely unexplored continent called Sothorios looms. The Narrow Sea also contains several islands on which some "Free Cities" can be found. It is not difficult to see in Westeros an adaptation of Britain, with Essos representing Europe, but also parts of Asia, while Africa is left blank. This impression is emphasized by the strategic use of Scottish-influenced expressions especially for the "Men of the North," those occupying the Northern part of Westeros. Already on the second page of the epic one encounters a ranger who is described as "a veteran of a hundred rangings by now, and the endless dark wilderness that the southrons called the haunted forest had no more terrors for him" (*AGoT* 2). "Southron" is Scottish for Southerners, i.e., Englishmen. It is also used by Tolkien for men from the South of Middle-earth.

All the same, in ideological terms already the name "Westeros" hints at the "West," here American culture and political identity, which is negotiated by means that often border on the xenophobic and indeed racist. Thus, Westeros is fought over by diverse factions, a feature that will occupy much of the second part of the present analysis. Yet in the "Free Cities" one finds different regimes already resembling European Renaissance city republics (and often ruled not by a monarch, but by an assembly of elected merchants). These are all depicted as decadent and corrupt, while in the vast deserts of Essos, the East, the nomadic Dothraki for a long time fight among themselves until they are united (a union so far not realized, but suggested from the first book) and become a threat to Westeros. The Middle East, Iraq and Afghanistan are certainly ghostly foils for such constructions, in the same way that the mysterious East of Essos ultimately imports a new and dangerous religion to the West.

Technology in *A Song of Ice and Fire* is tellingly medieval, too. Swords, axes, and spears dominate warfare (see *AGoT* 614), and when "wildfire," a form of Greek fire, is used for the destruction of ships during an attack on the capital of Westeros, King's Landing, it is shown to be the product of King's Landing's alchemists (see *ACoK* 308). All more powerful weapons, such as dragon fire or the use of malevolent spirits, are firmly relegated to the magical realm. Moreover, it appears that over the centuries this state of technology has remained unchanged, and neither in Westeros nor in Essos industry has emerged. The economic basis is solidly agricultural. Does this unpromising standard setup provide a basis for a more advanced or merely more differentiated view of politics?

The "Game of Thrones" that goes on in Westeros refers to the claim to a symbol of power that signals centralized rule over the constantly quarreling nine regions of Westeros. It is composed of swords of conquered rulers, which signals that it represents and continues a form of power based on superior military and personal strength: "The Iron Throne of Aegon the Conqueror was a tangle of nasty barbs and jagged metal teeth waiting for any fool who tried to sit too comfortably" (*ACoK* 400). Bloodlines also come into play, yet can be overruled by force. At the time of the start of the series, king Robert Baratheon, who has managed to get the previous mad king from the Targaryen dynasty slain, asks for the support of his ally Eddard Stark, himself the Lord of Winterfell, ruler of the North, a vast territory encompassing much of the North of Westeros. This territory borders on "The Wall," a vast construction manned by rangers of the so-called Night's Watch that keep at bay the Wildlings north of the Wall. Stark, who reluctantly assumes the role of "Hand of the King," a sort of steward, discovers a conspiracy by the king's wife that eventually costs Robert his life. So much, so standard, one might claim. But things become rather complicated afterwards.

Just when one expects Eddard Stark to become the reluctant hero who Hamlet-like is born to set the world *right again*, he himself becomes the victim of the conspiracy and is executed at the end of the very first volume (*AGoT* 727). The reader is left to attach his or her interest and sympathies elsewhere, as indeed the narrative had offered before when it started to narrate the story through multiple focalization, first through Eddard's second legitimate son Bran, then his wife Catelyn, but then suddenly via a strange female character called Daenerys Targaryen, one of the surviving children of the mad king deposed by Robert Baratheon. By volume five of the tale, the number of such focalizers has reached thirty-one.[3]

The text leaves it deliberately unclear who its hero or heroine will be and continues to offer the reader more and more candidates (including a dwarf, a young girl, a former pirate, and a coward). In the same way the text purposely withholds clear evidence of the supernatural. After the first possible encounter with undead beings in the prologue of the first volume (see *AGoT* 8–11), the reader has to wait a few hundred pages for their next appearance. Only the strange empathic connection of the children of Eddard Stark to their direwolf pups might be seen as supernatural, though it might also have psychological causes. In the same vein it takes Daenerys Targaryen many chapters to mutate from a stereotypical dumb blonde sold into sex slavery to a leader of the Dothraki barbarians to a self-determined potential ruler who through fire magic manages to hatch three dragons.

The Proliferation of Forms of Power in *A Song of Ice and Fire*

The text clearly toys with genre conventions, and this becomes relevant for politics when it concerns the question of ethics. Right and wrong are usually clearly demarcated in fantasy. No one would for an instant worry about Sauron's claim to Middle-earth in Tolkien or apply the concept of legitimate political rights to the White Witch of Lewis's Narnia stories. Yet who is right and who is wrong in *A Song of Ice and Fire*? This is not merely a question that troubles Eddard Stark until his demise. Every character has a different—and usually convincing—justification for his or her actions. Daenerys is the last scion of the previous dynasty. But they had been usurpers too, and their rule had resulted in madness and cruelty. Robert, the subsequent usurper, ends his days as a fat drunkard with a limited interest in his dominion. His son Joffrey is the offspring of the incestuous relationship of Robert's wife Cersei and her brother Jaime and merely represents the dynastic interests of the Lannister family, the biggest money lenders in Westeros. The story even permits Cersei and Jaime a narrative perspective and troubles the reader by justifying their actions as well, which include attempting to kill and permanently crippling Eddard Stark's son Bran. This clearly shows that a more abstract categorization of political concepts in *A Song of Ice and Fire* is called for, and it can be attempted through a structured view of the different kinds of power that are at work in the epic.

The first most obvious and easily expected form of power is physical and military prowess. This is what wins Robert Baratheon (in his younger and fitter days) the throne of Westeros. It marks out Jaime Lannister, too, until he loses one of his hands (another shock to the reader, who has just been groomed to accept Jaime as a shining knight manqué). Yet this form of power is transient and can be subverted—by technical means (as during the assault by a superior naval force on King's Landing that is quenched by wildfire) or by changing allegiances (the troops of one of the contenders to the throne after Robert's death, his brother Renly, quickly change sides and join his older brother Stannis after Renly's mysterious death).

The surest way to achieve such a change of sides is the second most potent form of power in *A Song of Ice and Fire*: money. The Lannister family is the banking dynasty in Westeros, and it is knowingly employed irony that the text emphasizes that all Lannisters are blond and blue-eyed—as if to make the cliché of the Jewish moneylender clash with its Aryan counterpart. "A Lannister always pays his debts" is the unofficial family motto, and it also implies that a Lannister can buy whatever he or she wants, for example the hired mercenary who becomes the personal bodyguard of Tyrion Lannister, Cercei and Jaime's dwarfish brother (see *ACoK* 319), or military and political alliances.

Bloodlines have already been mentioned and are a third form of power in the novels. Yet as the example of Robert's son Joffrey shows, they are an unstable one. Bastard children are so frequent in *A Song of Ice and Fire* that there is even a system for giving them generic surnames according to the region in which they are born. Eddard Stark's bastard son Jon indeed acts as one of the dominant narrative perspectives and as an important military leader at the Wall. Moreover, bloodlines—in Westeros as in all other parts of the world of *A Song of Ice and Fire*—count little when superior military or economic force are employed, or the next form of power worth investigating: diplomacy, allegiances, and conspiracy.

These forms of power are often identified with politics as such, and indeed they feature prominently in the plotlines of *A Song of Ice and Fire*. In the King's

Council in King's Landing, the Councilors (including Lord Petyr Baelish, who is the greatest brothel-keeper in the capital, and the eunuch Lord Varys) compete in a game of reciprocal spying and bribery. Spying relates to knowledge and information, important political features in the novels, for which even a form of communication via ravens has been invented. Bribery links this form of politics to the previous one of finance. That conspiracy and bribery can easily backfire becomes evident when Baelish's plan to save Eddard Stark by having him imprisoned leads to Stark's execution on the orders of the vengeful young king Joffrey. Allegiances between aristocratic houses are also important, as the vast appendix after every volume of the epic attests. Yet they can quickly change, too.

Gender and sexuality become crucial political forces when *A Song of Ice and Fire* makes an incestuous relationship central to the plotline, but also grants wives of rulers, female rulers and contenders, and even a prostitute, influence on decisions and developments, although, as a rule, patriarchal structures dominate and remain largely unchallenged. Arya Stark, Eddard Stark's youngest daughter, who is something of a tomboy, provides another central focalizer. She survives becoming imprisoned in the civil war that follows King Robert's demise, travels to distant shores and even undergoes a mysterious religious training there. Brienne of Tarth, a huge woman without stereotypical feminine attributes, emerges as one of the most competent fighters in the tale (see *ACoK* 343). Her physical abnormality unites her with the dwarf Tyrion Lannister, who compensates his deformity (and therefore low standing with his powerful father and others) by book learning. Tyrion becomes an unlikely carrier of the readers' sympathies and indeed a crucial protagonist in the later volumes when he, Oedipus-like, kills his own father and thus interferes drastically with his family's ambitions. He also upholds a very different political ideology from all other characters: that of justice. When he is made "Hand of the King," the following dialogue with his lover Shae takes place: "'So what will you do, m'lord, now that you're the Hand of the King?' [...] 'Something Cersei will never expect,' Tyrion murmured softly against her slender neck. 'I'll do ... justice'" (*ACoK* 69). Yet his attempt at an ethical approach to power ultimately proves frustrating: "it rankled, to sit here and make a mummer's show of justice by punishing the sorry likes of Janos Slynt and Allar Deem" (*ACoK* 129). Tellingly, in contrast to Tyrion's scruples, in institutional terms "justice" in Westeros is merely unthinkingly embodied in the post of "King's Justice," the royal executioner. For most other characters, "justice" simply means revenge, as in the speech by the foolish Ser Dontos to the hostage Sansa, whom he promises to free with the help of some precious gems: "It's justice you hold. It's vengeance for your father" (*ACoK* 915).

Religion also plays a role in the novels. The reader learns from the start that there are at least two, an old and a new religion, that exist in an uneasy truce. The "Old Gods" are forces of nature and are venerated in so-called "weirwoods," while the new "Faith of the Seven" has divided crucial aspects of human civilization into symbolic figures that share the adoration of the believers, the Father, the Mother, the Warrior, the Maiden, the Smith, the Crone, and the Stranger. Yet other religions abound and are tolerated, such as that of the Drowned God on the Iron Islands, the Horse God of the Dothraki, or the mysterious fire god R'hllor, whose cult originates in the East and whose powers are used by the manipulative Melisandre for Stannis Baratheon. That religion is a powerful political force becomes evident when Cersei wants to employ religious radicals for her cause and ends up imprisoned by them with her head shaved and a death sentence hanging over her (see *AFfC* 931-39).

Race and ethnicity play a further part in the political setup of *A Song of Ice and Fire*. It is very striking that all central characters in Westeros share the same racial identity. They are all white and Caucasian. Even the otherwise excluded Wildlings in the North form part of this pattern. In contrast to them are the Dothraki nomads in the deserts of Essos, whose politics are simply the rule of the physically fittest and most powerful in combat and whose only permanent dwellings serve ritual functions. They are also not interested in economy. Instead they have a concept of "gifts," which means a mixture of expected presents or simple theft and robbery when a Dothraki sees something he or she wants. Although they are looked down upon by the Westerosi as barbarians, they themselves cherish their own racial superiority over another people in their roaming ground, whom they call "Lamb Men." Nonetheless, a group of them adopts Daenerys Targaryan as their leader once she has shown her supernatural strength by surviving the heat of a funeral pyre and by hatching her dragons. In stark contrast to Dothraki and Westerosi alike stand the population of the "Free Cities" and the big slaving and trading towns on the Western coast of Essos. Here, racial background is irrelevant, while economic prowess is all, a fact that finds expression in Xaro Xhoan Daxos, a rich merchant who becomes Daenerys Targaryan's host and suitor in the city of Quarth. He "was not himself of the Pureborn, but he had told her whom to bribe and how much to offer" (*ACoK* 576). Moreover, he is one of "the Thirteen" (*ACoK* 577), the rulers of the city.

The last, and perhaps most pervasive power in the novels, one that is so evident that it is easily overlooked, is that of the seasons. In Westeros, these do not follow the pattern of spring, summer, autumn and winter in one year. Instead, there are periods of summer and periods of winter, and these can last for years or indeed decades—with foreseeable consequences on the agrarian economy and on power relations. "Winter is coming" is the family motto of the Lords of Winterfell, and the threat of coming winter hangs over the entire epic, only counterbalanced by the threat of fire embodied in the recently hatched dragons

(dragons had been extinct for centuries) and perhaps also by the fire god R'hllor.

Conclusion: A Postmodern Politics of Openness— Or Tolkien Revisited?

What we see in *A Song of Ice and Fire* is therefore a double strategy concerning power and politics. On the one hand, the novels reiterate in prolific abundance all structures familiar from previous fantasy novels and their generic ancestors. They modernize some of the features, for example by making sex scenes explicit and by granting female characters greater scope. Yet the overall motivation for power, symbolic leadership and control of all significant territories, has not changed. The books, in other words, still function in accordance with imperialist ideology, something that has shaped fantasy from its inception in the late nineteenth century (see Durst 158ff.).

On the other hand, the texts also challenge many of the assumptions concerning power and politics from within their own frameworks. A good example is power through sexuality. Its standard form in human civilization is the patriarchal model of heterosexual procreation with the aim of securing power in dynasties. This is also the model behind many of the conflicts surrounding the Iron Throne in Martin's novels. Yet Renly Baratheon, the pretender to the crown after the death of his brother Robert, is clearly marked as homosexual in the books. His own brother responds to Renly's boast that his wife came to him a virgin: "In your bed she's like to die that way" (*ACoK* 478). Bastardy and incest have already been mentioned as subversions of patriarchal power structures.

In connection with religion, this is true as well. On the one hand, the texts are brimming with colorful and exotic rites. Yet which religion is to be taken more seriously than another? Not even Arya Stark's temporary service to the Many-Faced God, who represents death, once she has reached a temporary exile in Braavos, signals the eventual triumph of one religion. Her paralyzed brother Bran seems to enter a mystical union with some spirits of the Old Religion once he is taken to the North, yet this could be part of the vivid dreams from which he has been suffering ever since being pushed out of a window by Jaime Lannister.

The quest for the Iron Throne, for which thousands are sacrificed in gory battles, indeed often appears ridiculous, for instance when a disoriented Daenerys stumbles across the desert with her Dothraki followers who have no idea of her pretensions to the throne of Westeros, while she mainly has legends on which to feed her ambition. It is no coincidence either that her most reliable support is an exiled traitor. Yet the other pretenders' motivations are equally dubious: Stannis Baratheon acts out of duty and ignores that he is allowing himself to be manipulated by Melisandre, who wants to use the war to make the fire religion of R'hllor the only accepted faith (see *ACoK* 18). The Lannisters want the throne because they think that, as the richest dynasty, they deserve it. Yet they have to learn that this might be a very unwise investment, since they in succession lose the young king Joffrey, then the paterfamilias Tywin, who falls victim to his own son, while Jaime loses a hand and Cersei's daughter Myrcella an ear. The Starks are perhaps the most troubled family as far as motivation is concerned. Already Eddard had been reluctant to become the "Hand of the King." His widow Catelyn wants to see her oldest son Robb avenge his father and liberate her daughters, yet Robb only grudgingly allows himself to be called "King in the North" (*AGoT* 797) by his followers, because he rightly sees that in doing so he only enters the ever-growing list of pretenders to the throne. This proliferation of claims to power enters an interesting dialectic with what Cersei had spelled out to Robb's father Eddard: "When you play the game of thrones, you win or you die. There is no middle ground" (*AGoT* 488).

It is this dialectic of what Jean-François Lyotard calls the grand narrative of power versus its self-inflicted fragmentation that is at the core of the political ambivalence of a text like *A Song of Ice and Fire*—and perhaps contemporary fantasy in general. Their plots are generally about a struggle for unified power, something seemingly guaranteed by a feudal structure. Yet this struggle more often than not leads to the very opposite, a diversification of interests that prove mutually subversive and undermining.[4] Minor families, such as those of the Greyjoys and the Freys, then use the destabilized state of affairs for their own advantage. For Christine Brooke-Rose, structural contradictions or gaps between two conflicting stories are in fact the very definition of fantasy. To her, these gaps are "situated in both *fabula* [story] and *sjuzet* [discourse], and are prevented from being filled in by two mutually exclusive systems of gap-filling clues" (228). Nonetheless, even Brooke-Rose continues to think in binaries, whereas Martin's epic thrives on multiplying the mutually challenging positions more and more.

A Song of Ice and Fire, despite its mock-medieval setting, responds to the political situation of the world at the start of the twenty-first century, where old Cold War powers are a thing of the past and new imperial ones are only gradually making their impact felt. There, hotbeds of instability challenge both old and new powers, while forces beyond politics, such as global warming, reshape the world (see Berg 4). Similar claims could be made about the books' depiction of religion as plural, but also as eager to achieve dominance in some fundamentalist forms.

Yet the text goes further than this in its simultaneous assertion and challenge of generic and ideological structures. The unruly and seemingly anarchic Wildlings of the North, who, like the Dothraki, only know "kings" as temporary strategic appointments, actually follow an ideology all of their own, which differs radically from that upheld by the rest of Westeros. Jon Snow, Eddard Stark's illegitimate son, who wishes to put an end to dynasties and bastardy in his own world by remaining celibate, fails abysmally in his plan when he meets the Wildling girl Ygritte. She introduces him to more than sex, though, since she explains to him the thinking of the Wildlings. For the Wildlings, all forms of political submission are inherently wrong and against the "nature" of human beings. This is why they call themselves the "Free Folk" (*ACoK* 744), and the people of the South "kneelers" (*ASoS* 203). Ygritte confronts Jon and the reader with a basic message of *A Song of Ice and Fire* through a traditional song of the Wildlings:

> "Bael the Bard made it," said Ygritte. "He was King-beyond-the-Wall a long time back. All the free folk know his songs, but might be you don't sing them in the south."
> "Winterfell's not in the south," Jon objected.
> "Yes, it is. Everything below the Wall's south to us."
> He had never thought of it that way. "I suppose it's all in where you're standing."
> "Aye," Ygritte agreed. "It always is" [*ACoK* 745].

Exposure to the Free Folk makes Jon realize the relativity of his convictions in a way that postcolonial scholarship calls "going native": "It was easy to lose your way beyond the Wall. Jon did not know if he could tell honor from shame anymore, or right from wrong. *Father forgive me*" (*ASoS* 218). Only the last phrase, emphasized in the text and certainly a reference to Eddard Stark, Jon's great idol, since Jon is not a believer in the new religion, shows that his ties to the dominant ideology of Westeros are not yet broken.

The verdict must in fact remain out on *A Song of Ice and Fire* when one wishes to determine its ultimately conservative and stable or subversive and potentially progressive implications (see Schenkel 138). The final two volumes of the epic are still to be published. What will happen when winter comes and the anarchy of the Free Folk is let loose in Westeros (see Gelder)? Are the undead Others simply zombie-like revenants of dead Wildlings and rangers, or do they bring a more complex message? What will occur when Daenerys Targaryen, a blast from the past in a very literal sense if she manages to turn her dragons into precision weapons, hits the troubled political and military set-up of Westeros? The story still has many cards up its sleeve.

Notes

1. An exception is Peter E. Firchow's essay "The Politics of Fantasy: *The Hobbit* and Fascism" (2008). Richard Matthews's *Fantasy: The Liberation of Imagination* (2002) lists politics only in relation to socialism, and T. H. White and power only in connection with magic (see 215). More typical is Brian Attebery's "The Politics (If Any) of Fantasy" (1991).

2. Neil Cornwell also believes the gothic tradition to be the starting point of modern fantasy. Matthews claims that the history is much longer and touches on the Romantics, but uses William Morris's *The Well at the World's End* (1896) as his first example (see 37–53). Uwe Durst offers a slightly different categorisation (see 17–18).

3. On the destabilization of the narrator in fantasy, see Durst 198.

4. This, I believe, is what Neil Cornwell aims at in the very tentative conclusion of his monograph *The Literary Fantastic* (see 217–18).

Works Cited

Attebery, Brian. "The Politics (If Any) of Fantasy." *Journal of the Fantastic in the Arts* 4.1 (1991): 7–28. Print.

Berg, Stephan. *Schlimme Zeiten, böse Räume: Zeit- und Raumstrukturen in der phantastischen Literatur des 20. Jahrhunderts*. Stuttgart'sche Diss. Stuttgart: Metzler, 1991. Print.

Brooke-Rose, Christine. *A Rhetoric of the Unreal: Studies in Narrative & Structure, Especially of the Fantastic*. Cambridge: Cambridge University Press, 1981. Print.

Cornwell, Neil. *The Literary Fantastic: From Gothic to Postmodernism*. New York: Harvester Wheatsheaf, 1990. Print.

Durst, Uwe. *Theorie der phantastischen Literatur*. Rev. ed. Literatur Forschung und Wissenschaft 9. Berlin: Lit Verlag, 2007. Print.

Firchow, Peter E. "The Politics of Fantasy: The Hobbit and Fascism." *Midwest Quarterly: A Journal of Contemporary Thought* 50.1 (2008): 15–31. Print.

Gelder, Ken. "Epic Fantasy and Global Terrorism." *From Hobbits to Hollywood: Essays on Peter Jackson's* Lord of the Rings. Ed. Ernest Mathijs and Murray Pomerance. Contemporary Cinema 3. Amsterdam: Rodopi, 2006. 101–18. Print.

Lyotard, Jean-François. *The Post-Modern Condition: A Report on Knowledge*. Trans. Geoff Bennington and Brian Masumi. Theory and History of Literature. Manchester: Manchester University Press, 1984. Print.

Martin, George R.R. *A Clash of Kings* [1999]. New York: Bantam, 2011. Print. [*ACoK*]

_____. *A Dance with Dragons* [2011]. London: Harper Voyager, 2012. Print. [*ADwD*]

_____. *A Feast for Crows* [2005]. New York: Bantam, 2011. Print. [*AFfC*]

_____. *A Game of Thrones* [1996]. New York: Bantam, 2011. Print. [*AGoT*]

_____. *A Storm of Swords* [2000]. New York: Bantam, 2011. Print. [*ASoS*]

Matthews, Richard. *Fantasy: The Liberation of Imagination*. London: Routledge, 2002. Print.

Mendlesohn, Farah. *Rhetorics of Fantasy*. Middletown, CT: Wesleyan University Press, 2008. Print.

Nietzsche, Friedrich. *On the Advantage and Disadvantage of History for Life* [German original 1874]. Trans. Peter Preuss. Indianapolis: Hackett, 1980. Print.

Schenkel, Elmar. "Die Macht des Ungeschehenen: Phantastische Geschichtsschreibung in *alternative histories*." *Fantasy in Film und Literatur*. Ed. Dieter Petzold. Anglistik und Englischunterricht 59. Heidelberg, Winter, 1996. 129–42. Print.

Todorov, Tzvetan. *The Fantastic: A Structural Approach to a Literary Genre*. Cleveland: Case Western Reserve University Press, 1973. Print.

The Politics of Post-Apocalypse: Interactivity, Narrative Framing and Ethics in *Fallout 3*

MATTHIAS KEMMER

Post-apocalyptic settings are quite the rage in our post-millennial age of ecological, financial and political crisis. Novels such as Margaret Atwood's *Oryx and Crake* (2003), Cormac McCarthy's Pulitzer Prize-winning *The Road* (2006), or Suzanne Collins's *The Hunger Games* (2008), including their film adaptations, have met with critical acclaim, as have comic-book series such as Robert Kirkland's *The Walking Dead* (2003–2013) or Brian Vaughan's *Y—The Last Man* (2002–2008). From Hollywood blockbusters, such as the Wachowski siblings' *The Matrix* trilogy (1999–2003) or the Hughes brothers' *The Book of Eli* (2010), to widely popular video games, these texts explore moral, political, anthropological and philosophical concerns that are believed to present themselves to scrutiny once the fetters of civilization have been cast off. Recently, developers have been particularly interested in post-apocalyptic settings, with the releases of free-to-play online title *Fallen Earth* (2009), Ninja Theory's *Enslaved: Odyssey to the West* (2010), 4A Games' *Metro 2033* (2010), Id Software's *Rage* (2011), Gearbox Software's *Borderlands* series (2009–2012) and Naughty Dog's *The Last of Us* (2013) following in brief succession.

For a discussion of the politics of fantasy texts in general and fantasy video games in particular, Bethesda Softworks' *Fallout 3*, elected Game of the Year in 2008 by various media outlets and having sold over 4.7 million copies (see Graft), still presents an exciting case, as it allows for a comparatively high degree of freedom of interaction with the game world and consequently its politics—even in comparison to more current titles. As the interactive nature of the medium allows the player to interfere in the game world's narrative progress, it may foreground the role of individual agency for larger societal developments, thus enabling the playful exploration of politics in all the senses of the word.

The discussion of *Fallout 3* that follows will treat post-apocalyptic texts as a subgenre of fantasy. The theoretical basis for this premise is provided by Todorov's model of fantastic forms of literature. He calls mimetic, i.e., realist or naturalist modes of writing *uncanny*, as seemingly supernatural events have to be explained rationally at some point in these texts, e.g., as a trick played by a villain, a misperception or hallucination. If this were not the case, the respective text would immediately cease to be a valid representation of the reader's extra-textual reality, which is understood as the realm of the empirically possible, fully subject to the laws of physics. Metaphysical or magical events are explicitly excluded, rendering inexplicable events (before their eventual rational explanation) merely uncanny. Opposed to the uncanny is the *marvelous*, Todorov's term for fantasy texts. In these texts elements may occur that are inexplicable from the perspective of the reader's empirical world view, since they contradict physical laws, as dragons or magic spells do. The reader's incredulity is not shared by characters inside the textual world, however: for Gandalf or Bilbo from Tolkien's *Lord of the Rings* (1954), dragons or giant spiders are an accepted part of reality. Science fiction, then, is understood to be a specific mode of fantasy, which not only represents events or elements yet to arrive with future technology, but often depends on an "idiom of 'pseudo-science'" (Roberts 9) to speculate about technology that might never see the light of day, such as time travel. In the "scientific marvelous," as Todorov calls sci-fi texts, "the supernatural is explained in a rational manner, but according to laws which contemporary science does not acknowledge" (61). Sci-fi texts may start "from irrational premises," but they "link the facts they contain in a perfectly logical manner" (61). For Todorov, the "logical manner," i.e., the pseudo-scientific idiom, enables science fiction to explain that which science itself would deem impossible. Post-apocalyptic texts, then, can be situated at the intersection of horror texts (also a subcategory of fantasy) and science fiction. A recent example for the former would be the AMC television series *The Walking Dead*, in which the cause of the zombie apocalypse deliberately remains unknown to science; as convenient example for the latter serves *The Book of Eli*, in which the apocalypse has been brought about by nuclear holocaust. In both texts, apocalypse is caused by supernatural events or scientific overreaching, placing them in the realm of the marvelous, i.e., fantasy texts.

Before embarking on a case study of *Fallout 3*, I will briefly illustrate some of the issues at the core of public discourses around video games as they relate to two defining aspects of the medium: interactivity and immersion. Against this background it will be possible to isolate the function of fantasy elements at odds with presentational realism, as well as functions of the titular narrative framing in its tension with interactivity. Both of these vectors form the basis of the game's political dimensions.

In 2014, the relevance of video games for contemporary mass media can hardly be overstated. Economically, video games have become twice as big as the music industry (see Anderson), and about half as big as the film industry (see "Games v. Movies"). Video games as a medium are no longer restricted to video game consoles and personal computers, having extended their natural habitat to smart phones, tablets and the living rooms of so-called casual gamers. Blizzard's *World of Warcraft* (2004), offering a complex game world, at peak times even harbored roughly 10 million subscribers (see Karmali), who can be found meeting online regularly to role-play as orcs, elves, and other creatures. This has provided a certain heft to debates around the influence of simulation on real life, especially as the virtual and the real begin to overlap in unforeseen ways. The increasing monetary flow reallocated from the real economy's tangible products via microtransactions to virtual goods such as lightsabers or magic wands sold in virtual stores located in-game has drawn the attention of financial administrators and economists alike (see Plumer). Meanwhile, developers such as Valve are employing trained economists to calculate exchange rates for their individual virtual game worlds' currencies.

Technologically, the medium has undergone a drastic evolution, substituting the moving dots of the infamous table tennis simulation *Pong* (1972) with the nearly photorealistic 3D environments found in current games such as *Heavy Rain* (2012). Its sequel *Beyond: Two Souls* (2013) features Hollywood's rising star Ellen Page, faithfully recreated as a lifelike 3D polygon model. Their economic impact on the entertainment sector, in conjunction with rapid technological advancements, has helped to elevate video games from the status of a marginalized toy for children and geeks to that of a powerful mass cultural force. Titles such as Konami's *Silent Hill 2* (2002) or Bethesda Softwork's *Skyrim* (2011) feature elaborate worlds and narratives on par in complexity with those found in art house films or multi-volume epics; where *Silent Hill 2*'s plot reminds one of David Lynch's *Lost Highway* (1997) and quotes the iconography of Adrien Lyne's *Jacob's Ladder* (1990) extensively, *Skyrim*'s lore and world have been heavily inspired by Tolkien's *Lord of the Rings* cycle. The most popular games eventually make their way to the big screen, the *Silent Hill* franchise being a case in point, having spawned two full-length movie adaptations so far.

Philosophically, the amount of time invested into what is considered mere play seems disconcerting to many conservative observers who bemoan the allegedly eroding effects of video game consumption on the social aptitude of players. If more and more individuals are content to withdraw to the realm of the virtual, evading the bio-power of the disciplinary system by relocating into *other spaces*, to apply Foucauldian terms, how does this affect productivity and social coherence? It is telling that during the 2012 U.S. presidential election, Maine's state senator Colleen Lachowicz was accused of compromising her personal probity as a representative of the people by "leading a bizarre double life" in online fantasy worlds, role-playing as a level 68 rogue orc girl (Lee). Despite the fact that other politicians indulge in chess or golfing, also games after all, the concept of someone staring at a screen and enjoying herself in virtual and consequently seemingly irrelevant fantasy worlds remains a provocation.

Even more polarizing has been the question of the psychological side effects of video games. In many cases, games employ a first-person view, or ego-perspective, enabling the player to experience simulated environments as if through his own eyes. This perspective is especially common in games in which the player wields guns and engages in simulated combat, which has incited furious debate over the possibly corrupting influence of video games on the minds of players. This is illustrated by the controversies around so-called killer games in the U.S. after the Columbine High School shootings in Colorado in 1999 and in Germany after the shootings at a secondary school in the city of Erfurt in 2002. To many critics, playing video games seems disconcertingly close to actually living the onscreen representations. The mere degree of today's games' realism, in conjunction with the fact that the player actively engages in the action onscreen supported by a camera perspective that visually places him inside the body of the avatar he is playing, lend themselves to a neo-behaviorist understanding of interactive media. Radically put, for these critics, the repeated enactment of virtual killings resembles a training camp for soon-to-be high-school killers. A disturbing view, considering the fact that major titles may reach an audience of several million players. Such a strictly behaviorist perspective of course has to be rejected as a simplification. Instead, the individual game, just like any fictional text regardless of its medium, has to be understood as embedded in various discourses, either reproducing, or transforming them. It is of relevance to analyze how the actions of the player are contextualized by a game's narrative, how he or she impacts the situation represented onscreen, and whether this allows for a re-contextualization of the narrative.

In addition to economic, technological, philosophical and psychological concerns, much public attention has been given to issues more closely related to the classic fields of cultural criticism and its focus on racial or gendered stereotyping, as well as other forms of ideological myth-making. In 2008, Capcom's *Resident Evil 5* pitched its protagonists against the warriors-turned-zombies of an African warlord in a fictional Central African region. After the presentation of the first trailers of the game, N'Gai Croal criticized in a *Newsweek* column how the game echoed racial stereotypes by putting players into the role of a white agent who has to kill mindless hordes of black zombies, thereby "othering" blacks as a hormone-driven threat ("Newsweeks' N'Gai Croal"). The debate that followed centered on the question whether the game's iconography was in fact perpetuating racist stereotypes. This core concern was exacerbated by *Resident Evil 5* being a video game, as it seemingly forced the consumer to actively engage in the in-game killings. The counter argument went that the fantastic nature of its locations, plot and characters removed the game far enough from reality that such accusations had to be seen as an oversimplification.

Gender stereotyping in video games similarly received attention in 2013, when feminist cultural critic Anita Sarkeesian crowd-funded a series of online video blogs about the representations of women in a medium dominated by men—both on the production side and regarding its core audience aged 15–30. According to her examination of major games series, women usually function as either helpless damsels-in-distress, or are represented in a highly sexualized fashion. The publication of her project incurred rather drastic forms of online harassment from parts of the male gaming demographic, with one of her critics even uploading a game on the internet where the player's aim is to repeatedly punch a representation of Sarkeesian (see O'Leary). Such a harsh backlash only highlights that the analysis of video games' processes of signification is as relevant as it is political.

This brief glance at some major concerns about video games in public discourse helps to identify three binaries which will function as a guideline for the case study. Firstly, in current games, immersion is often fostered by a high degree of *realism*, which helps suspend disbelief. This informs conservatives' fear of players confusing the real and the virtual, a line of argument that represses the fact that the realism of games often merely takes place on the surface level of graphical and auditory presentation, and ignores the role fantastic elements or a *fantasy* setting might play. Secondly, *interactivity*, as the defining criterion of video games, enables the player to experience and perform actions otherwise not at his or her disposal in real life. This informs the conservatives' fear of gamers learning and training certain violent or antisocial forms of behavior, a line of argument that represses the *narrativity* of the game, which may very well comment on, satirize, offset, subvert or otherwise transform the avatar's actions via narrative contextualization. Thirdly, from the perspective of cultural studies methodology, the symbols and narrative structures *internal* to the game are of necessity intertwined with discourse structures *external* to the individual game. It is here that the political comes into sight in all its forms: stereotyping, gendering, national myth-making, economic, anthropological and ethical ideologies, representations of ways of living, and so forth. An analysis of these interfaces between discourses inside and outside the text corresponds to the approach employed by critics such as Sarkeesian. The awareness of such discourses may or may not be repressed by the immersion or entertainment the player derives from the game. In addition, such structures may or may not have been implemented deliberately by the developers of the game, who represent the Foucauldian author function. The following case study will take into account the interconnection between the three binaries outlined above.

In *Fallout 3*, set in a post-apocolyptic Washington D.C., the player tries to survive among the hostile remnants of American civilization, free to choose the means to his survival unobstructed by law. As *The Walking Dead* or *The Road*, *Fallout 3* exploits the post-apocalyptic setting to problematize human nature, as it is believed to show itself once it has been freed from the shackles of civilization—a recurring paradigm in the history of ideas. In fact, the main binary at work in many post-apocalyptic texts is the Rousseauian notion of man as an inherently good being, all his corruptions deriving from civilization, a notion thrown into sharp relief with the Hobbesian dictum of *homo homini lupus*, which in turn has been adopted in Freud's seminal culture critique *Civilization and Its Discontents* (1929). Freud understands civilization as both, the effect of the repression of innate animalistic drives, making possible human cooperation in the first place, and simultaneously as the cause of repression, thus effecting the titular discontents of man. Post-apocalyptic texts usually examine this binary and its implications for anthropology, ethics, authority, legislation, discipline or constructions of difference on the level of gender, race, or nation building, among others, and thus are concerned with politics in its broadest sense. A recurring device is the exposure of protagonists to moral dilemmas insoluble by turning to societal norms, common law, or capable institutions, as these no longer exist. *Fallout 3* shares the genre's ambitions and similarly confronts its protagonist with moral dilemmas, the specific potential of video games being that it is the player who is being exposed to these dilemmas.

Fallout 3 is commonly categorized as an open world single player role-playing game (RPG), and indeed its relevance for the following case study consists in its open gameplay structures, i.e., its role-playing mechanics and open world, which are designed so as to immerse the player in these ethically far-reaching scenarios as deeply as possible. Its openness and flexibility allow for a transparent conceptual juxtaposition of interactive and narrative elements, as the greater the player's freedom of action is, the lesser are the restrictions by a given game's narrative structure. Taking a closer look at the role-playing mechanics, it is evident that *Fallout 3* takes pains to immerse the player not merely in the playing of a game, but rather simulates living a life. Consequently, the player experiences his or her avatar's birth through the eyes of the latter, watching the doctor from between the raised legs of the mother in first-person perspective. The player may then select a name, which the game will pretend the virtual father is just now giving the child. Freedom of choice quickly becomes political, as the player, in addition, may choose the avatar's biological sex and its looks by selecting among a wide range of hairstyles, eye colors and skin tones. Even race may be determined by selecting among Asian, African American, Caucasian or Hispanic facial patterns. On the one hand, such rather strict demarcations between racial schemas foreclose hybridity and repress the historicity of racial categories. On the other hand, these options nevertheless harbor a specific dialectics by foregrounding the performative character of gender behavior and ethnic consciousness, since the player may play a male or female character and an ethnic background any way he or she sees fit. Since the narrative of the game does not actually change in relation to the race selected and none of the gameplay mechanics are exclusive to one of the races, *Fallout 3* suggests that individuals of any of the four predefined racial backgrounds alike are capable of holding their own in the game's world. The fact that the gameplay is not impacted by the selected gender can similarly be taken as an implicit statement about the equal ability of the two historically distinguished biological sexes. As with the race selector, however, hybridity on the physical side is being repressed, as certain facial shapes can only be selected if the appropriate sex has been chosen in the first place. Intersexuality, transsexuality or merely cross-dressing are no part of *Fallout 3*.

In contrast to Black Isle Studio's prequel *Fallout 2* (1998), Obsidian's follow-up *Fallout: New Vegas* (2010), or Bethesda Softworks' own *Skyrim* (2011), the latter even featuring interracial and homosexual marriage, homosexual roleplaying is *not* directly supported in *Fallout 3*, even if the player befriends gay and lesbian NPCs (the acronym stands for *non-player characters*) over the course of the game, all of whom are represented without referring to clichés such as cross-dressing. In fact, in the case of gay NPC couple Flak and Shrapnel, who own a weapons store, the player learns only from other NPCs of their sexual orientation, e.g., when Flak is derogatively being called a "queen" by a slaver named Grouse upon enslavement by the hands of the player (*Fallout 3*). Homosexuality as a topic is being treated in a rather unagitated fashion, but issues of real-life discrimination are not completely avoided by the game, as such examples illustrate.

After the player has finished determining his character's gender, race and looks, he may distribute a limited number of points among several talents and skills such as charisma, strength, intelligence, dexterity, barter, lock-picking, or science, which enable him to solve problems in the game in different ways. To avoid breaking immersion, this process is represented in-game as learning, i.e., the player's avatar skims a children's book as a toddler, distributing points to each stat described on one of the book's pages. Depending on the distributed skills and talents, a given in-game objective can be solved, for instance, by talking to NPCs, stealing things, picking the locks of doors to gain access to restricted areas, or hacking computers etc. If the player has prioritized speech skill, he or she will occasionally have extra options at his or her disposal while in dialogue with NPCs, but may not be able to hack more highly secured doors. Conversely, if the focus lies on lockpicking, the avatar may open such doors to steal ammunition, acquire sensitive data, or even open a shortcut to the prison cell of a kidnapped NPC, but will not be able to exhaust all options in conversation.

The skill system opens up a tremendous range of possibilities to interact with the game world, which is supplemented by an equally flexible open world structure. *Fallout 3* does not force the player down a linearly scripted path, i.e., from point A to point B, but rather enables access to different locations of the game world from the get-go. This can be taken quite literally, as the player is controlling a virtual body made of polygons and is free to navigate this avatar to almost any location in the realistically rendered, 3D virtual environment right after the first couple of introductory minutes.

The gameplay mechanics of character creation, skill system and open world work together with the lawless setting to provide for a degree of flexibility rarely found in other games, narrativity included. In contrast to so-called persistent game worlds of massively multiplayer online RPG titles such as *Fallen Earth* or *World of Warcraft*, *Fallout 3* is an offline, single player experience. All of the player's interactions are with artificial intelligences, i.e., NPCs. By talking to the various NPCs residing in *Fallout 3*'s world, the player can start so-called *quests*. Regarding the narrative flow of the game's story, these quests are best understood to represent subplots, as it is only inside of quests that the story progresses, as opposed to situations when the player aimlessly roams the wastelands to explore the map, or to collect different loot. While this may impact the environment, e.g., by killing a gang of raiders, a traveling merchant or animals, it does not have lasting consequences for the game's story (but it *does* affect *karma point distribution*, see below). There is no fixed order in which the player has to take on these subplots, which could consist in having to find stolen goods, to rescue kidnapped townsfolk, or to locate a group of vampires that slaughter villagers' cattle at night. Whereas several outcomes to most quests exist, of course all of the possible variants must have been predesigned by the game's developers. Once an individual quest is started, it can be abandoned at any point and taken up later in the course of the game. Interactivity and narrativity thus are co-dependent: the decisions of the player during the different quests shape the fate of NPCs and the game world, and consequently also the story that is being related to him. This includes both its syntagmatic dimension, i.e., the order in which events take place, and its paradigmatic dimension, i.e., the different possible outcomes of quests—a dimension that is rather difficult to reproduce in literary texts or films (Akira Kurosawa's *Rashômon*, 1950, or Tom Tykwer's *Run Lola Run*, 1998, could be cited as examples for successful cases).

Much of the flexibility regarding the outcome of certain quests depends on the skillset of the avatar. Still, solving a quest is not merely a technical question of which door to open, which computer to hack, or which dialogue option to choose. Instead, they are always tied to moral issues, as many of the items in *Fallout 3* belong to some NPC or other. If the player steals something, the owner will object. If the player hacks a computer, the owner will violently insist on his privacy. If the player wants to cannibalize an NPC, he will defend his life, and so forth. Conversely, if the player helps someone, this NPC will reward him or her, financially or otherwise.

The plethora of options not only permits the player to form a unique character, it also encourages him or her to consider the continuity of his decisions and their underlying moral principles. If interested in a consistent subjectivity, in a self that acts on principles rather than randomly, in short, in an actual *identity*, the player has to consider how the avatar shall be thought of and remembered by NPCs. One could also say that the player has to consider the biography others will write about the avatar, and is thus induced to behave consistently. This presupposes two things: firstly, NPCs need to remember the avatar's actions. Secondly, at the end of the game some form of moral review of the avatar's life, e.g., a biographical narration including some form of moral judgment, has to be constructed by some entity other than the player. Without such a device the player would never have to worry about consistency as the player would never receive a final assessment of the moral quality of the avatar's actions. Of course, this entity would need the authority to make such a verdict. The game fulfills both premises by employing a feedback system (the *karma system*) that keeps track of the player's actions and allowing a narrative instance to judge the avatar's life at the end of the game, bringing the binary of interactivity and narrativity into close proximity to ethical considerations. In order to understand the role of this narrator, it is necessary to understand *Fallout 3*'s karma system.

Considerations of moral consistency and identity are being reinforced by an immediate feedback regarding the moral value of one's actions. Stealing from an NPC or helping someone leads to an increase in positive or negative karma, as many interactions with the game world are being rewarded with karma points, which can take the form of a positive or a negative value. Karma points are used by the game to calculate the avatar's reputation with certain groups within the game world, in a sense simulating the aggregated individual memories of NPCs of one's actions. Whether NPCs will help the avatar with his quests, try to intercept his actions, or even kill him, depends on his reputation. Since different factions are at war in *Fallout 3*, a positive reputation will secure the support of the avatar by one faction while incurring the scorn of their enemies, and vice versa. At first glance, the karma system seems to be based on classic notions of good and evil, as helping brutal, exploitative factions such as the slavers will incur negative karma. A negative karma balance will result in a negative reputation, indicated by a clearly negative so-called karma title, such as "Devil" or "Wasteland Destroyer," which is displayed on the in-game menu screen.

This karma mechanism lends itself to the view of *Fallout 3* as a moral simulator, an educative tool, as it were, which allows the player to experiment with the consequences of certain forms of behavior. By being awarded "good" and "evil" karma, the player might, in this view, even train how to behave morally. Schulzke, who proceeds from a concept of Aristotelian virtue ethics called *phronesis*, i.e., the practical wisdom of knowing how to act morally in particular situations, indeed argues that *Fallout 3* represents such a kind of tool. According to Schulzke, the player learns "how to be good by strengthening one's practical wisdom to the point that it is capable of resolving moral dilemmas as they arise." A convincing hypothesis, especially considering the fact that the developers of the game were in full control regarding the amount of positive or negative karma that the avatar is being awarded for a given action when they implemented the game. In fact, similar virtual moral dilemma simulators have been designed and employed by educators like Moshe Sherer and Avner Ziv for years (see Schulzke). However, while I *do* think that *Fallout 3* allows for experimentation with different forms of action and their moral consequences, I do not believe that the player necessarily may learn about the virtuous, "good" life, but rather that the game's ethical implications are more open-ended. As I will show below, instead of subscribing to the classical good/evil binary, *Fallout 3* subtly foregrounds the relativity of ethical systems as well as any form of moral behavior while at best merely *recommending* a deontological ethics.

Interestingly, negative karma will never be punished by the game in metaphysical or objective terms, nor incur any disadvantages for the player. Certain factions, whom we would instinctively describe as evil, will even respect a negative karma title or negative karma, as it is a sign of recklessness and prowess. For them, what others consider "evil" is synonymous with "good," which suggests that the opposition of "good" and "evil" represents merely words without actual meaning outside of that which is given to them by local discourses. The question is, who determines what is "good" and what is "evil" and how this authority is legitimized. The game thus resonates with views of philosophical skepticism that reduce ethical systems to the status of subjective morality, i.e., as based on premises which the respective philosopher or group may have prioritized, but which are unfounded, as they cannot be empirically demonstrated:

> [Moral skepticism] was fuelled initially by the logical positivists who dismissed moral statements as meaningless. Such statements failed the test of the verificationist principle that divided the realm of meaningful discourse into either logical tautologies ("A bachelor is a married man") or statements based on empirical observation. They were best construed not as statements at all but rather the expressions of feelings, like "Hurrah!" [...] At a logical level, it was argued that there was an unbridgeable gap between factual and ethical statements, summarized in the Humean slogan that one cannot infer an "ought" from an "is" [Fisher 31].

Jean-Francois Lyotard refines this line of argument by providing a poststructuralist analysis of the legitimations underlying conflicting moral statements and colliding ethical or political views, which he calls *differends*, defined as "a case of conflict between (at least) two parties, that cannot be equitably resolved for lack of a rule of judgment applicable to both arguments" (xi). He illustrates his concept by presenting a vast number of paradoxes, such as the following:

> Either the Ibanskian witness is not a communist, or else he is. If he is, he has no need to testify that Ibanskian society is communist, since he admits that the communist authorities are the only ones competent to effectuate the establishment procedures for the reality of the communist character of that society. He defers to them then just as the layperson defers to the biologist or to the astronomer for the affirmation of the existence of a virus or a nebula. If he ceases to give his agreement to these authorities, he ceases to be a communist. We come back then to the first case: he is not a communist. This means that he ignores or wishes to ignore the establishment procedures for the reality of the communist character of Ibanskian society. There is, in this case, no more credit to be accorded his testimony than to that of a human being who says he has communicated with Martians [4].

This paradox illustrates how the definition of *communist* renders any criticism of the practices of communism impossible *for anyone pertaining to this category*, i.e., from the *inside* of its moral/political discourse, since he, as a result of the definition of the status communist, would cease to be a communist in the instant he questions the (communist) authorities. Someone from the outside, say, an American liberal, could very well criticize communism, but no communist would treat his criticism as valid, as it is a part of this world view that only the communist authorities *have the ability* to assess the nature of communism, just as only the trained astronomer has the ability, the knowledge and the authority to determine the nature of specific astronomical phenomena. Of course, the difference between the astronomer and the communist is that the former possesses an external criterion for his assessment, namely the empirical in reality (the Humean "is"), whereas the latter operates on wholly normative terms (the "ought"), which refers any judgment about its object back to the status of normative discourse. As such, it is always dependent on the participants of discourse, the power relations among them, subjectivity and historicity, but never on truths *a priori* to it.

Ethical systems in *Fallout 3*'s game world are presented as precisely such normative constructions dependent on locally and historically contingent legitimations for certain modes of behavior. One faction will never accept the moral values and norms of another faction, as the legitimizing principle underlying the other group's ethical system is being rejected. The problem, again in Lyotard's words, is the following: "A case of differend between two parties takes place when the 'regulation' of the conflict that opposes them is done in the idiom of one of the parties while the wrong suffered by the other is not signified in that idiom" (9). The idiom of these local discourses, then, prevents signification of the wrong suffered by the respective other group, as the members of this group are not understood to be of equal value at all. For the slavers, enslaving people is an act commanding respect, as people too weak to defend themselves are not seen as worthy of the same status as the strong; instead, their status is akin to that of cattle. Membership of the slavers' faction is prioritized over shared physical traits between slavers and slaves; the status as slaves or even merely potential slaves precludes them from the right to life, liberty or property of oneself. For the slaver, unconditional, natural rights in the Lockean sense do not exist in the first place. As the weak escape the slaver's definition of dignity, enslaving them is not an evil for the slaver. Karma titles therefore only function as indicators of reputation but do not objectively tell whether the player's actions are objectively good or bad, despite the temptation to view them as such. Recourse to legitimations on the level of absolute, metaphysical values outside of that of the local discourses presented in-game is impossible since such values simply do not objectively exist; as in Nietzsche's famous dictum of the death of God, the game lacks a moral center. There is no transcendent authority in the game to ever sanction or punish the player's actions by referring to a universal idiom preceding that of the different ethical principles that the player may use to rationalize actions, i.e., to provide consistency to them. Punishment is instead administered by NPCs according to the respective arbitrary standards of the faction they belong to, and never on an absolute level. Often, it is merely self-defense or revenge instead of judgment based on principles. To produce examples for how such a metaphysical good/bad binary might be realized in video games, it suffices to take a look at RPGs by Japanese developers, e.g., the *Final Fantasy* (1987–2012) and *Dragon Quest* (1986–2012) series. Very often, metaphysical beings such as gods or angels are real entities in these games and possess the authority to judge human behavior or the avatar's actions from the outside of discourse; in most of these games, metaphysical values *are* founded and do exist as well.

An interesting question arises around the fact that children in *Fallout 3* are invincible. It is clear that this limitation of the player's freedom does not represent a universal metaphysical law in *Fallout 3*'s world, as it is never mentioned or recognized by any in-game character over the course of the game, be it in in-game dialogue or elsewhere. While the player is surprised to find out that one cannot slay children in the game, the inhabitants of *Fallout 3* do not ever recognize this special status of children, and neither does the player's avatar (curiously enough, it is still possible for the avatar to sell a six-year-old girl into slavery). The question remains, however, whether this limitation has to be understood as an overarching moral statement of the game. I would hold the following two statements to be true: firstly, the player, in contrast to the avatar, is made aware of the fact that children have a different status in the game than any other entity and that killing them is not desired by the developers. This possibly reinforces the player's moral predilections, as they are most likely based on the special status children and adolescents enjoy in most law systems as well as in most cultures' discourses on childhood (children as innocent, in need of protection etc.). Secondly, due to the fact that the status of children in *Fallout 3* is not part of the laws of the world recognized by characters in the Todorovian sense, and considering that children are the only entities escaping the karma mechanic, it is clear to the player that children are *not representative* for whatever statements can be extracted from the rest of the game. Regarding its mechanics as well as its ethics, the status of children represents an *anomaly*. Consistency on the level of both gameplay and ethics would presuppose that either all NPCs should be killable and be subject to the karma system or no NPCs at all. I will therefore ignore this anomaly and illustrate how the karma mechanic foregrounds the relativity of ethics rather than the good/evil binary.

In addition to the karma mechanic at work at all times, the game self-consciously intensifies the impossibility of a centered system of ethics in the form of pre-designed moral dilemma scenarios which enable the player to experience the difficulties of political/moral decisions first hand, as the actions are forced into the moral contexts of different groups of NPCs. It is here that the game also links the abstract problem of ethics with a mapping of more concrete *real-life discourses* on otherness and racism with *in-game discourses*. This mapping corresponds to the third of the three main binaries outlined in the introduction.

In the quest "Tenpenny Tower," an obvious homage to George A. Romero's zombie flick *Land of the Dead* (2005), for example, a powerful man called Alistair Tenpenny occupies a tower in the capital wasteland to turn it into a safe haven featuring most of the conveniences of the pre-nuclear era for the few remaining well-to-do. A group of ghouls, living in an old subway station nearby, is not welcome to cohabitate the highly secured tower, despite the fact that they could provide the financial means to do so. Ghouls are humans who have been irradiated, and, while mentally unchallenged, have a leprous skin condition which incurs discrimination. The player has several options to apply himself or herself in the conflict at hand. Firstly, in the hope of peaceful cohabitation, one can try to persuade Tenpenny and other influential tower dwellers in lengthy dialogues to let the ghouls in. Here, however, the player is being reminded of the fact that political negotiation has its limits: if successful in persuading enough dwellers to subscribe to a policy of integrating the ghouls, individual NPCs refusing to accept the new status quo will immediately leave the tower. Secondly, the player can follow the security chief's recommendation to exterminate all ghouls, thus prioritizing the security of the humans while implicitly accepting the construction of difference based on superficial physical traits (the condition of the skin), which ostracizes ghouls as non-human, even though they once belonged to the category of humans. Thirdly, one can side with the ghouls, and, depending on the avatar's skills, either let them in by picking the appropriate locks, resulting in the ghouls massacring of the tower's inhabitants, or kill the tower dwellers himself as an assassin for the ghouls.

Central to any decision of the player is his definition of humanity. Will he or she foreground sameness—consciousness and reason which both ghouls and men share? Or will the player focus on the differences—the visual markers of otherness? Even if the player recognizes the sameness, the question remains whether revenge for the discrimination is in order and whether to administer it violently. Interestingly, siding with any of the two factions will be rewarded with negative karma; only a truce results in positive karma. This, however, does not render the truce the ultimate solution, as positive karma always leads to a negative reputation with other factions, e.g., the slavers.[1] On a completely different level, the solution to kill any of the two groups will be rewarded with loot and bounty payments, and is by far the quickest way to proceed, rendering it economically attractive. Exterminating no group will also not prevent future conflicts between both parties as, after a couple of days, the ghouls and tower dwellers living together in the tower after the player has chosen the truce-solution will in fact massacre each other. This shows how the unpredictability of the consequences of certain actions complicates ethical principles or motivations on the level of practice.

The ghoul-scenario echoes historical segregation, which was equally dependent on visual markers of difference of the skin, obviously playing on the situation of African Americans before the legal abolition of segregation in the Supreme Court's Brown v. Topeka ruling in 1954, or the ostracizing of the infected during the AIDS-crisis of the 1980s. By displacing historically, politically and ethically charged conflicts from real life to the fantasy realm of a post-apocalypse roamed by humans-turned-ghoul, the game's narrative allows for the interactive exploration of the consequences of moral decision-making. It avoids triggering the learned reflexes around real-life discourses, e.g., on racism, while keeping intact the recurring ideological patterns underlying such conflicts, which may draw from religion, history, philosophy or politics, but always legitimize constructions of sameness and difference. This, then, is the precise function of fantasy in *Fallout 3*, bringing us back to the first binary outlined in the introduction: *realism*, enabling immersion and suspension of disbelief, is needed for the player to care about moral consistency while *fantasy* allows him to analyze the dynamics behind real-life conflicts while steering clear of stereotypical thought patterns.

In another moral dilemma scenario titled "Head of the State," the legacy of America's peculiar institution is directly addressed, but separately from visual markers of difference and thus from blackness and racial schemas, instead focusing on the historico-political dimension of myth-making—maybe to avoid controversy about racism in games as it arose around Capcom's *Resident Evil 5* in the following year, or to avoid losing African American gamers' support for *Fallout 3*. As in McCarthy's *The Road*, the unscrupulous strong enslave the weak, with gender or skin color *not* playing a role in the process. Escaped slaves hiding outside of Washington's ruins plan to reconquer the destroyed Lincoln Memorial from the hands of the slavers to rebuild it. Both slavers and slaves are aware that the symbolic legacy of the Lincoln Memorial is key in the slaves' liberation. The player has the choice to side with either faction and to aid in the extermination of the respective enemy. If siding with the slaves, the player can assist in the restoration of the Lincoln Memorial, which then becomes a beacon of freedom for the enslaved throughout the country. Conversely, if siding with the slavers, the player may destroy the Memorial and sell its parts to an antiques dealer for significant monetary compensation. In "Head of the State," the player consequently not only has to focus on the continuity of morals in the eyes of others—in other words, the avatar's biography. The player also positions the continuity of the avatar's life alongside that of American history. Individual agency thus becomes intertwined with the narration of the nation's (the Wasteland's) fate, as well as with the historical fate of the U.S. around the time of the Civil War (1861–65).

The importance of continuity of the individual life for the fate of the nation is expressed in the retelling of Lincoln's biography by one of the slaves. The rebel slave's leader, Hannibal, explicitly stresses the fact that young Lincoln felt pity for chained animals. He constructs a specific altruistic continuity around the historical Honest Abe:

> As a child, he could not bear to see any animal chained or imprisoned. [...] As a youth, Lincoln fought raiders in the Black Hawk War. When the war ended, he settled down to rule Illinois, a small tribe of free men. He grew so famous, that one day he was made president. [...] When he declared that all slaves must be freed, the slavers rebelled against his rule. They fought a great war, which Lincoln won. [...] We will restore his vision, where all men are created equal, and all men can live free! [*Fallout*].

Here, biographical narration constructs a consistent moral identity ignoring any further motivations that might have played a role for the historical Abraham Lincoln, fusing individual morality with a whole nation's liberation from amorality, as Hannibal understands it. Altruism in this view is taken as an essential quality of certain individuals, a quality that the slavers do not possess, thus permitting their extermination.

In a manner comparable to Lincoln's life, the life of the avatar and thus the interactive dimension of *Fallout 3* receive closure through narrative framing, which corresponds to the second binary outlined in the introduction, i.e., interactivity vs. narrativity. As demonstrated above, the game does not ever punish anti-social behavior outside of the reaction of NPCs to ensure immersion by simulated freedom. This, however, changes after the final quest of *Fallout 3*, in which the player may save mankind from a so-called "forced evolution virus," which is about to be injected into the water supply of Washington by the Enclave. The Enclave are the followers of self-proclaimed president Henry Eden, who turns out to be an artificial intelligence. Alternatively, the player may side with Eden and inject this virus. The virus will wipe out all irradiated and mutated life forms, including the settlers of the Capital Wastelands, whose genetic code has been exposed to radiation, rendering it impure, i.e., prone to all kinds of mutations. Only groups of people who had escaped nuclear warfare by withdrawing to underground vaults, such as the player's character or Enclave members, would be spared, as they survived the nuclear apocalypse insulated from radiation. The Enclave is the only faction with access to the highly advanced technologies of pre-apocalypse civilization, which Eden wants to use to rebuild the "glory of pre-war America" (*Fallout 3*). After the ultimate decision of whether to expose the wastelands to the virus or not, an ending sequence plays out automatically, during and after which the player is unable to interact with the game any further. It consists of *PowerPoint*-like slides depicting the consequences of the individual moral decisions the player made in the moral dilemma scenarios and elsewhere. Considering the large number of quests and their possible solutions, this allows for more than 200 different combinations of this final cutscene, in which a narrative voice recounts the avatar's life and his decisions. In a sense, it is the biography of the avatar that is being narrated in this cutscene by an unknown narrative voice (in Genette's terms comparable to an overt, reliable, heterodiegetic narrator employing external focalization in his retelling of the avatar's life); its account clearly featuring a temporal distance between the retelling and the actions of the avatar by using the past tense. Although the slides and their description would suffice as an ending for the story, they are also being morally evaluated. The narrator/biographer is implicitly voicing discontent with some of the player's choices, while praising others by using terms like "sadly" or "thankfully." Thus it becomes obvious that the wording of karma titles such as "Wasteland Destroyer" does have an author, and hence a moral center is being established, against which the concepts of *negative* and *positive* karma become meaningful: this choice of words represents the evaluative perspective of the biographer; his narration consequently provides a framing to *Fallout 3*'s events.

This biographer is particularly critical if it was the final decision of the player to inject the virus into the water supply. To repeat, injecting it will "cleanse" the human genetic pool by killing off anyone whose percentage of genetic mutation is higher than that caused by the normal biological processes (i.e., recombination and crossing over of chromosomes during meiosis), thus "restor[ing] the glory of this great nation," as "[t]he good people of this country cannot regain control while mutation runs rampant through our land," according to Eden (*Fallout 3*). Even though such a radical measure is reminiscent of the fascist fantasies of Third Reich eugenicists, it is in line with less contested ethical perspectives of consequentialist ethics in the vein of Benthamite utilitarianism, which applies the principle of the "greatest happiness for the greatest number" as "the measure of right and wrong" (Bentham 93). This involves a *hedonic calculus*—the assessing and weighing of the consequences of actions on a happiness/pain balance sheet, as it were. Any action, then, is morally good if it maximizes the total sum of happiness in a given society—right and wrong are being determined by looking at the consequences of a given action rather than its motives. Objectively, saving mankind by wiping out ghouls, mutants and other irradiated folks to restore civilization might indeed, over time, provide greater happiness for more individuals than if these individuals were permitted to procreate and possibly compete for resources in a violent fashion.

Eden's reasoning, however, is sound only as long as the definition of who or what counts as human excludes hybridity, since all of the aforementioned were *human* at some point even according to Eden's definition. Only then is it possible to measure the sacrifice of the irradiated versus the happiness of the healthy, as mutants, ghouls and so on might very well experience happiness in their future generations just as (other) humans do, if such a distinction were not upheld. Even when hybridity is being excluded, however, one might refuse the sacrifice of minorities for the welfare of the majority by prioritizing different moral principles over the maximizing of happiness. In fact, objections to utilitarianism usually criticize precisely the fact that the hedonic calculus—the calculating of the aggregated sum of happiness in a society, *does* provoke a similar reasoning as that of president Henry Eden when taken to its logical conclusion (Bentham himself would most likely consider any reading which allows for the sacrifice of minorities a perversion of his intentions, though).[2] Opponents of utilitarianism therefore often illustrate their criticism by constructing similar moral dilemmas as those faced by the avatar, and, by proxy, the player, such as the following:

> A surgeon has five patients who will die unless they are provided with certain essential bodily parts. A young man has just come in for his yearly check-up, and his parts will do: the surgeon can cut him up and transplant his parts among the five who need them. The surgeon asks the young man if he is willing to volunteer his parts, and thus his life; the young man says, "Sorry, I deeply sympathize with your five patients but no." Would it be morally permissible for the surgeon to proceed anyway? Hardly! [Thomson 257–60].

Commenting on the case, Thomson contends that "[if utilitarianism] does not come to the wrong conclusion about the example, [utilitarianism] will be embarrassed to say why the right conclusion is to spare the young man's life" (Braybrooke 80). Thomson argues that utilitarianism would clearly have the surgeon proceed, as the young man's death would save 5 lives, creating an excess of 4 happy lives. If utilitarianism came to another decision (i.e., advising the surgeon against proceeding, for Thomson the right decision), utilitarianism would be "embarrassed" to justify it—one would have to resort to non-utilitarian values such as the right of the young man to his own life (a libertarian argument). This is because in utilitarianism, happiness, as a magnitude, becomes itself an entity, more important than its "carrier," the individual experiencing it. Consequently, happiness can freely be shifted between individuals—provided the sum of happiness increases.

The line of reasoning in Thomson's example, which is based on the same utilitarian principles *Fallout 3*'s Henry Eden adheres to, can of course be attacked from the vantage point of a deontological, Kantian ethics, which is legitimized by a wholly different principle based on the construction of the sameness of all human beings. This sameness in turn is derived from the proposition that every human being is a rational being, the implicit precondition of deontological ethics. The ubiquitously cited formulation of the categorical imperative—"Act only on that maxim whereby you can at the same time will that it become a universal law"—however, only implies this underlying criterion of sameness (Kant 421). Fortunately, Kant provides an alternative formulation which highlights this point. Sandel retraces the argumentative steps of this alternate version of the categorical imperative: according to Kant, "we can't base the moral law on any particular interests, purposes or ends, because then it would be only relative to the person whose ends they were," as the premise of the categorical imperative is precisely that it remains unconditional (Sandel 121).

> "But suppose there were something whose existence has in itself an absolute value," as an end in itself. "Then in it, and in it alone, would there be the ground of a possible categorical imperative." What could possibly have an absolute value, as an end in itself? Kant's answer: humanity. "I say that man, and in general every rational being, exists as an end in himself, not merely as a means for arbitrary use by this or that will." This is the fundamental difference [...] between persons and things. Persons are rational beings. They don't just have a relative value, but [...] an intrinsic value. That is, rational beings have dignity. This line of reasoning leads Kant to the second formulation of the categorical imperative: "Act in such a way that you always treat humanity, whether in your own person or in the person of another, never simply as a means, but always at the same time as an end" [Sandel 121, quotes within the quote from Kant 428].

The dignity of any being featuring the faculty of reason can thus be defined as sacrosanct, very much like in the first article of the German *Grundgesetz*, which proclaims the "inviolability of human dignity," or the U.S. Declaration of Independence's "unalienable rights." Still, the Kantian approach ignores the issue of maximizing happiness, instead focusing on imposing limits to certain forms of behavior (even the Declaration leaves it up to the individual to *pursue* his own happiness but does not deal with its intensity or its societal distribution). Furthermore, it simply represses the fact that human beings differ from each other, and presupposes any human to be a rational being, with all the problems this implies.

Eden is a super computer not by coincidence, and quotes the common sci-fi trope of the logically superior, but cold scientific rationality of the A.I. depending on precise mathematical calculations (such as utilitarianism's hedonic calculus), at odds with human sympathy or ethical systems as that of Kant, according to whom a rational being may never be treated as the means to an end *only*, even if this end would mean a significant increase in welfare of other beings. It is telling that Eden has to depend on the avatar, after his subordinate, Enclave's General Autumn, "has allowed his subjectivity to cloud his objectivity" and refused to follow through with Eden's plan, i.e., having prioritized the protection of any rational being over the long-term maximization of happiness (*Fallout 3*).

Both approaches, the utilitarian and the deontological, as well as their principles of legitimation, the greatest happiness of the many versus the dignity of rational beings, can be taken to be equally valid contenders in a Lyotardian *différend* for a universal ethics. The narration of the chronicler of the player character's actions in *Fallout 3* explicitly confirms this view in his discussion of the consequences of the forced evolution virus after its injection:

> *Sadly*, when selected by the sinister president to be his instrument of annihilation, the Wanderer agreed. Humanity will be preserved, but only in its purest form. The waters of life flowed at last, but the virus contained within soon eradicated all those deemed unworthy of salvation. The Capital Wasteland, *despite its progress*, became a graveyard [...] [*Fallout 3*, emphasis added].

Here, the biographer explicitly shows his awareness of this conflict when he admits that the virus *did* in fact accelerate the "progress" of mankind and might consequently lead to a greater amount of happiness for a greater number of individuals in the long run—even if under a uniform, technocratic and fascist regime. Still, he clearly prefers Kant's uncompromisingly humane vision, as he commiserates the sacrifice of the individuals too weak to survive the effects of the virus as being a "sad" affair and likens the game world to a "graveyard."

For the player, the narrative voice represents an attempt at reconstructing the moral center of *Fallout 3* and thus to solve its main *différend* of conflicting ethical perspectives in a unifying perspective, comparable to that of an authorial narrator. The narrator's account seems to represent the ultimate verdict of the avatar's life—and thus of the player's decision-making during playtime. This is also due to the narrator's rather condensed account, which inevitably has to ignore inconsistencies of the avatar's behavior, for example killings that the player committed outside of quests. Quite literally, the biographer has the last word, and it is this prominent position as the frame to the player's actions which, in conjunction with the artificial consistency of his narrative, provides credibility to his moral authority. His authority might not seem unlike the authority of Nietzsche's God, yet at the same time it is not quite that of this God—it is not absolute in the sense that it could reconcile the *differends*. The fact that the narrator has to relativize his own verdict by acknowledging the progress that came with the "evil" ending (and with it the possible prosperity of future generations) highlights this. While not diminishing his authoritative position, this acknowledgment nevertheless restores the *differends* at the heart of *Fallout 3* which any absolute moral judgment would inevitably have to repress. The narrator's seemingly universal verdict therefore is reduced to the status of a mere *recommendation* to the player. The game thus develops a meta-ethical discourse while taking a stand all the same: even if the narrator is finally unable to solve *Fallout 3*'s fundamental *differends*, he embraces this moral uncertainty consciously and employs his position to advocate his preferred ethical system all the more credibly. Bertrand Russell's famous dictum, quoted by an NPC in the game, sums this up nicely: "War does not determine who is right, only who is left." When the avatar leaves Washington after the end of the game, it is the biographer's retelling that is left, rendering his evaluation of the player's decisions and the avatar's actions uncontestably right—or so it may seem.

Notes

1. This solution is furthermore complicated by the fact that in a quest called "The Power of the Atom," the player may assist Tenpenny in his endeavors to ignite an unexploded nuclear warhead at the center of a nearby town ironically called Megaton. Tenpenny's interests, and those of his crew, are obviously in stark contrast to those of Megaton's inhabitants.

2. For a thorough discussion of the various variants of the classic utilitarianism of Jeremy Bentham, Henry Sidgwick, Francis Ysidro Edgeworth and John Stuart Mill, which accept the sacrifice of the happiness of minorities to promote that of the majority, see Braybrooke 80–130. According to Braybrooke, of the original proponents, the most extreme stance is taken by Edgeworth, who nevertheless stops short of life-sacrifices: "To give more means of happiness to people with larger capacities, Edgeworth is willing, in principle, to have those less favoured in capacity driven below the point of zero happiness, but he thinks it an empirical certainty that well before the less capacious are pushed to the point of starving, 'the pleasures of the most favoured could not weigh much against the privations of the least favoured.' Thus he did not contemplate the privations' being carried so far as to endanger the lives of the least favoured. Moreover, Edgeworth contemplates 'mitigating' the conditions of the least favoured class by having them emigrate. No lives are sacrificed; the emigrants are happier than they were, or at least as happy; and, if the home population is happier in the absence of their infelicible former neighbours and companions, the score for the whole group, divided, will be greater than the score for the whole group undivided" (Braybrooke 82; quotes within the quote from Edgeworth 63–75).

Works Cited

Anderson, Nate. "Video Gaming to Be Twice as Big as Music by 2011." *Ars Technica*. Condé Nast. 30 Aug. 2007. Web. 5 April 2013.
Bentham, Jeremy. *A Fragment on Government*. Oxford: Clarendon Press, 1891. Print.
Braybrooke, David. *Utilitarianism: Restorations; Repairs; Renovations*. Toronto: University of Toronto Press, 2004. Print.
Edgeworth, Francis Ysidro. *Mathematical Psychics*. London: C. Kegan Paul & Co., 1881. Print.
Fallout 3. Bethesda Softworks. 2008. Game.
Fisher, David. *Morality and War*. New York: University of Oxford Press, 2011. Print.
"Games v. Movies: The Numbers." gamepolitics.com. Entertainment Consumers Association. 28 Dec. 2010. Web. 5 April 2013.
Graft, Kris. "Fallout 3 Ships 4.7 M." *Edge Online*. Future Publishing. 6 Nov. 2008. Web. 5 April 2013.
Kant, Immanuel. *Groundwork for the Metaphysics of Morals*. New York: Harper Torchbooks, 1964. Print.
Karmali, Luke. "Mists of Pandaria Pushes Warcraft Subs Over 10 Million." IGN.com. IGN Entertainment Inc. 4 Oct. 2012. Web. 5 April 2013.
Lee, Kristen A. "World of Warcraft Player Colleen Lachowicz Captures Seat in Maine State Senate Despite Republican Attacks on Her 'Bizarre Double Life' as a Gamer." *New York Daily News*. NYDaily.com. 7 Nov. 2012. Web. 5 April 2013.
Lyotard, Jean-Francois. *The Differend: Phrases in Dispute*. Minneapolis: University of Minnesota Press, 1988. Print.
"Newsweek's N'Gai Croal: RE5 Trailer Imagery is Racist." *gamepolitics.com*. Entertainment Consumers Association. 12 April 2008. Web. 5 April 2013.
O'Leary, Amy. "In Virtual Play, Sex Harassment Is All Too Real." NYTimes.com. New York Times. 1 Aug. 2012. Web. 5 April 2013.
Plumer, Brad. "The Economics of Video Games." washingtonpost.com. The Washington Post. 28 Sept. 2012. Web. 5 April 2013.
Roberts, Adam. *Science Fiction*. New York: Routledge, 2010. Print.
Sandel, Michael J. *Justice: What's the Right Thing to Do?* London: Penguin, 2010. Print.
Schulzke, Marcus. "Moral Decision Making in *Fallout*." *Game Studies* 9.2 (2009). Web. 5 April 2013.
Thomson, Judith J. *Rights, Restitution, and Risk*. Cambridge: Harvard University Press, 1986. Print.
Todorov, Tzvetan. *The Fantastic: A Structural Approach to a Literary Genre*. New York: Cornell University Press, 1975. Print.

The Atheist Believer: *Harry Potter* and the Politics of Religion

BÄRBEL HÖTTGES

"Ein Buch ist ein Spiegel, wenn ein Affe hineinguckt,
so kann freilich kein Apostel heraussehen."[1]
[Christoph Georg Lichtenberg]

If readers of J.K. Rowling's *Harry Potter* series were asked to summarize the books, most would probably answer that the series is about a boy wizard fighting evil; some people would maybe also claim that the novels are about friendship and loyalty, or that the narrative is an epic coming-of-age story. Judging from the secondary sources available on the Potter phenomenon, however, we obviously have to revise this statement. Instead, we could assume, *Harry Potter* is about nothing but religion. How else could we explain that dozens of books, scores of articles, hundreds of web pages, and thousands of Internet forum entries are dedicated to the religious world view depicted in the *Harry Potter* series? Interestingly enough, though, there is no consensus concerning the religious orientation of the novels—while some critics accuse Rowling of propagating witchcraft and dark magic, others take exception to Rowling's allegedly atheistic agenda; others again celebrate Rowling's fundamentally Christian worldview and point to an abundance of Christian themes, motifs and biblical parallels that permeate Rowling's novels. The following discussion will analyze this controversy and reveal that Rowling's writing is neither religious nor areligious in itself. Rather, the religious orientation of the series shifts with the readers' ideological world view and their ability to negotiate content and context.

Lucifer's Assistant: *Harry Potter* and the Satanist Conspiracy

The most active faction concerning the *Harry Potter* controversy probably is the Christian right.[2] For many fundamentalist Christians, Harry is a representative of the Antichrist, and the series is nothing but a witchcraft manual that leads innocent children from fictional Polyjuice Potion to real-life Satanist practices. Pastor David J. Meyer of *Last Trumpet Ministries International*, for instance, claims on his website that the books

> are training manuals for the occult. Untold millions of young people are being taught to think, speak, dress and act like witches by filling their heads with the contents of these books. [...] By reading these materials, many millions of young people are learning how to work with demon spirits. [...] These books were taken into homes everywhere with a real evil spirit following each copy to curse those homes.

Similarly, Cindy Jacobs, a right-wing Christian author and journalist, argues that the *Harry Potter* books "are entry-level occult tools that introduce readers to witchcraft"; the series, Jacobs claims, "is clearly demonic in nature. [...] What begins as fantasy leads to real spells and potions. They are open doors for a person to become a practitioner of magic." For many fundamentalist Christians, *Harry Potter* is thus not a children's book but a dangerous starter drug. A Christian educational video entitled *Harry Potter: Witchcraft Repackaged—Making Evil Look Innocent* openly warns, accordingly, that "children as young as kindergarten are being introduced to human sacrifice, the sucking of blood from dead animals, and possession by spirit beings" through *Harry Potter* (McGee [0:05:50–0:06:15]). And Pastor Mike Norris of the *Franklin Road Baptist Church* concludes that allowing your kid to read *Harry Potter* is "just like giving a child a cigarette, then getting him hooked on pot, then taking him to crack cocaine, then on to heroine. These books are just the starting place for evil."

As if millions of newly converted Satanists were not bad enough, some critics even go further and read the *Harry Potter* series in the context of the Apocalypse. Pastor Joseph Chambers of *Paw Creek Ministries*, for example, is convinced that "the Harry Potter series is a creation of hell helping prepare the younger generation to welcome the Biblical prophecies of demons and devils led by Lucifer himself." In a similar manner, the writers of the website *The Cutting Edge* conclude:

> Antichrist can appear, and Harry Potter might just be instrumental in preparing the children of the world for him. [...] Henry [*sic*] Potter books are so overtly Satanic they are designed to quickly put Satan's key in the lock of your children's hearts! [...] Truly, the overwhelming popularity of occult books like Henry [*sic*] Potter plus all the occult themes in TV and movies, tell us that the necessary pre-

conditioning of the population has reached the point where Antichrist can arise. Truly, the End of the Age is upon us ["Book Covers"].

In some cases, the reasoning behind these statements borders on satire. Even though J.K. Rowling has repeatedly stated that she is a Christian, some critics have implied that Rowling's real alliances can be deduced from her statement that she likes Halloween (see "Harry Potter 'A Sorcerers Tale'"; Allan; cf. Soulliere par. 39). Others, such as Pastor Norris, see their assumption that Harry Potter is in league with the Antichrist confirmed by the fact that book-launching parties all over the world took place at *midnight*: "If this has nothing to do with the occult, why do they put it on sale at midnight? Why not at eight o'clock in the morning?" Pastor Chambers even sees the series' genesis as a case in point:

> It all began on a train ride in which the whole idea just dropped in Rowling's head. The very manner in which the series came to her would suggest "spirit influence." She stated, "Harry, as a character, came fully formed as did the idea for his sidekicks, the character of Ron and Hermione, who is the brain of the threesome." [...] Such language sounds familiar to the world of the occult.

Furthermore, Chambers adds on his website, "Harry Potter Takes Drugs," a claim he supports by pointing out that the Potions Master, Severus Snape, mentions "an infusion of wormwood" in one of his classes (see Rowling, *Stone* 102). Since wormwood can be "used to make Absinthe, a hallucinogenic liqueur," Chambers deduces that students at Hogwarts both produce and consume drugs.

While critics such as Chambers are comparatively easy to dismiss,[3] the *Harry Potter* series has been the object of more serious criticism from the Christian right. The most popular objection to the series is the claim that the books violate biblical rules. The biblical book that is most often quoted in this context is Deuteronomy, which explicitly rejects practices such as divination and sorcery: "There shall not be found among you anyone who makes his son or his daughter pass through the fire, one who uses divination, one who practices witchcraft, or one who interprets omens, or a sorcerer, or one who casts a spell, or a medium, or a spiritist, or one who calls up the dead. For whoever does these things is detestable to the Lord" (*KJV*, 18.9–12). Most of the activities mentioned in this passage are indeed on display in the *Harry Potter* universe.[4] While one might point out that there is a decisive difference between reading about and practicing witchcraft (see Koukl), the description of these activities is enough for many critics to condemn the series. As Kimbra Wilder Gish, a comparatively moderate critic, puts it: "Portraying something that we consider to be dangerous as harmless or ineffective is conceptually as perilous as saying it is good or efficacious, if not more so" (266).

The biblical rejection of witchcraft is closely related to another claim that is often brought forward to denounce Rowling and her books—the claim that the series not only portrays but also endorses and promotes witchcraft and the occult. While only few critics such as Berit Kjos, Marcia Montenegro, Glen Spencer, and Matthew J. Slick accuse Rowling of portraying real-life occultism, even more moderate Christian critics often voice the concern that Rowling's fictional spells "could easily present a spiritual danger to children and teens, or even adults, who are either leaning toward occultism or who may be vulnerable to its attractions" (Abanes, *Bible* 24; also see Leap; cf. Soulliere par. 20). While these accusations are usually brought forward by Protestant evangelicals, they are not necessarily restricted to this group; two years before he became Pope Benedict, the Catholic cardinal Joseph Ratzinger also cautioned against the "subtle seductions" of *Harry Potter* which, he claims, "act unnoticed and by this deeply distort Christianity in the soul, before it can grow properly."[5] Most of these critics simply advise their audience to be cautious, implying that *Harry Potter might* negatively influence already insecure adolescents, but some authors also claim that books such as *Harry Potter* are not only *potentially* dangerous but actually responsible for an increase of occult practices among teens.[6]

While only comparatively few critics directly blame Rowling for the alleged popularity of New Age and Wicca practices, many conservatives nevertheless worry about other potentially harmful influences of the *Harry Potter* series on children and teens. Pointing out that Harry and his sidekicks Ron and Hermione often are disobedient, routinely break rules, and sometimes lie and steal to reach their ends, critics such as Richard Abanes and Marsha West argue that Rowling violates Christian virtues and provides bad role models for her teenage audience (see Abanes, *Bible* 68; also see West; cf. Soulliere par. 27). Furthermore, some critics declare, Harry's world does not provide clear boundaries between good and evil, is morally ambiguous, and thus encourages ethical confusion (see Abanes, *Bible* 35; cf. Griesinger, "Deeper Magic" 464; Soulliere par. 27).

While those who bring forward the points mentioned above find fault with the things that can be found in the books (images, actions, characters, world view, plot etc.), others have linked the supposedly anti–Christian orientation of the series to a thing that is *absent* in Harry's world—institutionalized religion. There might be Christmas parties, these critics argue, but Christian services and rituals are consciously absent in Harry's world. William Schnoebelen, a self-appointed Satanist-turned-fundamentalist-Christian, claims, for example, that "[t]he Harry Potter books [...] present a godless universe, one in which the most powerful wizard wins. They are books in which the hero is a wizard who shows no evidence of belief in God and does not use the power of prayer to combat evil." Similarly, Lev Grossman remarked in a *Time Magazine* article in 2007 (at a point when everyone was wondering which character was going to die in the final installment of the series):

> If you want to know who dies in Harry Potter, the answer is easy: God. Harry Potter lives in a world free of any religion or spirituality of any kind. He lives surrounded by ghosts but has no one to pray to, even if he were so inclined, which he isn't. [...] In choosing Rowling as the reigning dreamer of our era, we have chosen a writer who dreams of a secular, bureaucratized, all-too-human sorcery, in which psychology and technology have superseded the sacred.

In a similar manner, the absence of Christian and conservative values in the series is often criticized, an accusation which generally stems from the claim that Rowling portrays conservatives—most notably the Dursleys, who firmly reject the supernatural, but also other Muggles—as ridiculous and ignorant fools (see, for example, O'Brien, "Paganization"; O'Brien, "Death"). Linda Harvey, president and founder of the right-wing organization *Mission: America,* even detects traces of "Anti-Christian Bigotry" in Rowling's series and concludes:

> The message that screams from these pages for children to absorb is that these despicable people who object to "magic" are worthy of the worst scorn. [...] Our children quickly figure out that Muggles equate to traditional conservatives. And who are the most fervently "anti-magic" in real-world America? Christians [cf. also Soulliere par. 23].

In the light of the often extreme accusations described in the previous paragraphs, it is not particularly surprising that many opponents of Rowling's series did not restrict their criticism to verbal protest. Some of them also organized public book-burning parties and similarly extreme measures to display their disgust concerning everything Potter.[7] In addition to public exhortations not to read *Harry Potter*, many right-wing opponents of the series also tried to remove the books from the shelves of libraries and to ban them from classrooms. As a result, *Harry Potter* topped the American Library Association's (ALA) list of the most frequently challenged books in America for several years in the late 1990s and early 2000s, and the series also took first place of the ALA's list of the "Top 100 Banned/Challenged Books: 2000–2009" (see "Frequently Challenged"; "Top 100").[8] Not all attempts to ban *Harry Potter* books from public and private institutions were successful, of course, but the series has been removed from a number of school libraries in the past few years; in some cases, the books as such are still available, but restrictions (such as parental permission) apply (see Elizabeth; Kennedy; "Harry Potter Series"). The official completion of both the book and the movie series in 2007 and 2011, respectively, has somewhat cooled down the zeal to ban Potter from our children's lives, but the controversy, it seems, is by no means over yet, as countless articles, books, websites, and forum entries suggest that continue the discussion even more than five years after the publication of the last installment of the series.

Christ's Companion: *Harry Potter* and the Christian Subtext

Considering these extreme religious objections to the *Harry Potter* novels, one might be surprised to learn that Rowling's series has also been hailed as inherently *Christian* by critics. Analyzing the novels' imagery, their plot structures, and their world view, critics such as John Granger, John Killinger, Gregory Koukl, Connie Neal, Alan Jacobs, Dave Bruno, Ari Armstrong, and Emily Griesinger celebrate the series' deeply Christian orientation. John Granger, for example, a Christian author who home-schools his children "to keep them on course with biblical values and virtue" (*Looking* 183), detects a "profoundly Christian meaning at the core of the series" and stresses the "implicit Christian content of the books" (*Looking* xviii, xx). Similarly, Ari Armstrong claims that "Rowling's novels promote important Christian themes" (51), and Connie Neal maintains that the "general themes of each book uphold and promote foundational beliefs and Judeo-Christian values emphasized throughout the Bible" (*Gospel* 4). Rev. Dr. John Killinger even goes a step further, arguing that "the Potter mythology [...] is not only dependent on the Christian understanding of life and the universe, *but actually grows out of that understanding and would have been unthinkable without it*" (11).

To support this view, critics point to a number of plot details, images, and references that evoke and support a Christian context and world view. Dan McVeigh, for instance, sees Rowling's series in line with "a Christian Romantic tradition" (199), among other things because she incorporates Christian views and symbols into her narrative: "Dumbledore rescues Harry from destruction with a Phoenix [...]. As far back as A.D. 200 and throughout the Middle Ages the Phoenix symbolized the resurrected Christ, who set a pattern for all in His conquest of that which is 'Full of Death'" (210). Derek Murphy reveals in his analysis that many of the novels' images also have a biblical origin: Voldemort and the Slytherins are associated with the snake, a biblical symbol of temptation and evil, while Harry and Gryffindor—like Christ—are associated with the symbol of the lion (see Murphy 4). Furthermore, there are major similarities between Harry's and Christ's stories. Especially in *Harry Potter and the Deathly Hallows*, it is hard to miss these parallels, and Harry's sacrificial death—Harry is willing to lay down his life so that others may live—has been interpreted as a deeply Christian gesture and as a tribute to Christian values by various critics as a result (see, for example, Adler; Griesinger, "Why" 311; Granger, *How* 233, 240–41). Analyzing Rowling's intertextual allusions to the Bible, Dave Bruno even suggests that "Harry Potter 7 Is Matthew 6," arguing that Rowling not only quotes the Bible verbatim in *Harry Potter and the Deathly Hallows* but also uses Matthew's gospel to provide the novel with meaning.[9]

To support their claims, Christian advocates of Rowling's series also directly address the accusations brought forward by the Christian right. While the right-wing critic Richard Abanes argues, for example, that Rowling propagates "ethical and moral subjectivism" because Harry does as he pleases and is usually rewarded rather than reprimanded for his disobedience (see *Bible* 39, 35–38), Emily Griesinger points out that Harry generally *is* punished whenever he breaks school rules and that there are "definite moral and ethical ground rules" in Rowling's world ("Deeper Magic" 464). In a similar manner, Alan Jacobs rejects the claim that Rowling's world is morally ambiguous and thus harmful for kids: "The clarity with which Rowling sees the need to choose between good and evil is admirable, but still more admirable, to my mind, is her refusal to allow a simple division of parties into the Good and the Evil. Harry Potter is unquestionably a good boy, but, as I have suggested, a key component of his virtue arises from his recognition that he is not *inevitably* good." It is thus *choice* rather than nature that determines what is good and what is evil in Rowling's world, and even though Rowling offers realistic and round characters—"good" characters such as Dumbledore or Harry have negative sides, "bad" characters such as Malfoy or Dudley show moments of compassion—she nevertheless clearly differentiates between good and evil and the need to fight for what is right even at the risk of one's life. Even though the books contain witchcraft, critics such as Griesinger conclude, Harry thus is a wonderful role model for Christian children, as the books celebrate values such as love, friendship, compassion, loyalty, and self-sacrifice and thus offer a profoundly Christian world view at their core.

Perspective's Ally: *Harry Potter* and the Aesthetics of Reception

Those who condemn *Harry Potter* for religious reasons have little sympathy for critics such as Griesinger, Granger, and Killinger. As Richard Abanes puts it: "There is this whole movement within Christianity where people are trying to say that the Harry Potter books are Christian novels. And that is just untrue. You can't interpret it that way" ("Harmless"). Such a dualistic view, which clearly differentiates between valid and invalid readings, may be convenient because it makes being right so much easier. This view, however, ignores the fact that literature is always open to interpretation and that different views *are* legitimate as long as they are based on textual evidence.

A theory which analyzes this phenomenon—and which can be used to explain the religious controversy concerning the interpretation of the *Harry Potter* series—is Wolfgang Iser's aesthetic response theory, a model that tries to explain the interactions between readers and texts. Iser assumes that the meaning of the text is neither determined by its author nor can it be found "encapsulated" in a text; rather, it *develops* between text and reader:

> a literary work has two poles, which we might call the artistic and the aesthetic: the artistic pole is the author's text and the aesthetic is the realization accomplished by the reader. In view of this polarity, it is clear that the work itself cannot be identical with the text or with the concretization, but must be situated somewhere between the two. It must inevitably be virtual in character, as it cannot be reduced to the reality of the text or to the subjectivity of the reader, and it is from this virtuality that it derives its dynamism. As the reader passes through the various perspectives offered by the text and relates the different views and patterns to one another he sets the work in motion, and so sets himself in motion, too. [...] Thus, the meaning of a literary text is not a definable entity but, if anything, a dynamic happening [21-22].

There is, in consequence, no "correct" meaning of a text, as the meaning of a text develops and redevelops with every individual reading. This sounds like a call for interpretative anarchy, but Iser is actually not propagating total subjectivism. "However individual may be the meaning realized in each case," Iser insists, "the act of composing it will always have intersubjectively verifiable characteristics" (22). Put differently, an interpretation must be based on and justified by certain aspects of the text, but as long as it is, a text will nevertheless inevitably produce different interpretations in different readers.

Iser finds an explanation for this phenomenon in the nature of fictional texts. A literary text, according to Iser, is not a monolithic structure containing a predetermined meaning but rather a fabric consisting of various segments (characters, plot, narrator, etc.), which become meaningful in relation to each other only (see 195–96). Segments are coherent units, but between the segments, breaks and gaps, which Iser calls *blanks*, become visible: "Between segments and cuts there is an empty space, giving rise to a whole network of possible connections which will endow each segment [...] with its determinate meaning" (196). Blanks, Iser claims, "mark the suspension of connectability between textual segments" (195), requiring the reader to negotiate the various segments in order to fill the blanks coherently. "[W]henever the reader bridges the gaps," Iser claims, "communication begins. The gaps function as a kind of pivot on which the whole text-reader relationship revolves. Hence the structured blanks of the text stimulate the process of ideation to be performed by the reader on terms set by the text" (169). One and the same text will thus produce different readings in different readers because each reader fills the blanks and negotiates the segments of a text according to his or her own perception, experience, and world view.

This theory makes sense concerning the religious controversy concerning *Harry Potter*, as it explains why the books can be considered Satanic and Christian at the same time—the reading depends on the reader and his or her way of negotiating blanks and segments in Rowling's narrative. I would argue, however, that the theory can only in part account for the religious controversy and the extremely different religious perception of the series. Two other constellations come into play here as well: the readers' ideological orientation and their ability to negotiate text and context.

The ideological factor in the reception of the *Harry Potter* series is comparatively easy to spot because people who reject *Harry Potter* for religious reasons usually do not only share a religious but also a political and ideological world view. In the U.S., for instance, those who condemn *Harry Potter* are usually members of evangelical Christian organizations and the Christian right. Religious, political, and ideological attitudes are inextricably intertwined in these circles, and peer pressure is high. Once a consensus concerning a certain issue is reached, members are expected to conform, and those who voice doubts are quickly targeted by their former allies.[10] To endorse *Harry Potter* in public is as unthinkable for many evangelical leaders as supporting abortion, gay rights, or evolution. This is a *political* rather than *religious* phenomenon, and the rejection of everything Potter has nothing to do with blanks or segments in this case but rather with ideological conviction.[11] In this respect, it is the community *around* the reader—rather than the reader him- or herself—that determines or at least decisively influences the perception of a text.

One of the few scholars who acknowledge and describe this phenomenon in theoretical terms is the critic Stanley Fish. The reader, he claims, is not an independent agent in his reception of a text because the strategies that he or she employs to understand a text

> proceed not from him but from the interpretive community of which he is a member. [...] Indeed, it is interpretive communities, rather than either the text or the reader, that produce meanings and are responsible for the emergence of formal features. Interpretive communities are made up of those who share interpretive strategies not for reading but for writing texts, for constituting their properties. In other words these strategies exist prior to the act of reading and therefore determine the shape of what is read rather than, as is usually assumed, the other way around [14].

These considerations certainly make sense concerning the *Harry Potter* controversy because they explain why the individual reception of the series so often corresponds with the political, religious, and ideological convictions of certain communities. I would argue, however, that among less radical readers, Fish's theory can account for the different perceptions of the series in part because more moderate Christian groups generally lack a clear consensus concerning *Harry Potter*. There are individual Catholic leaders such as Cardinal Ratzinger, for example, who caution against the series, but there is no public consensus concerning the novels among Catholics. In less political circles, it seems, the perception of the series is much more determined by the individual reader than by group convictions, and the influence of interpretive communities seems to decline. In these cases, a force comes into play that probably has to be located somewhere *between* the reader and his or her interpretative community: whether one perceives the series as Christian, atheist, or anti-Christian depends, I claim, mainly on the reader's ability—or willingness—to negotiate text and context.[12] Put differently, how much institutional context do we need to perceive something as Christian? Or, metaphorically speaking, do we recognize coffee if it is served in a soup bowl, or is the container a necessary prerequisite in our perception of its content?

The last installment of the series, *Harry Potter and the Deathly Hallows*, can be most easily used to illustrate this claim because it contains a scene that is prototypical of the series' religious world view. The scene I am referring to takes place roughly in the middle of the narrative, when Harry and Hermione go to a village called Godric's Hollow to pay a visit to the grave of Harry's parents. They approach the village square in the dark one late winter afternoon:

> Strung all around with coloured lights, there was what looked like a war memorial in the middle, partly obscured by a windblown Christmas tree. [...] They heard a snatch of laughter and pop music as the pub door opened and closed; then they heard a carol start up inside the little church.
> "Harry, I think it's Christmas Eve!" said Hermione.
> "Is it?"
> He had lost track of the date; they had not seen a newspaper for weeks. [...]
> The singing grew louder as they approached the church. It made Harry's throat constrict, it reminded him so forcefully of Hogwarts, of Peeves bellowing rude versions of carols from inside suits of armor, of the Great Hall's twelve Christmas trees, of Dumbledore wearing a bonnet he had won in a cracker, of Ron in a hand-knitted sweater... [358–60].

The two teenagers enter the dark graveyard and soon find familiar names on the snowy headstones, even though they do not find the grave of Harry's parents right away:

> Harry stooped down and saw, upon the frozen, lichen-spotted granite, the words *Kendra Dumbledore* [...] *and her daughter Ariana*. There was also a quotation: *Where your treasure is, there will your heart also be.* [...] He did not understand what these words meant. [...]
> "Harry [...] Look at this!" The grave [Hermione was pointing to] was extremely old, weathered so that Harry could hardly make out the name. Hermione showed him the symbol beneath it.
> "Harry, that's the mark in the book!"
> He peered at the place she indicated: the stone was so worn that it was hard to make out what was engraved there, though there did seem to be a triangular mark beneath the nearly illegible name. [...]
> The darkness and the silence seemed to become, all of a sudden, much deeper.

Harry looked around, worried, thinking of Dementors, then realized that the carols had finished, that the chatter and flurry of church-goers were fading away as they made their way back into the square. Somebody inside the church had just turned off the lights [361–63].

Finally, Harry and Hermione spot James and Lilly's grave. The headstone immediately catches Harry's attention:

> Harry did not have to kneel or even approach very close to it to make out the words engraved upon it: [...] *The last enemy that shall be destroyed is death.* [...] A horrible thought came to him [Harry], and with it a kind of panic. "Isn't that a Death Eater idea? Why is that there?"
> "It doesn't mean defeating death in the way the Death Eaters mean it, Harry," said Hermione, her voice gentle. "It means... you know... living beyond death. Living after death."
> But they were not living, thought Harry: they were gone. The empty words could not disguise the fact that his parents' mouldering remains lay beneath snow and stone, indifferent, unknowing. And tears came before he could stop them. [...] He should have brought something to give them, and he had not thought of it, and every plant in the graveyard was leafless and frozen. But Hermione raised her wand, moved it in a circle through the air and a wreath of Christmas roses blossomed before her. Harry caught it and laid it on his parents' grave [363–65].

In a way, this short scene contains everything there is to say about religion in the *Harry Potter* universe, and it also allows a brief, if indirect, glimpse at the series' religious makeup. Like the books in general, the scene offers three different religious perspectives. The first shows a thoroughly atheist narrative, as religion does not seem to play a role in this scene: Harry does not even remember that it is Christmas, and when he does, he thinks of secular rather than religious rituals. Furthermore, Harry and Hermione are, both literally and metaphorically, *outside* of the church—they are not part of the community of believers, and they obviously also do not feel the desire to join the churchgoers. At his parents' grave, Harry cries but does not pray, and Christian symbols are either missing (there are no crosses or other Christian symbols adorning the headstones) or they have become empty signifiers (like, for example, Hogwarts' twelve Christmas trees). Examined from this angle, the scene echoes Lev Grossman's statement that "Harry Potter lives in a world free of any religion or spirituality of any kind. He lives surrounded by ghosts but has no one to pray to, even if he were so inclined, which he isn't. [...] [P]sychology and technology have superseded the sacred."

In addition to this supposedly atheist makeup, evangelical readers are likely to see traces of the occult in this scene. Rowling not only sends Harry to the graveyard at nighttime, she also adorns the graves of wizards with occult rather than Christian symbolism. Hermione does not yet recognize the triangular symbol she encounters on one of the ancient graves, but it is, as she will find out later, a symbol signifying the belief in deathly hallows, three magical objects which, according to a wizard legend, make their owner the master of death. Death is, in consequence, not conquered by Christ and divine grace in Rowling's world, but rather by magical objects and occult practices. For the undiscerning reader, the inscription on Harry's parents' grave also seems to be connected to this occult desire to master death, and even Harry senses danger and dark magic from the words he reads there. From this perspective, Harry is not only outside of the church that night but also *opposed* to it.

A third, albeit more hidden, perspective offers an altogether different approach. While the scene appears to leave the Christian faith behind, a closer look reveals that Christianity still permeates the scene and provides it with meaning. On a more abstract level, one could argue that the scene endorses Christian values such as love and charity. Harry does not enter the graveyard to celebrate a black mass, after all, but because his love for his dead parents draws him to the place. Furthermore, he stands at the grave of two people who sacrificed their own lives so that their son might live, which could be interpreted as the highest and purest form of brotherly love. But even if one ignores these comparatively abstract implications, the passage is much closer to Christian traditions than many people might think, because the inscriptions on the two graves are neither references to the occult nor the product of Rowling's imagination: even though traditional markers such as references to chapters and verses are absent, the inscriptions are direct Bible quotations.

The passage on Ariana's grave is taken from Matthew 6: 19–21: "Lay not up for yourselves treasures upon earth, where moth and rust doth corrupt, and where thieves break through and steal: But lay up for yourselves treasures in heaven, where neither moth nor rust doth corrupt, and where thieves do not break through nor steal: For where your treasure is, there will your heart be also" (*KJV*). Harry assumes that Dumbledore must have chosen the words. Considering that Dumbledore inadvertently contributed to his sister's death because he was busy seeking power and fame rather than taking care of his family, one might interpret the inscription as a painful realization—Dumbledore's thirst for power was indeed an earthly treasure, and it had corrupted his heart. After his sister's death had opened his eyes, Dumbledore started to collect different treasures: instead of fighting for power and his personal advantage, he started fighting for the good of others, protecting the weak and opposing evil. One might argue that Dumbledore does not become a nominal Christian after his sister's death (whether he is a nominal Christian or not, we do not know); the values he espouses, however, certainly are Christian in nature.

The inscription on the grave of Harry's parents is taken from 1 Corinthians and deals with the question of life after death. Since Christ has risen from the dead, Paul insists in this letter, we may all hope to rise from death as well:

> For since by man came death, by man came also the resurrection of the dead. For as in Adam all die, even so in Christ shall all be made alive. But every man in his own order: Christ the firstfruits; afterward they that are Christ's at his coming. Then cometh the end, when he shall have delivered up the kingdom to God, even the Father; when he shall have put down all rule and all authority and power. For he must reign, till he hath put all enemies under his feet. The last enemy that shall be destroyed is death [*KJV*, 1 Cor. 21–26].

The passage, thus, does not refer to occult practices and the deathly hallows, as one might assume, but rather to the Christian hope of resurrection. Harry might be hopeless at this point, but Rowling obviously is not, and Harry, too, will later find out that death is not the end of things and that his parents are still with him. While Harry and Hermione are not *in* the church that night, they are thus—both literally and metaphorically—still in its vicinity (literally because they are in the churchyard, i.e., still on hallowed ground, and metaphorically because the Bible quotations evoke a Christian context).[13]

This observation brings us back to the image of coffee served in a soup bowl: why do some people detect Christian foundations in this scene while others do not? I think the answer to this question can be found in that churchyard: Rowling and Harry have left *institutionalized* religion behind. Christianity clearly is still there—the Bible quotations, the values, the world view—but the indicators that usually mark a religious perspective (the references to particular Bible passages, the church services, the creed) are absent. Rowling, who has stated several times that she *is* a Christian, serves a Christian world view in a non–Christian context.

In a way, the religious makeup of the entire series is contained in this scene in *Harry Potter and the Deathly Hallows* because Rowling discusses Christian themes and motifs in a very similar manner in the other books as well. Rowling introduces Christian values and concepts,[14] she uses Christian images and symbols,[15] and she incorporates biblical parallels into her narrative.[16] Rowling may play around with these concepts, and she certainly avoids mono-dimensional, flat characters and situations, but she never rejects, undermines, or mocks Christianity in her novels—if anything, she endorses concepts such as love, self-sacrifice and tolerance, and she clearly rejects self-centeredness and injustice. Ultimately, even magic remains a literary backdrop—it is not a superior spell that allows Harry to triumph in the end but his *moral choices*; similarly, the deathly hallows and the horcruxes, which could be read as an occult counterdraft to the Christian concept of immortality, are exposed as spiritually empty, dangerous, and ultimately ineffective cul-de-sacs.

Religion, thus, clearly is there in *Harry Potter*. Despite the many references to Christianity, however, Rowling never openly connects her story to institutionalized religion or religious doctrine, and the series is certainly not meant to be a Christian allegory (like, for example, the *Chronicles of Narnia*, whose Christian context is hard, if not impossible, to miss). Rowling's story consequently is religious but not *about* religion—it offers a religious *content* but not a religious *context*. For those who need a clear creed, the series thus will remain inacceptable, no matter how many biblical parallels or values it contains, because the context is a necessary prerequisite in the evaluation of the content for these individuals.

The issue of religion in *Harry Potter*, thus, boils down to the following question: do we need the institutionalized container to recognize its religious content? Or are we able to recognize the content for what it is even in a different context? In this respect, it is not only the blank that turns *Harry Potter* into a controversial series but also the world view of its audience, which does or does not allow readers to assume a certain perspective. The discussion of religion in Rowling's series can thus never come to a satisfying conclusion by relying on literary analyses alone; it needs to take personal, political, and ideological considerations into account, too, because these issues shape the perception of that topic as much as—or even more than—traditional categories such as plot and imagery do.

If we consider these implications, all questions concerning the religious orientation of the *Harry Potter* series can easily be answered: Is *Harry Potter* a Christian narrative? Absolutely. Is it Satanist? For sure. Is it atheist? No doubt. This realization does not, of course, tell us anything about the spiritual consequences of reading *Harry Potter*. So the more accurate question would probably be what reading *Harry Potter* will do to our children. Will some kids wear fake glasses and wave plastic wands after reading *Harry Potter*? Certainly. Will they play wizard and enter Hogwarts in their dreams? Many will. Will they become Satanists? Considering that there are millions of *Harry Potter* readers all around the world, we probably cannot completely eliminate that possibility. But if Rowling has produced a generation of "Satanists" who like reading and endorse values such as tolerance, compassion, loyalty, friendship, and selflessness, I, for my part, would take the risk.

Notes

1. Quoted in Gallmeier 74. Translation: "A book is like a mirror. If a monkey looks in, you cannot expect an apostle to look out."

2. As Gemmill and Nexon note, opposition to Rowling's series is a worldwide phenomenon with important strongholds in the U.S., Australia, Canada, Russia, and Thailand (see 79). The following analysis will focus on the reception of *Harry Potter* in U.S.-American culture.

3. Chambers does not seem to be too familiar with the *Harry Potter* series; he once refers to "young Henry" when talking about Harry, and also freely admits that he only read "the first chapter [of *The Goblet of Fire*] as it appeared in the Newsweek magazine," which does not stop him from diagnosing "a glorification of the devil" in that book. Many other self-appointed evangelical *Harry*

II. The Politics of Fantasy

Potter experts reveal similar weaknesses in their analyses. The anonymous *Harry Potter* authority on the website of *The Cutting Edge*, for instance, also calls Harry "Henry" several times (see "Book Covers"), and Mike Norris summarizes the dangerous activities in *Harry Potter* as follows: "Three times a week the students went out to the greenhouses to study potions. The history of magic class was taught by a ghost, and it is very evident that he taught about out-of-body experiences. Harry thought transfigurations were difficult to learn: teachers could change children into animals and then back again." While Norris gets some things right—the History of Magic classes are indeed taught by a ghost—people who have actually read the books will know that out-of-body experiences are not on the students' syllabus at Hogwarts and that the students do not study Potions in the greenhouses. Similarly, teachers do not turn children into animals in Rowling's series, at least not in Transfiguration classes. (The only possible exception might be the scene when Barty Crouch, disguised as Prof. Moody, transforms Draco Malfoy into a ferret, but this does not take place in a Transfiguration class and, according to Prof. Minerva McGonagall, clearly violates the rules of Hogwarts [see Rowling, *Goblet* 180–82].)

    4. Shortly before he faces Voldemort in *Harry Potter and the Philosopher's Stone*, Harry walks through a wall of fire after drinking a potion that allows him to proceed unharmed (see 208); Divination is an elective course (third years and up) which includes interpreting omens and star-gazing/astrology (see *Harry Potter and the Prisoner of Azkaban* and *Harry Potter and the Order of the Phoenix*); witchcraft and casting spells are, of course, a daily business at Hogwarts; furthermore, Trelawney, one of the teachers of Divination, considers herself a seer, which at least brings her close to being a medium and to spiritist activities, even though her predictions only very rarely come true; finally, the Resurrection Stone allows Harry to talk to the dead in *Harry Potter and the Deathly Hallows*.

    5. In a letter to Gabriele Kuby, a conservative Christian critic from Germany, Ratzinger wrote in 2003: "Es ist gut, daß Sie in Sachen Harry Potter aufklären, denn dies sind subtile Verführungen, die unmerklich und gerade dadurch tief wirken und das Christentum in der Seele zersetzen, ehe es überhaupt recht wachsen konnte" (Ratzinger, "Letter"). In a second letter, Ratzinger explicitly allowed Kuby to publish his statement concerning *Harry Potter* (see Ratzinger, "Permission").

    6. Mark Nash, a contributor to theTRUMPET.com claims, for example, that "[s]ince the advent of Harry Potter, the inquiries to occult related organizations have skyrocketed. Many such associations have added a 'youth' adviser to handle the increased interest from children." Similarly, Linda Harvey, president of the conservative Christian organization *Mission: America*, claims that "[m]any teens say their interest was initially sparked by reading Harry Potter books" (also see "Harry Potter's Influence").

    7. Daniel Schwartz of the Canadian CBC News Network reports that there were at least six public book-burning parties involving the Harry Potter series between 1998 and 2011. Since permission to burn books in public was not granted by the authorities in some cases in the U.S., there were also some public book cuttings that allowed participants to express their disdain for the Harry Potter books by publicly destroying them with knives and scissors (see Serchuk; Elizabeth; "Satanic Harry").

    8. A challenge, according to the ALA, "is an attempt to remove or restrict materials, based upon the objections of a person or group. Challenges [...] are an attempt to remove material from the curriculum or library, thereby restricting the access of others"; a banning "is the removal of those materials" ("About").

    9. That Bruno's interpretation is not as far-fetched as it may sound was confirmed by Rowling during a press conference in October 2007, about two months after the publication of *Harry Potter and the Deathly Hallows*. During this press conference, Rowling stated that the Bible quotations in that novel "almost epitomize the whole series. I think they sum up all the themes in the whole series" (reported in Adler). I will address these Bible quotations and their meaning in my discussion of the graveyard scene in Deathly Hallows in section III of this essay.

    10. At the very beginning of the *Harry Potter* controversy in the late 1990s, a few Evangelicals started out supporting *Harry Potter*. In 1999, for example, Chuck Colson endorsed the *Harry Potter* series in his *Breakpoint* broadcast. Harry and his friends, he claimed, "develop courage,

loyalty, and a willingness to sacrifice for one another—even at the risk of their lives. Not bad lessons in a self-centered world." In the years that followed, Colson was violently attacked for his opinion. In 2007, Colson departed from his original view and rejected the series: "Now personally, I don't recommend the Potter books. I'd rather Christian kids not read them. [...] Dare them to have [biblical] Daniel as their role model, not Harry Potter." The evangelical Christian author James Dobson faced similar problems. Several sources attributed the following statement to Dobson: "Harry Potter is a standard tale of good vs. evil, and good always wins in the end. Harry, the hero, often triumphs because of his upright character and pure motives. Unconditional love and courage are held as ideals of great importance. By following Harry and his best friend Ron, the reader gets a glimpse of true loyalty and friendship, as well as self-sacrifice" (see, for example, "James Dobson"). Even though Dobson claims that he has never made this statement (see Jackson), a number of critics subsequently attacked Dobson—Pastor David Meyer, for instance, insults both Dobson and Colson on his website and sheds doubts on their Christian orientation: "Sadly enough, this blatant witchcraft has been endorsed by well-known and respected 'Christian' leaders, such as Dr. James Dobson and Chuck Colson who have proven themselves to be modern day Judas Iscariots." These examples show that one's attitude toward *Harry Potter* is not a matter of personal opinion in fundamentalist circles but rather a yardstick of character and, most importantly, true faith.

11. Hence Richard Abanes' statement that "You can't interpret it [*Harry Potter*] that way [i.e., as a book endorsing Christianity]." Abanes is not concerned with literary considerations or interpretative questions here, but rather takes an ideological and political stance.

12. The *ability* to negotiate text and context, I would argue, mainly depends on the readers' world view and their mental flexibility; the *willingness* to play with these categories, by contrast, is probably influenced by interpretive communities as well.

13. Harry also unknowingly reenacts a medieval nativity play in this passage, which further enforces the Christian implications of the scene: according to a folk legend, a poor shepherd girl wanted to greet the newborn savior along with the other shepherds and the Three Kings at the stable in Bethlehem. Realizing that she had nothing to give to Jesus, the girl started crying. An angel appeared and pointed to the frozen ground. Suddenly, Christmas roses started to blossom at the girl's feet so that she finally had something to offer to the baby (see Foley 84).

14. That Rowling introduces (and endorses) values such as love, selflessness, compassion, and self-sacrifice in her series is easy to discern, but especially in *Harry Potter and the Deathly Hallows*, she also discusses concepts such as sin and redemption: after his sacrificial death, Harry sees Voldemort's mutilated soul represented by a wounded, whimpering, and agonized creature resembling a newborn child. This, Rowling implies, is Voldemort's spiritual destiny. The only way for Voldemort to escape this hellish fate, Hermione states, would be "[r]emorse [...] You've got to really feel what you've done" (119). Spiritually, you thus clearly pay for your sins in Rowling's world, and the concept of true remorse is not so different from that of confession and atonement.

15. In addition to comparatively obvious Christian symbols such as the snake, the lion, and the phoenix, Rowling also includes some less obvious Christian images. The Dark Mark, for instance, a brand that Death Eaters bear on their left forearms, is reminiscent of the mark of the beast mentioned in chapter 13 of the Book of Revelation, which the followers of the beast bear on their hands or foreheads (see Neal, "Harry Potter"). Furthermore, when Harry sacrifices himself, Voldemort uses the *Cruciatus* curse—which derives from the Latin word *crux* (as in crucifixion)—on Harry, and Harry spends the minutes after his "death" at King's *Cross*. Both images further enforce the connection between Christ's and Harry's sacrificial death.

16. Derek Murphy lists a number of parallels between Jesus and Harry: "Magic Father, human mother. Miraculous birth, foretold by prophesy. Threatened by an evil ruler, had to go into hiding as a baby. Power over animals, time, and matter. Symbolized by a lion / enemy symbolized by a snake. Descended into the underworld. Broke seven magical seals. Went willingly to his death. Suffered and died (or appeared to die) willingly, was mourned. Came back to life. Defeated his enemy in a glorious final battle" (4).

WORKS CITED

Abanes, Richard. *Harry Potter and the Bible: The Menace Behind the Magick*. Camp Hill: Horizon Books, 2001. Print.

_____. "Harry Potter: Harmless Christian Novel or Doorway to the Occult?" Interview with Belinda Elliott. Christian Broadcasting Network. Web. 1 Oct. 2012.

"About Banned & Challenged Books." *American Library Association*. Web. 1 Oct. 2012.

Adler, Shawn. "'Harry Potter' Author J.K. Rowling Opens Up About Books' Christian Imagery: 'They Almost Epitomize the Whole Series,' She Says of the Scripture Harry Reads in Godric's Hollow." Mtv.com. 17 Oct. 2007. Web. 1 Oct. 2012.

Allan, Sterling D. "Harry Potter: Satanic Godsend Mainstreaming Witchcraft." *Greater Things*. 19 Dec. 2011. Web. 1 Oct. 2012.

Armstrong, Ari. "Religion in Harry Potter." *Skeptic* 17.1 (2011): 51–53. Print.

"Book Covers of Two Harry Potter Books Display Occult Symbols of the Antichrist!" *The Cutting Edge*. Web. 1 Oct. 2012.

Bruno, Dave. "Harry Potter 7 Is Matthew 6: The Young Wizard May Not Have Read the Bible, But Someone Else Certainly Did." *Christianity Today*. 2 Aug. 2007. Web. 1 Oct. 2012.

Chambers, Joseph. "The Harry Potter Series: A Vision of the Antichrist." *Paw Creek Ministries*. 26 Oct. 2009. Web. 1 Oct. 2012.

Colson, Chuck. "Witches and Wizards: The Harry Potter Phenomenon." *BreakPoint*. 2 Nov. 1999. Web. 1 Oct. 2012.

Elizabeth, Jane. "Like Magic, Harry Potter Draws a Record Number of Complaints." Postgazette.com. 17. Nov. 2001. *Pittsburgh Post-Gazette*. Web. 1 Oct. 2012.

Fish, Stanley. *Is There a Text in This Class? The Authority of Interpretive Communities*. Cambridge: Harvard University Press, 1980. Print.

Foley, Michael P. *Why Do Catholics Eat Fish on Friday? The Catholic Origin to Just About Everything*. New York: Palgrave Macmillan, 2005. Print.

"Frequently Challenged." *American Library Association*. Web. 1 Oct. 2012.

Gallmeier, Michael. *Georg Christoph Lichtenberg: Leben und Vermächtnis*. Hamburg: Johann Trautmann Verlag, 1948. Print.

Gemmill, Maia A., and Daniel H. Nexon. "Children's Crusade: The Religious Politics of Harry Potter." *Harry Potter and International Relations*. Ed. Daniel H. Nexon and Iver B. Neumann. Lanham, MD: Rowman and Littlefield Publishers, 2006. 79–100. Print.

Gish, Kimbra Wilder. "Hunting Down Harry Potter: An Exploration of Religious Concerns about Children's Literature." *The Horn Book Magazine* 76.3 (2000): 262–71. Print.

Granger, John. *How Harry Cast His Spell*. Carol Stream: Tyndale House, 2008. Print.

_____. *Looking for God in Harry Potter*. Carol Stream: Tyndale House, 2006. Print.

Griesinger, Emily. "Harry Potter and the 'Deeper Magic': Narrating Hope in Children's Literature." *Christianity and Literature* 51.3 (2002): 455–80. Print.

_____. "Why Read Harry Potter? J.K. Rowling and the Christian Debate." *Christian Scholar's Review* 32.3 (2003): 297–316. Print.

Grossman, Lev. "Who Dies in Harry Potter? God." *Time*. 12 July 2007. Web. 1 Oct. 2012.

"Harry Potter 'A Sorcerers Tale.'" *Let Us Reason Ministries*. 2009. Web. 1 Oct. 2012.

"Harry Potter Series—Selected Challenges." Jan. 2008. Web. 1 Oct. 2012.

"Harry Potter's Influence Goes Unchallenged in Most Homes and Churches." *Barna Group*. 1 May 2006. Web. 1 Oct. 2012.

Harvey, Linda. "Harry Potter and Anti-Christian Bigotry." *WND*. 18 July 2007. WordNetDaily. Web. 1 Oct. 2012.

Iser, Wolfgang. *The Act of Reading: A Theory of Aesthetic Response*. Baltimore: Johns Hopkins University Press, 1978. Print.

Jackson, Kevin. "Dobson Officially Denounces 'Harry Potter.'" ChristianPost.com. 23 July 2007. *Christian Post*. Web. 1 Oct. 2012.
Jacobs, Alan. "Harry Potter's Magic." *First Things* 1 (2000). Web. 1 Oct. 2012.
Jacobs, Cindy. "What's Wrong with Harry Potter?" *Charisma Magazine*. 30 Nov. 2001. Charisma Media. Web. 1 Oct. 2012.
"James Dobson." conservapedia.com. 30 May 2011. Web. 1 Oct. 2012.
Kennedy, Elizabeth. "The Harry Potter Controversy: Book Banning and Censorship Battles." about.com. Web. 1 Oct. 2012.
Killinger, John. *God, the Devil, and Harry Potter: A Christian Minister's Defense of the Beloved Novels*. New York: Thomas Dunne Books, 2002. Print.
Kjos, Berit. "Harry Potter and the Postmodern Church." Newswithviews.com. June 2004. Web. 1 Oct. 2012.
Koukl, Gregory. "Musings on Harry Potter." *Stand to Reason*. 2001. Web. 1 Oct. 2012.
Leap, Dennis. "Parents, Get to Know Harry Potter." *Philadelphia Trumpet* 10.9 (1999). The TRUMPET.com. Web. 1 Oct. 2012.
McGee, Robert S., and Caryl Matrisciana. *Harry Potter: Witchcraft Repackaged—Making Evil Look Innocent*. Jeremiah Films, 2001. Web. 1 Oct. 2012.
McVeigh, Dan. "Is Harry Potter Christian?" *Renascence* 54.3 (2002): 97–214. Print.
Meyer, David J. "Harry Potter? What Does God Have to Say?" *Last Trumpet Ministries Online*. Web. 1 Oct. 2012.
Montenegro, Marcia. "Occult: Harry Potter—Sorcery and Fantasy." *Reachout Trust: Building a Bridge of Reason*. 1 Jan. 2004. Web. 1 Oct. 2012.
Murphy, Derek. *Jesus Potter Harry Christ: The Fascinating Parallels Between Two of the World's Most Popular Literary Characters*. Portland: Holy Blasphemy Publishers, 2011. Print.
Nash, Mark. "What Is It about Harry?" *Philadelphia Trumpet* 12.10 (2001). TheTRUMPET.com. Web. 1 Oct. 2012.
Neal, Connie. "A Harry Potter Villain Beat His 'Dark Mark': So Can We." *Beliefnet*. Web. 1 Oct. 2012.
Neal, Connie. *The Gospel According to Harry Potter: The Spiritual Journey of the World's Greatest Seeker*. 2nd ed. Louisville: Westminster John Knox Press, 2008. Print.
Norris, Mike. "Harry Potter: A Dangerous Hero for Our Children!" jesus-is-savior.com. Web. 1 Oct. 2012.
O'Brien, Michael D. "Harry Potter and 'the Death of God.'" LifeSiteNews.com. 20 Aug 2007. Web. 1 Oct. 2012.
_____. "Harry Potter and the Paganization of Children's Culture." LifeSiteNews.com. 31 July 2001. Web. 1 Oct. 2012.
Ratzinger, Joseph. "Letter." LifeSiteNews.com. Web. 1 Oct. 2012.
_____. "Permission." LifeSiteNews.com. Web. 1 Oct. 2012.
Rowling, Joanne K. *Harry Potter and the Deathly Hallows*. 2007. London: Bloomsbury, 2008. Print.
_____. *Harry Potter and the Goblet of Fire*. London: Bloomsbury, 2000. Print.
_____. *Harry Potter and the Order of the Phoenix*. 2003. London: Bloomsbury, 2004. Print.
_____. *Harry Potter and the Philosopher's Stone*. London: Bloomsbury, 1997. Print.
_____. *Harry Potter and the Prisoner of Azkaban*. London: Bloomsbury, 1999. Print.
"'Satanic' Harry Potter Books Burnt." *BBC News*. 31 Dec. 2001. British Broadcasting Corporation. Web. 1 Oct. 2012.
Schnoebelen, William. "Straight Talk on Harry Potter." *Educate-Yourself: The Freedom of Knowledge, the Power of Thought*. 30 Jan. 2004. Web. 1 Oct. 2012.
Schwartz, Daniel. "The Books Have Been Burning: A Timeline of 2,200 Years of Book Burnings, from Ancient China to *The Book of Negroes*." *CBC*. 22 June 2011. Canadian Broadcasting Corporation. Web. 1 Oct. 2012.

Serchuk, David. "Harry Potter and the Ministry of Fire." Forbes.com. 12 Jan. 2006. Web. 1 Oct. 2012.
Slick, Matthew J. *"Harry Potter and the Sorcerer's Stone."* CARM: *Christian Apologetics & Research Ministry.* Web. 1 Oct. 2012.
Soulliere, Danielle M. "Much Ado about Harry: Harry Potter and the Creation of a Moral Panic." *Journal of Religion and Popular Culture* 22.1 (2010): 1–37. Web.
Spencer, Glen, Jr. "The Wicked World of Harry Potter." Thy World Is a Lamp to My Feet. Web. 1 Oct. 2012.
"Top 100 Banned/Challenged Books: 2000–2009." *American Library Association.* 1 Oct. 2012.
West, Marsha. "Harry, Yoda, and Yoga." *RenewAmerica.* 2 Aug. 2007. Web. 1 Oct. 2012.

Political Rhetoric as a Structural and Ideological Instrument in *Star Wars* and *Harry Potter*

CHRISTINA FLOTMANN

Though seemingly unrelated fields of culture, political rhetoric of war and fantasy tales, with their recurrent focus on a fight between good and evil forces, are subtly connected and mutually influence each other. Both more or less explicitly comment on and react to "real-life" trends and events. This paper will compare the approach taken on the good/evil dichotomy by politicians, specifically former president George W. Bush, British ex-prime minister Tony Blair, and President Barack Obama, to its representation in *Star Wars* and the *Harry Potter* series by J.K. Rowling, two of the most popular contemporary fantasy stories. The resemblance between chosen extracts from the politicians' speeches and the two stories takes two forms, both of which are interrelated and contribute to the ideological messages put forth by the political discourse and fantasy discourse, respectively. Firstly, the general structures of political rhetoric resemble the overall structures of the fantasy tales. Secondly, the rhetoric of the political speeches is directly taken up and mirrored in the actual political speeches featured in *Star Wars* and *Harry Potter*. To unravel the complex interplay of these different cultural texts and the ways in which they question, subvert and, I will argue, finally reinforce each other, several cultural theories will be employed. Claude Lévi-Strauss' approach to myth lays open the way in which formulaic tales such as the fantasy story are structured. Roland Barthes explains how cultural representations of any kind influence people and shape the way in which they perceive the world. Finally, John Fiske's work on the popular makes clear how popular stories are open to critical readings that question their ideological assumptions and evaluate their cultural contributions. The paper will be an attempt at a "producerly" reading in the vein of Fiske (see Fiske, *Understanding* 104) and will try and dismantle the manner in which political rhetoric on good and evil, as well as its equivalent in fantasy stories, is meant to work.

Although one function of the fantasy formula is providing escape (see Cawelti 6), i.e., helping consumers to distance themselves from everyday (political) "reality," if just for a short time, fantasy fiction and film are often much closer to "reality" than is apparent at first glance (see e.g., Neumann and Nexon 1, 6). Theorists such as John Fiske have already pointed out the fundamental ambiguity of popular stories (see "British" 122). This ambiguity chiefly lies in the fact that formulaic tales follow two contradictory impulses: on the one hand their fixed structures, usually organized around a conflict between good and evil, tend to reduce the complexity of the world, as every element of the story and all discourses treated are subordinated to the central dichotomy. On the other, by their very acts of drastic reduction, they draw attention to the deliberate simplicity of much real-life discourse and open it up for "producerly" readings (see Fiske, *Understanding* 104). If a reader approaches a popular text in a "producerly" fashion, s/he does not remain passive and simply accepts its ready-made meanings but tries to uncover its gaps and inherent contradictions, and questions the ideologies it represents (see Fiske, *Understanding* 103–104). The reader becomes active, "produces" new and possibly unintended meanings, and thus has the chance of discovering the mechanisms of popular fiction and the ways in which it shapes the cultural imagination.

Formulaic stories are extremely structural and tend to embody what Derrida calls nostalgia for unspoiled and harmonious origins and unity (see *Writing* 369). This might express itself in a search for unitary selfhood (see Steveker 77 for *Harry Potter*) or the urge to stand united in the face of evil and evoke shared human values. Lévi-Strauss has described the structure of myth as always oscillating between two mutually exclusive principles which need a third term as an intermediary (see 130). In fantasy stories, these structural principles are commonly embodied by the main characters. *Star Wars* and *Harry Potter*, the two stories analyzed here, are interesting cases in point, because they do not always neatly split these positions between three different characters. For *Star Wars* it can be argued that Anakin Skywalker fills all three positions: that of the good side in his childhood self, evil in his persona as Darth Vader, and that of the mediator, as he unites both good and evil within his character and fulfills the ominous prophecy of one bringing balance to the Force. In *Harry Potter* the character of Voldemort is a representative of pure evil, while Harry Potter embodies the good. However, at the same time, it might be argued that Harry fills the mediating position as he contains a grain of evil in the form of a Horcrux, part of Voldemort's soul attached to his own. It can be seen that although the dichotomy between good and evil applies to both stories and its treatment forms an integral part of the tales' (moral) messages, the validity of strict separations between good and evil, right and wrong is questioned already in the set-up of characters, which makes the stories ambiguous in the sense of Fiske. Both stories eliminate moral grey zones and reinstate security in the end by killing off the villains and freeing the protagonists (Harry and Vader) from their less ideal parts. Still, questions about the nature of good and evil and moral fundamentalism remain.

While Lévi-Strauss describes the structure of myth and thus provides us with a tool for analyzing popular formulaic stories, Roland Barthes shows how any kind of discourse, from photography to media coverage, can be mythical, i.e., use ideology to manipulate people (see Barthes 2). According to Barthes, much that is depicted, written or said is designed to fulfill a certain purpose. Very often this involves persuading people to buy something, literally or figuratively. Mythical discourse does not present people with "reality" but with a certain picture of reality. The reason for people to accept this "distorted" representation of reality is that myth works via the principle of naturalization (see Barthes 21). This means that the points important to the advertiser, media representative, photographer or politician are presented as seeming facts, which people often accept as a priori truths, not realizing that they are in fact dealing with ideology.

Fantasy fiction and film as well as political speeches, the objects of this paper, can be taken as examples of the kind of discourse Barthes describes. While Barthes is rather pessimistic about our ability to step out of ideology, Fiske has more confidence in "readers." He challenges them to question texts, particularly those that seem to be simple and self-evident, such as formulaic ones, and to become active and fill the gaps that popular artifacts produce (see Fiske, *Understanding* 104).

In the following, it will be shown that both fantasy stories, such as *Star Wars* and *Harry Potter*, and political rhetoric are informed by the paradoxical double strategy of incorporating containment and subversion at the same time. The comparison will be based on the narrative of good and evil that underlies much fantasy fiction and film, as well as political speeches, and the subject of war that emerges from this central binary. The popularity of *Star Wars* and *Harry Potter* turns them into potential meaning-makers, which makes it profitable to take a closer look at how the stories position themselves ideologically.

The basic assumptions feeding the good-evil dichotomy in the tales already show Barthesian naturalization at work. The fact that the tales are told from a white Western perspective naturally affects the value system they purport. The view of good as, simply put, everything which affirms individual freedom and promotes the integrity of each person's body and soul is contrasted with notions of evil, as that which works against these humanistic principles, i.e., cruelty, racial hatred, totalitarianism, and other threats to freedom of mind, body and soul. In *Star Wars*, the Emperor, aided and abetted by Anakin Skywalker, later Darth Vader, violates freedom of mind and physical integrity by manipulating and enslaving people for his purposes. He further disregards the principles of moral integrity by corrupting Anakin, who stands as representative for countless others who also fall prey to the Emperor's manipulations. Lord Voldemort in *Harry Potter*, too, defies all of the basic Western assumptions about citizen- and fellowship. He manipulates people both mentally and physically by possessing and torturing them, and he has taken many lives on his way to power. The particular view of good and evil put forth here is generated from the history of Western civilization, which has seen the Enlightenment, the French Revolution, American Independence, two world wars, totalitarian regimes and, most recently, threats by Islamic fundamentalists. All of these events have contributed to shaping Western values centered on the freedom of the individual.

As much as these positions on good and evil are simply taken for granted in Western fantasy stories, so they are in political speeches following the terrorist attack on the World Trade Center, as some examples from Tony Blair's and George W. Bush's reactions to the event show.

> Be in no doubt: Bin Laden and his people organised this atrocity. The Taliban aid and abet him. He will not desist from further acts of terror. They will not stop helping him.
> [...] Look for a moment at the Taliban regime. It is undemocratic. That goes without saying. There is no sport allowed, or television or photography. No art or culture is permitted. All other faiths, all other interpretations of Islam are ruthlessly suppressed. Those who practice their faith are imprisoned. Women are treated in a way almost too revolting to be credible. First driven out of university; girls not allowed to go to school; no legal rights; unable to go out of doors without a man. Those that disobey are stoned [Blair].

This excerpt from Tony Blair's Labour Party Conference speech of 2 October 2001 reinforces the Western idea of good just outlined for the fantasy stories by a negative example: democracy, freedom of religion and speech, education, self-fulfillment in art or culture, as well as physical well-being, are missing in Afghanistan according to Blair. The division between the lifestyles of the West and those of countries supposedly supporting terrorists is simplified and exaggerated. This is not to say that this division does not exist; rather, Blair's treatment of it exemplifies Barthes's notion of myth as distorting rather than actively falsifying reality (see Barthes 21). Western political and religious freedom and equality are naturalized as eternal givens, although in many Western countries they have only taken effect as essential rights in the last couple of decades. The association of us/the West with good, and them/the terrorists with evil is also naturalized. The excerpt shows how dependent we are on binary oppositions to define our values and ideals and how good and evil are not a priori states that can be positively defined in themselves (see Derrida, *Positions* 41).

A further interesting point about Blair's speech is its attempt at constructing a certain emotional framework within which to perceive the terrorist attacks and then establishing it as the only valid one in this context.

> Think of the cruelty beyond our comprehension as amongst the screams and the anguish of the innocent, those hijackers drove at full throttle planes laden with fuel into buildings where tens of thousands worked.
> They have no moral inhibition on the slaughter of the innocent. If they could have murdered not 7,000 but 70,000 does anyone doubt they would have done so and rejoiced in it? [Blair].

Without doubt, 9/11 caused unspeakable suffering and produced strong emotional responses around the world. However, the exploitation of these emotions for political reasons is questionable, and the benefit of an emotional narrative about "evil" dubious. In fact, there are scholars who have argued for a less emotionally charged approach to evil which focuses on understanding the reasons for its generation and possible solutions for its prevention in the future (see Seibold 93). Blair expressly dismisses this more balanced view of the situation: "Understand the causes of terror. Yes, we should try, but let there be no moral ambiguity about this: nothing could ever justify the events of 11 September, and it is to turn justice on its head to pretend it could" (2001). Indeed, nothing justifies the killing of thousands of people. However, the part of the statement which asserts this draws listeners' attention away from its other, more problematic assertion. How are we really supposed to understand the causes of terror without taking the complexity of the situation in countries such as Afghanistan or Iraq into account? How can we understand anything if we are conditioned by a worldview that makes clear-cut distinctions between white and black and unquestioningly positions the West at the good end of the spectrum and the terrorists at the evil end? Although Blair wishes for moral clarity, questions of good and evil are ambiguous by necessity as they are always dependent on point of view. At the end of the statement, he even implicitly discourages a more balanced opinion on the subject by accusing those who might be inclined to adopt it of furthering injustice and rejecting Western notions of right and wrong. In this he is less explicit than Bush in his memorable statement: "Every nation in every region now has a decision to make: Either you are with us, or you are with the terrorists[,]" but still implicitly dictates the way right and wrong, good and evil are supposed to be perceived. Both Blair's and Bush's statements show a blunt structuralism and can very obviously be read as myths in the sense of Barthes, as they rely on people's readiness to accept ideological narratives, such as the positioning of the West as good and the terrorists as evil, as natural and pre-given.

In the following I will show how *Star Wars* and *Harry Potter* enter into a dialogue with, challenge and finally reconfirm the basic moral assumptions of these reactions to terror, questioning but ultimately endorsing Blair's request: "let there be no moral ambiguity [...]." The power of language to shape people's perceptions of reality plays a role in both the stories analyzed and political rhetoric after 9/11. Particularly in the U.S. in the first few months after the terrorist attacks, there was a tendency in politics to create (religiously tinted) narratives of a fight between the forces of good and those of evil which was eagerly taken up by the media (see Edgerton, Hart, and Hassencahl 198). The realm of popular culture then again reacted to and commented on this trend in a variety of ways. *Star Wars* and *Harry Potter* contain statements rather similar to those by Blair and Bush. In *Star Wars*, episode III, *Revenge of the Sith*, Senator Palpatine, the clever and cunning politician later to become the Emperor, confronts his mentee Anakin with the following remark: "Good is a point of view, Anakin. The Sith and the Jedi are similar in almost every way including their quest for greater power" (*Revenge of the Sith* 00:43:33). On a meta-level, the assertion directly exposes the structuralist logic around which the tales themselves are organized as non-natural. In post-structuralist fashion, Palpatine deconstructs the seemingly fixed entity of moral goodness and establishes it as what Derrida calls a "floating signifier" (see Sarup 33). At second glance, however, the complexity of the series' position becomes clear. Palpatine only posits good as a point of view to confound Anakin's moral judgment and to get him to see his (Palpatine's own) "evil" outlook as good. He takes evil out of the equation here, only implying that it might be a point of view, too. Instead, it becomes clear that by equating the Sith and the Jedi, he simply wishes to discredit the latter in Anakin's eyes. Thus, he does not intend to make Anakin see the complexities of the world but rather to get him on his side. It is significant that it is the evildoer who makes this morally relativizing statement. This finally reinforces clear-cut binary oppositions instead of truly challenging them, as the villain stands for the destruction of the "good order" and everything that is cherished by the Jedi, so that his dictums are "naturally" rejected by the audience (see Flotmann 115).

However, this is not the end of the story. The scene between Palpatine and Anakin is closely linked to, mirrored and extended in a further scene between Anakin and his "good" mentor, Jedi Obi-Wan, towards the end of *Revenge of the Sith*. Anakin has been seduced by evil, murdered countless Jedi and now turns against Obi-Wan on a volcanic planet. While the two are fighting, Obi-Wan confronts Anakin with what he has done and tells him that he is deeply disappointed by him. Anakin, who has read the claim that "good is a point of view" exactly as Palpatine intended, believes himself to be in the right and thinks that his acts will bring freedom to the galaxy. In his wrath he exclaims: "If you're not with me then you're my enemy" (*Revenge of the Sith* 1:43:14). The similarity to Bush's statement from his speech on 20 September 2001 cannot be overlooked and is probably not accidental, as the film was released in 2005 (see also Kellner 179). It induces audiences to ponder the easy assignation of binary categories, as Bush is compared to a fictional character whose strong belief in the moral rectitude of his actions has turned him from good to evil. The rather explicit (and again partly distorting) comparison of Bush with someone killing innocents possibly implies a criticism of Bush's military exploits in Afghanistan and Iraq.

Obi-Wan's reaction to Anakin's angry remark is "Only a Sith deals in absolutes" (*Revenge of the Sith* 1:43:13). This emphasizes two points. First of all, it recalls the earlier scene between Palpatine and Anakin and the fact that Palpatine, as a Sith, was actually the one who did *not* deal in absolutes, the one who relativized and problematized the easy categorization into good and evil, albeit briefly and driven by his own aims. Secondly, by his statement, Obi-Wan makes clear that he has in fact by this time identified and categorized Anakin as a Sith. So his remark shows that it is not merely Sith, i.e., evil characters, who are prone to classification. "Good" Obi-Wan, too, needs the safety of clear categorizations and cannot accept that a human being might not be simply good or evil (see also Flotmann 161–62).

This becomes even clearer in the following. The fight between Anakin and Obi-Wan continues until Obi-Wan manages to cut off Anakin's legs with his lightsaber, causing him to slide towards a lava-filled crate and slowly catch fire. Obi-Wan leaves Anakin with the words: "You were my brother, Anakin. I loved you" (*Revenge of the Sith* 1:55:26), making sure the audience knows that he is not his brother anymore. Here "good" Obi-Wan finally suits his actions to his words. As much as Anakin can only see him as either friend or enemy, Obi-Wan can only see Anakin as good or evil. He deals in absolutes by leaving a badly injured person to what he must know to be a terrible death. The film blurs the boundaries between good and evil, exposing the simplistic world view behind the strict division of people according to these categories (see also Flotmann 163).

The original *Star Wars* trilogy, which chronologically follows upon the more recent one, introduces a character, Luke Skywalker, who renounces binary thinking. Although he knows what Vader has done, he constantly affirms his belief that "[t]here is still good in him" (*Return of the Jedi* 00:45:03). This forgiving stance, which takes grey zones in between good and evil into account, nevertheless leads back to categorization in the end. Vader is reclaimed for the good side and then has to die, presumably as atonement for his more horrible deeds. To cater to people's escapist needs, it seems, formulaic works have to restore order in the end (see also Cawelti 10), an order that is built around the clear separation of binary categories such as good and evil. In accordance with Fiske, however, this dominant reading exists side by side with the more subversive one questioning strict categorization. While all six movies directly engage with the discourse on good and evil, the more recent trilogy completed after the terrorist attacks of 9/11 seems to be slightly more ambivalent about the evaluation of the dichotomy and about taking a clear-cut stance on what constitutes the two sides to the binary. This perfectly reflects the general insecurity after the attacks and their potential to change perceptions of "reality" which the politicians then countermanded by making their speeches as morally and ideologically clear as possible. Although the movies finally cement Western humanist values, they still tend to ask the question of perspective more strongly than the politicians whose remarks were discussed. The movies can teach viewers to be more critical of absolutist categories, especially if these are brought forth in a political context in which they are often evoked to reach certain aims.

Harry Potter separates good and evil more clearly than *Star Wars*, while questioning the Western notions underlying the dichotomy far less intensely. This becomes clear already when we look at the difference in focus. In *Star Wars* attention is directed towards the main character's fickleness, while in *Harry Potter* the protagonist's rather unchanging goodness is highlighted. Harry Potter is a thoroughly good character that is not even seriously tainted by the part of the villain's soul attached to his own. He constantly embodies values such as love, charity, friendship and bravery, which also help him overcome the villain in the end. He is also a very "Western" hero who represents the values of individual freedom and integrity of body and soul outlined above.

The *Harry Potter* novels nevertheless contain political and ideological statements which are very similar to those in *Star Wars* and also recall the treatment of the good-evil binary. As early as the end of the first book in the series, *Harry Potter and the Philosopher's Stone*, Harry's nemesis Voldemort, in the guise of Defense Against the Dark Arts Professor Quirrell, gives the readers his view on good and evil. In the confrontation between Harry and Quirrell, the elder wizard tells the boy how he adapted his view on good and evil when he became Voldemort's henchman: "A foolish young man I was then, full of ridiculous ideas about good and evil. Lord Voldemort showed me how wrong I was. There is no good and evil, there is only power, and those too weak to seek it" (*Harry Potter and the Philosopher's Stone* 313). As in the case of *Star Wars*, this statement comes from the villain and is finally rejected as such. However, when we look at it more closely, we can see that in contrast to the Emperor, who explicitly destabilizes the binary opposition of good and evil for a short time, Quirrell/Voldemort upholds binaries. He dismisses the distinction between good and evil but replaces it with another opposition, namely the one between power and weakness (see Flotmann 124–25). As the readers learn more about Voldemort's childhood and adolescence mainly in novels four and six, the statement becomes understandable: Voldemort is depicted as almost genetically unable to distinguish between right and wrong (see also Hibbs 91). He does not have any notion of good and evil, because he has not learned that relationships with other people can be based on something other than power and domination. He does not love and he treats people as objects, disposing of them as soon as they are no longer of use to him (see also Rothman 206).

Quirrell's/Voldemort's remark thus shows that the treatment of evil in *Harry Potter* differs from *Star Wars*. While *Star Wars*, especially the more recent trilogy, depicts the generation of evil in one individual, *Harry Potter* asks questions about the nature of evil and good respectively. The novels raise questions such as whether good and evil are partly genetic and to which degree evil can be condoned and pardoned. As in *Star Wars*, evil acquires a political dimension as both Darth Vader and Lord Voldemort strive for unlimited power. Much like Darth Vader, Voldemort kills numerous people on his way to the top, including children and Muggles. In contrast to *Star Wars*, in which Darth Vader's victims are largely passed by, every death is a catastrophic event in *Harry Potter*. The emotionality thus produced is partly due to the narrative perspective. The readers see everything through the eyes of Harry himself, and as most of the deaths that occur are those of people close to Harry, he is prone to feel strongly about them. Much more than in *Star Wars*, the readers get the victim's perspective, and evil is closely connected to human suffering. The emotion involved, as Seibold says (see 93), often makes a more neutral approach to evil harder. By letting the readers see bits of Voldemort's past and his bleak childhood in novel six, *Harry Potter and the Half-Blood Prince*, Rowling makes an attempt at explaining from whence evil might derive. She also implies that Voldemort is mentally unstable. However, in contrast to *Star Wars*, where Anakin's story in part serves to exonerate him, Voldemort's sad childhood and possible madness never suffice as a criterion for exculpating him. In fact, he is utterly condemned: he has a bad childhood, he is probably mentally unhinged and he has no true notion of right and wrong, and can thus never feel what he has done and never reach forgiveness or atonement.

As his nihilistic outlook and his pure desire for power for its own sake (remember the way he discriminates between power and weakness) have totalitarian tendencies, they cannot be condoned. In his wish for power he overthrows what is considered to be the natural order in the novels, completely disregarding fundamental Western humanistic ideas. He violates the physical and mental integrity of people and breaches the boundaries between here and there, past and present, self and other, as well as life and death. He embodies "play" in the sense of Derrida (see *Writing* 352, 365), but in the world of fantasy fiction, play is not desired. Voldemort has to be finished in the end to restore the "natural" order, i.e., the naturalized assumptions about good and evil (see also Flotmann 128–29). In this context it is also telling that the *Harry Potter* novels contain an absolutist statement very similar to Anakin's about being with him or being his enemy. In contrast to *Star Wars*, however, it is made by a character that, up to that point, has always appeared as the epitome of good, Hogwarts headmaster Albus Dumbledore. At the end of novel four, after Voldemort has returned, Dumbledore speaks to Cornelius Fudge, Minister of Magic, who does not want to believe that the wizarding world is faced with the villain once more. Dumbledore says: "The only one against whom I intend to work [...] is Lord Voldemort. If you are against him, then we remain, Cornelius, on the same side" (*Harry Potter and the Goblet of Fire* 615). Rowling, like George Lucas, shows that not "only Sith deal in absolutes" but that even "good" characters often know no better than to simplify matters. Still, since Dumbledore, in contrast to Anakin at his point of conversion, embodies supreme goodness, readers tend to accept his judgment and the categories he sets up, so that finally a black and white moral evaluation à la Tony Blair is advocated.

Although the *Harry Potter* novels are generally more clear-cut than *Star Wars* morally as well as ideologically, they, too, have an ambiguous element. More than *Star Wars*, Rowling's novels foreground the plight of people and creatures not well respected within the wizarding community. Representatives of these groups, such as Hagrid the half-giant, Lupin the werewolf, Dobby the house elf, and Griphook the goblin, get to voice their opinions on the wizarding community's politics which often undermine the wizards' hegemonic assumptions (see e.g., Saxena 137–39).[1] As the hero Harry, although he personally treats other creatures with respect, ultimately caters to the needs of the dominant hegemonic group, and restores the "good" order in their image, the *Harry Potter* novels, too, and more so than *Star Wars*, finally leave Western hegemonic assumptions untouched. Nonetheless, the creatures who form the subordinate group of society are still there, and the ending leaves a bitter aftertaste, because their plight is unresolved. So although the stories do reinstate the dominant hegemonic order, they also, albeit in an implicit way, feature those who do not profit from it (see also Flotmann 362–64). In this sense the *Harry Potter* novels, like the *Star Wars* films, show their subversive potential under the traditional structural corset that restores an order based on strictly separated categories of good and evil. The novels criticize the assumption also put forth by the politicians cited earlier that there is one essential view on good and that the vanquishing of evil in the name of this particular understanding of good is beneficial for everyone. They show what politicians frequently veil in their flashy speeches: that the good they are promoting is often a white Western idea that only benefits the dominant hegemonic group, which is mostly rather small.

In a speech after Bin Laden's death on 2 May 2011 Barack Obama said:

> For over two decades, bin Laden has been al Qaeda's leader and symbol, and has

continued to plot attacks against our country and our friends and allies. The death of bin Laden marks the most significant achievement to date in our nation's effort to defeat al Qaeda. Yet his death does not mark the end of our effort. There's no doubt that al Qaeda will continue to pursue attacks against us. We must—and we will—remain vigilant at home and abroad [Obama].

This quote shows Obama's approach to evil to be a bit more measured and careful than that of his predecessor Bush and of Tony Blair. Although he acknowledges the death of Bin Laden as a "significant achievement" in the war against terror, he also points to the fact that Bin Laden has served as a symbol, a symbol not only for al Qaeda but implicitly also for the terrorist organization's opponents. Bin Laden came to be the face of evil, a satanic projection foil. And the operation to have him killed is implicitly acknowledged to have been a symbolic operation of exorcism. Like the Emperor and Darth Vader in *Star Wars*, and even more like Voldemort in *Harry Potter*, Bin Laden becomes the (undoubtedly highly guilty) scapegoat who has to be finished in order for society to find its way back to normality. What is often forgotten or repressed is that the very real threat and evil emanating from a Bin Laden, a Darth Vader or a Voldemort, could never be so threatening or develop such a destructive potential if it did not fall on fruitful soil, if it were not for people who follow these figures of identification (see also Rothman 213). Exorcizing evil with the help of a figure such as Bin Laden is always also a psychological effort to exorcize the potential for evil within all of us. As *Star Wars* and *Harry Potter* imply, Obama's statement makes clear that evil cannot be completely rooted out by killing one person. In *Star Wars* it is at least questionable whether one good act on the part of Vader (saving his son) can redeem hundreds of murders, and in *Harry Potter* evil remains in the hegemonic social structures which disadvantage so many. The fact that Obama keeps up the "us versus them" rhetoric makes clear that despite an awareness of moral and social complexities and ambiguities, some binaries are hard to pass by or overcome, something that is also shown in both stories analyzed. Political rhetoric in the tales clearly has a double function. It holds a mirror up to reality, exposing real-life political discourse as at best ideology-ridden and at worst manipulative but it also naturalizes ideologies and reinforces binary structures. *Star Wars* and *Harry Potter* are both playgrounds for creative, producerly readings in the sense of Fiske and ideological influences according to Barthes's definition, and as such highly ambiguous.

Notes

1. Further critics pointing to the political potential of the *Harry Potter* novels are, for instance, Karin E. Westman, Steven W. Patterson, Brycchan Carey, and Jackie C. Horne.

Works Cited

Barthes, Roland. "Myth Today." *Structuralism in Myth: Lévi-Strauss, Barthes, Dumézil, and Propp*. Ed. Robert A. Segal. New York: Garland, 1996. 1–29. Print.
Blair, Tony. "Full Text: Tony Blair's Speech." Speech at the Labour Party Conference, 2 Oct. 2001. Theguardian.com. 2. Oct. 2001. Web. 28 Nov. 2013.
Bush, George W. Speech to Congress, 20 Sept. 2001. *The History Place: Great Speeches Collection*. Web. 28 Nov. 2013.
Carey, Brycchan. "Hermione and the House-Elves: The Literary and Historical Contexts of J.K. Rowling's Antislavery Campaign." *Reading Harry Potter: Critical Essays*. Ed. Giselle Liza Anatol. Westport, CT: Praeger, 2003. 103–15. Print.
_____. "Hermione and the House-Elves Revisited: J.K. Rowling, Antislavery Campaigning, and the Politics of Potter." *Reading Harry Potter Again: New Critical Essays*. Ed. Giselle Liza Anatol. Santa Barbara: ABC-CLIO, 2009. 159–73. Print.
Cawelti, John G. *Adventure, Mystery, and Romance: Formula Stories as Art and Popular Culture*. Chicago: The University of Chicago Press, 1976. Print.
Derrida, Jacques. *Positions* [French original 1972]. Trans. Alan Bass. Chicago: University of Chicago Press, 1981. Print.
_____. *Writing and Difference* [French original 1967]. Trans. Alan Bass. London: Routledge Classics, 2002. Print.
Edgerton, Gary R., William B. Hart, and Frances Hassencahl. "Televising 9/11 and Its Aftermath: The Framing of George W. Bush's Faith-Based Politics of Good and Evil." *The Changing Face of Evil in Film and Television*. Ed. Martin F. Norden. Amsterdam: Rodopi, 2007. 195–214. Print.
Fiske, John. "British Cultural Studies and Television." *What is Cultural Studies? A Reader*. Ed. John Storey. London: Arnold, 1996. 115–46. Print.
_____. *Understanding Popular Culture*. London: Routledge, 2006. Print.
Flotmann, Christina. *Ambiguity in Star Wars and Harry Potter: A (Post-)Structuralist Reading of Two Popular Myths*. Bielefeld: transcript, 2013. Print.
Hibbs, Thomas. "Virtue, Vice, and the Harry Potter Universe." *The Changing Face of Evil in Film and Television*. Ed. Martin F. Norden. Amsterdam: Rodopi, 2007. 89–99. Print.
Horne, Jackie C. "Harry and the Other: Answering the Race Question in J.K. Rowling's Harry Potter." *The Lion and the Unicorn: A Critical Journal of Children's Literature* 34.1 (2010): 76–104. Print.
Kellner, Douglas. *Cinema Wars: Hollywood Film and Politics in the Bush-Cheney Era*. Chichester, UK: Wiley-Blackwell, 2010. Print.
Lévi-Strauss, Claude. "The Structural Study of Myth." *Structuralism in Myth: Lévi-Strauss, Barthes, Dumézil, and Propp*. Ed. Robert A. Segal. New York: Garland, 1996. 118–34. Print.
Neumann, Iver B., and Daniel H. Nexon. "Harry Potter and the Study of World Politics." Introduction. *Harry Potter and International Relations*. Ed. Daniel H. Nexon, and Iver B. Neumann. Lanham, MD: Rowman & Littlefield, 2006. 1–23. Print.
Obama, Barack. "Osama Bin Laden Dead: Obama Speech Video and Transcript." Address to the Nation, 2 May 2011. Huffingtonpost.com. 2 May 2011. Web. 28 Nov. 2013.
Patterson, Steven W. "Kreacher's Lament: S.P.E.W. as a Parable on Discrimination, Indifference, and Social Justice." *Harry Potter and Philosophy: If Aristotle Ran Hogwarts*. Ed. David Baggett and Shawn E. Klein. Chicago: Open Court, 2004. 105–17. Print.
Rothman, Ken. "Hearts of Darkness: Voldemort and Iago, with a Little Help from Their Friends." *Essays on Evil in Popular Media: Vader, Voldemort and Other Villains*. Ed. Jamey Heit. Jefferson, NC: McFarland, 2011. 202–17. Print.
Rowling, J.K. *Harry Potter and the Goblet of Fire*. London: Bloomsbury, 2000. Print.

―――. *Harry Potter and the Philosopher's Stone*. London: Bloomsbury, 1997. Print.
Sarup, Madan. *Post-Structuralism and Postmodernism*. New York: Harvester Wheatsheaf, 1993. Print.
Saxena, Vandana. *The Subversive Harry Potter: Adolescent Rebellion and Containment in the J.K. Rowling Novels*. Jefferson, NC: McFarland, 2012. Print.
Seibold, Verena C. "Noch nie war das Gute so böse—Warum auch gute Menschen böse handeln." *Noch nie war das Böse so gut: Die Aktualität einer alten Differenz*. Ed. Franz Fromholzer, Michael Preis, and Bettina Wisiorek. Heidelberg: Universitätsverlag Winter, 2011. 91–106. Print.
Star Wars: Return of the Jedi. Dir. Richard Marquand. Perf. Mark Hamill, Harrison Ford, Carrie Fisher and Anthony Daniels. LucasFilm, 1983. Film. (DVD version: LucasFilm, Special Edition 2004.)
Star Wars: Revenge of the Sith. Dir. George Lucas. Perf. Ewan McGregor, Natalie Portman, Hayden Christensen and Christopher Lee. LucasFilm, 2005. Film.
Steveker, Lena. "'Your Soul Is Whole, and Completely Your Own, Harry:' The Heroic Self in J.K. Rowling's *Harry Potter* Series." *Heroism in the Harry Potter Series*. Ed. Katrin Berndt and Lena Steveker. Farnham: Ashgate, 2011. 69–83. Print.
Westman, Karin E. "Specters of Thatcherism: Contemporary British Culture in J.K. Rowling's Harry Potter Series." *The Ivory Tower and Harry Potter: Perspectives on a Literary Phenomenon*. Ed. Lana A. Whited. Columbia: University of Missouri Press, 2002. 305–28. Print.

Haven't I Been Here Before?
China Miéville's Uncanny Cities

Dirk Vanderbeke

Fantastic cities have a long pedigree including Plato's Republic, Camelot, Tommaso Campanella's City of the Sun, John Winthrop's programmatic and visionary City Upon a Hill, Jonathan Swift's Laputa, J.R.R. Tolkien's Minas Tirith, Italo Calvino's Invisible Cities and François Schuiten and Benoît Peeters' Obscure Cities. They can be constructed merely as background, i.e., an imaginary location for the rather more important action, but also as a focus for the reader's attention, a central aspect of the actual message. There are some standard images of the city that run through urban conceptualizations and also the depictions of urban landscapes in the arts and in literature. The most prominent is probably the personification of the city, which in recent times has also led to the perception of the city as an organic entity with its own specific forms of growth and development akin to the biological phenomenon of the superorganism (for the following brief account, see Vanderbeke). Steven Johnson writes about this concept of the city: "The city is complex because it overwhelms, yes, but also because it has a coherent personality, a personality that self-organizes out of millions of individual decisions, a global order built out of local interactions" (39). This idea has been around for quite some time—it has made its appearance in William Wordsworth's "Composed upon Westminster Bridge, September 3, 1802" and in Alfred Douglas's "Impression de Nuit: London" (1894), and it has invited not only highly creative concepts of city architecture and self-organizing environments (see Choo; Droege; Novak), but also various imaginative and fantastic literary responses.

In science fiction we can find Greg Bear's *Strength of Stones*, in which some intelligent and mobile cities, created by religious communities, ultimately find their inhabitants' spiritual and moral purity wanting, and chuck them out. After hundreds of years the inhabitants' descendants still live as exiles in the desert, bemoaning the failures of their fathers and the loss of the Edenic life in the moving habitats. Even more weirdly, in Robert Coover's postmodern Western *Ghost Town*, a cowboy riding through the desert is overtaken by a town which "closes upon him [...] until at last it glides up under his horse's hoofs from behind and proceeds to pass him by even as he ambles forward" (6). Compared to this, Terry Pratchett's account of the living city Ankh-Morpork in the Discworld novel *Reaper Man* sounds rather factual:

> A city is alive. Supposing you were a great slow giant, like a counting pine, and looked down at the city? You'd see buildings grow; you'd see attackers driven off; you'd see fires put out. You'd see the city was alive, but you wouldn't see the people, because they'd move too fast. The life of a city, the thing that drives it, isn't some sort of mysterious force. The life of a city is people. [...]
> So we have the cities, big sedentary creatures, growing from one spot and hardly moving at all for thousands of years. They breed by sending out people to colonise new land. They themselves just lie there. They're alive, but only in the same way that a jellyfish is alive [Pratchett 202].

And indeed, there are some maritime animals that resemble jellyfish but are actually colonies of extremely specialized, but nevertheless individual, zooids, the most famous being the Portuguese man-of-war. Pratchett obviously had done his homework before writing this passage.

But then there is another view of the city, in which it is not an integrated environment but rather a space that is divided, occasionally divided against itself. Here we find worlds of differences, of segregation, of inclusion and exclusion, of taboo zones and no-go areas. Only few people can move freely between the different locations, and, like the mythical hero, the protagonist usually has to obtain the ability to navigate successfully between the various regions within the urban jungle. A good starting point for this tradition in city writing would probably be Eugène Sue's *The Mysteries of Paris* and its depiction of the rich, poor and criminal locations within the city. In addition, the different parts of the city are occasionally ontologically separated; they exist in different realities or on different levels of reality. James Joyce's Dublin in *Ulysses* is predominantly a realistically described city, but in the "Circe" episode, night town is a place where men can be turned into women or swine or both, where a bar of soap rises in the sky and speaks, or where a father can meet his long dead son. When in Thomas Pynchon's *V.*, Benny Profane enters the sewers of New York to hunt alligators—a motif that will resurface in Neil Gaiman's *Neverwhere*—this is a location where a mad priest preached to the rats and possibly acquired a very eager female student among them, "a kind of voluptuous Magdalen" (*V.* 121), who actually wanted to take up holy orders. Just before he shoots at the alligator,

Profane expects a Pentecostal wonder: "Surely the alligator would receive the gift of tongues, the body of Father Fairing be resurrected, the sexy V. tempt him away from murder. He felt about to levitate ..." (Pynchon, *V.* 122). Similarly, Oedipa Maas in *The Crying of Lot 49* finds a counterworld during her passage through night town, in which children are playing in their nightclothes in central park telling her that they are only dreaming the gathering. Here, the CIA is a secret anarchist organization, the "Conjuración de los Insurgentes Anarquistas," and at the end of the night Oedipa will encounter her own Pentecostal miracle: a congregation of deaf-mutes dancing in perfect order. "Each couple on the floor danced whatever was in the fellow's head: tango, two-step, bossa nova, slop" (90), but without any collision and all ending the dance simultaneously "by mysterious consensus" (91). In Jeanette Winterson's *The Passion*, Venice is the antithesis of Napoleon's rational empire of straight lines. It is a city of mazes: "You may set off from the same place every day and never go the same route. If you do so, it will be by mistake. [...] Your course in compass reading will fail you. Your confident instructions to passers-by will send them into squares they have never heard of, over canals not listed in the notes" (49). One part of Venice still has a beautiful front that can easily be accessed and enjoyed, but then there is also:

> a city within the city that is the knowledge of a few. In this inner city are thieves and Jews and children with slant eyes who come from the eastern wastelands without father or mother. They roam in packs like the cats and the rats and they go after the same food. [...] There are exiles too. Men and women driven out of their gleaming palaces that open so elegantly on to shining canals. Men and women who are officially dead according to the registers of Paris. They are here [...] [Winterson 53].

Internal and mostly invisible frontiers divide these cities along the lines of classes or marginality, between the upright citizens and the beggars, prostitutes, exiles or anarchists, but also between the realistic world of our experience and the fantastic otherworld of dreams, hallucinations or magic. This becomes most obvious in Neil Gaiman's *Neverwhere* in which the city is divided into London Above, the familiar city of our own experience, and London Below, the place for people who have quite literally "fallen through the cracks" (136). London Below is governed by strange laws and practices, where rat-speakers carry out the will of the true rulers and where there is actually an Earl's Court, including a herald and a jester, held in a darkened underground train. Here, darkness itself can be a physical entity that may take a girl away forever; here, you have to "mind the gap" or else a smoke-like tentacled monster will pour out and try to drag you into it. Of course, all this only happens to those who are part of the Underside, and it happens without being noticed by the inhabitants of London Above. If for one reason or the other you enter London Below, you become more or less invisible to those above: people will not notice you, if directly approached they will not recognize you and immediately forget you afterwards, your credit cards will become invalid; you have fallen through the cracks. Most inhabitants of London Below seem to have been born there, but then there are also those who unexpectedly found themselves in the new—or rather old—place after some incident of transition. But then you cannot go back: "It's one or the other. Nobody ever gets both" (88). This sharp division is, of course, indicative of a rigid social and economic segregation, but also of different ways of constructing identities. It separates along two different lines, between the affluent and the destitute, and between the accepted history and the actual past. In London Above the past is relegated to museums, to be on display and to be used for self-promotion and social ritual. In London Below past and present are strangely interwoven, and all of history seems to exist simultaneously in bits and pieces: "there are still some Roman soldiers camped out by the Kilburn River" (89), the community is organized into fiefdoms, the economy is based on swapping and bartering, there are black friars at Blackfriars and shepherds at Shepherd's Bush—but "[p]ray you never meet them" (137).

And then there is China Miéville. He has quite obviously always been interested in cities and urban landscapes, and in his novels the city is quite frequently the most important character. Occasionally there seems to be a kind of cross-fertilization with the work of Neil Gaiman. *King Rat* (1998), *Un Lun Dun* (2007) and *Kraken* (2010) take up elements from *Neverwhere* (1996), but a spider god first appeared as Anansi in *Rat King* and as Weaver in *Perdido Street Station* (2000), and only then in Gaiman's *American Gods* (2001) and *Anansi Boys* (2005). The strangest and most perplexing vision of an urban environment, however, is presented in a work that radically departs from the fantastic examples briefly outlined above, and it is the very lack of the usual elements of the fantastic that renders this novel so inexplicably weird.

The City and the City

The novel opens rather realistically like a common detective novel with a murdered woman discovered in a run-down part of town. The case is investigated by a not particularly interesting police inspector, Tyador Borlú, who is also the autodiegetic narrator. His name, as well as those of his colleagues and the street names, indicates some vaguely Eastern European location with Austrian, Hungarian, Slavonic and Turkish elements. At the end of the first chapter, however, we get a few lines that are decidedly bewildering. Looking at an elderly woman on the next street, Borlú suddenly realizes that something is wrong:

With a hard start, I realised that she was not on Gunter-Strász at all, and that I should not have seen her.

Immediately and flustered I looked away, and she did the same, with the same speed. I raised my head, towards an aircraft on its final descent. When after some seconds I looked back up, unnoticing the old woman stepping heavily away, I looked carefully instead of at her in her foreign street at the facades of the nearby and local Gunter-Strász [...] [Miéville, *City* 14].

Over the next pages it is slowly unfolded that Borlú's city, Besźel, is only part of the location. Interwoven with it is another city, Ul Qoma, and the novel is something like a new *Tale of Two Cities* with various twists. The inhabitants of these two cities have to follow complicated rules and conventions that are equally strict and strange. For them it is obligatory not to notice anything outside their own city and to unsee everything that does not belong to it.

This construct could well be a city that Calvino forgot to mention in his book about the *Invisible Cities*. The city of Sophronia, for example, "is made up of two half cities" ("Thin Cities 4"),[1] and "if you move along Marozia's compact walls, when you least expect it, you see a crack open and a different city appear" ("Continuous Cities 4"). But then Miéville's cities are the ultimate paradox: they are invisible cities in plain view. That makes life rather tricky: "I walked by the brick arches: at the top, where the lines were, they were elsewhere, but not all of them were foreign at their bases. The ones I could see contained little shops and squats decorated in art graffiti. In Besźel it was a quiet area, but the streets were crowded with those elsewhere. I unsaw them, but it took time to pick past them all" (*City* 30–31). Of course, things can get very awkward in a world that requires a double vision and the ultimate form of Orwell's doublethink. There are, for example, minor accidents that cannot easily be unseen but need to be ignored, like body contact in a crowded street or domestic animals passing between the cities. But there are also more severe protubs, i.e., "protuberances from the other city" (*City* 80), e.g., the "death of an Ul Qoman bystander from a stray bullet in a stickup" (81). The narrator also remembers a rather weird situation that is reminiscent of Don DeLillo's *White Noise*: "There once had been a fire grosstopically close to my apartment. It had been contained in one house, but a house not in Besźel that I had unseen. So I had watched footage of it piped in from Ul Qoma, on my local TV, while my living room windows had been lit by the fluttering red glow of it" (*City* 81).

Moreover, the relationships between the cities are not exactly friendly, and the international affairs are complicated as the cities have quite different diplomatic affiliations—in addition, they were non-combatant supporters of opposing sides in World War II. Of course, there is also contact between the cities. In a building named Copula Hall, the Oversight Commission meets and discusses matters of mutual interest, and there is also an official border crossing, the only place where people can leave their city and country and then re-enter the same from the other side. It is Checkpoint Charlie with just another little twist, and, in fact, the inspector once attended a conference in West Berlin on "Policing Split Cities" (*City* 90). Before you can really enter the other city, however, you have to take a preparatory course in which you learn to unsee everything you are used to, and suddenly to notice all the buildings, people and objects you have always tried very hard to dismiss from every form of perception.

To add just a last bit of strangeness to this environment, Miéville also constructed the cities as economically imbalanced. While Ul Qoma is a flourishing metropolis with a financial and business district, Besźel is less prosperous, with rather shabby houses and streets, less flashy clothes, colors and shops. And of course they have two different languages, Besź and Illitan, and even alphabets (see *City* 50). Telephone connections have the low quality of long distance international calls.

Of course, such a complicated system of inclusion and exclusion has to be strictly monitored. First, there is a very rigid internal control. The inhabitants are conditioned from their earliest childhood not to perceive the "elsewhere" and to automatically unsee, unhear and unsense any intrusion. In addition, there is a rather mysterious institution called Breach that polices the invisible lines between the cities—I will return to this institution later.

If, however, the invisible dividing lines between the cities seem to be an insurmountable barrier, other more traditional forms of segregation and enmity are suspended. The word *ébru*, for example, is no longer only applied to Jews but also to the city's Muslim population after hundreds of years in which immigrants from the Balkan came to Besźel. And strangely enough, a very peaceful coexistence between these two groups has developed, they are united under a term which here is "ludicrously inexact for at least half of those to whom it applied" (*City* 25).

Of course, quite a lot of the weirdness in the novel derives from an exaggeration of living conditions in split cities like Berlin or Jerusalem, in internally divided locations like Belfast, or in segregated countries like the former South Africa, even if this idea would, of course, be strictly rejected by both cities' authorities under the doctrine that Besźel and Ul Qoma have never been a single city and thus also never split. It would, however, be too easy to leave it at that, and I want to suggest that the motif structures not only each aspect of life in the two cities but also various levels of reading.

On the lowest level, the human ability willfully not to notice something unpleasant that may or may not require some kind of response is rather well documented and also rather obvious. Dan Ariely, professor of psychology and behavioral economics at Duke University, writes about an experiment in which one of his students acted as a beggar and tried various postures (sitting and standing) and approaches (eye contact versus no eye contact) in order to find out what brings most money:

> Interestingly, while the eye contact approach was working in general, it was clear that some of the passers-by had a counterstrategy: they were actively shifting their gaze in what seemed to be an attempt to pretend that he wasn't there. They simply acted as if there was a dark hole in front of them rather than a person, and they were quite successful at averting their gaze [Ariely].

On the next level beyond individual encounters, there are the lines that divide cities into the respectable quarters and the no-go areas, the sights and the slums we tend to "unsee." This tendency, then, has its equivalent on larger scales, in the distinction between the places we visit and those we shun, and in the very visual differences between first and third world countries. From there it quickly passes into a domain where coordinated individual action would be required to solve major problems, like climate change, pollution, poverty or starvation, but fails because the respective problems are easily "unseen" in our daily life.

A funny version of this phenomenon can be found in Douglas Adams's *Life, the Universe and Everything* as an "SEP field," in which SEP stands for "Somebody Else's Problem." As Ford Prefect explains it: "An SEP [...] is something that we can't see, or don't see, or our brain doesn't let us see, because we think that it's somebody else's problem [...]. The brain just edits it out, it's like a blind spot" (Adams 26–27). In Miéville's city, the division is not between "above" and "below" but between "local" and "elsewhere," but then "elsewhere" is a rather fuzzy term which can mean anything from "not here" to "far away." And these two aspects merge in the novel, as "local" and "elsewhere" are intertwined within the same cityscape, but then the close proximity is conceptualized as large scale distance.

Of course, in a globalized world, "elsewhere" has become "local" as distances have decreased, but, even more, because cause and effect can no longer be calculated within traditional scopes of influence. Over the last years, this has become a topical issue in economics, politics, social studies and, of course, in the media. We have learned that it only takes a few intermediaries to link people in this world, no matter where they are. At the same time, a movie like *Babel* made it quite clear that globalized connections need not be friendly or supportive.

In addition, in Miéville's text the difference between the cities is loaded with terms like "alterity" (*City* 29) or "cultural differentiation" (51), and they cannot fail to evoke recent theoretical concepts and models of cultural interaction, interfaces, third spaces, hybridity and multiculturalism. In an abstract for a paper on "Mapping the New Europe in China Miéville's *The City & the City*,"[2] Elizabeth Ho suggests that Miéville's novel "mocks the discourse of multiculturalism by marking the interstice and the interzone, so valued in postcolonialism, as interdict and illegality." The almost complete absence of any kind of inbetweenness, hybridity or negotiation challenges the subversive power attributed to a discursive space that lies outside the dominant binaries.[3]

Such a reading is supported by the rather obvious intertextual reference to Salman Rushdie's *The Satanic Verses*, chapter 5 of which is titled "A City Visible but Unseen." In an interview, Rushdie elaborated on this title and said that

> it seemed to me at that point that [the London Indian community] really was unseen. It was there and nobody knew it was there. And I was very struck by how often, when one would talk to white English people about what was going on, you could actually take them to these streets and point to these phenomena, and they would somehow still reject this information [Quoted in Brians 49].

By evoking an urban environment, consisting of two segregated communities which willfully blank out each other as an essential part of the cultural and legal codes and conventions, Miéville confirms Rushdie's assessment and satirizes contemporary visions of multicultural environments.

Most importantly, between Besźel and Ul Qoma there is nothing like a contact zone. According to Mary Louise Pratt, who coined the term, contact zones are "social spaces where cultures meet, clash, and grapple with each other, often in contexts of highly asymmetrical relations of power" (34). Nevertheless, for her, the contact zone is a utopian space that can actually be realized and has been realized, and she offers the examples of one of her classes on "the Americas and the multiple cultural histories (including European ones) that have intersected here" (39). She then writes that: "Virtually every student was having the experience of seeing the world described with him or her in it. Along with rage, incomprehension, and pain, there were exhilarating moments of wonder and revelation, mutual understanding, and new wisdom—the joys of the contact zone" (39). The contact zone thus carries a potential for interaction and recognition, both of which may be painful but also productive. But then, a classroom may not be the perfect location for an exploration of cultures that clash with each other in highly asymmetrical relations of power. Instead, the multicultural urban environments or (post)colonial contexts in relation to which this concept has frequently been discussed are probably more suitable for an assessment of this phenomenon. In contrast to many hopeful and occasionally highly ideological accounts, this may yield results that are not quite as joyful as the intercultural discussion of the American histories.

Be that as it may, the novel completely eradicates all notions of a contact zone between the inhabitants of the cities. One could argue that Besźel and Ul Qoma are all contact but with no zone in which interaction could actually take place. There is no accessible third space and no element of hybridity. The centripetal or gravitational social forces that lead to intercultural exchange and creative mixture are suspended by the rigid us/them differentiation on which quite a lot of human psychology and often inharmonious interaction rests.

But while there is no accessible third space, the novel is persistently concerned with hypothetical third spaces for which the text, indeed, offers two possibilities. The first is a visionary concept, a mixture of old legends or fairy tales and recent theoretical explorations. It suggests utopian hopes and productive dissent as a counter-discourse to the hegemonic forces of the two cities. Some existing postmodern theorists are press-ganged into the pages of the novel, and they are here closely linked to the idea that within the cities there must be some kind of third space, another city between the cities, called Orciny. The murdered girl subscribed to that theory, and it is stressed that she also was "more interested in Foucault and Baudrillard than in Gordon Childe and trowels" (*City* 106)[4]; Žižek (slightly misspelled as Źiżiek) is then also mentioned a few pages later. Research into Orciny is, of course, forbidden in both cities, but then there are the few who still secretly pursue their investigations and suspect it to be a place of so-called *dissensi*, "places that everyone in Ul Qoma thinks are in Besźel, and everyone in Besźel thinks are in Ul Qoma. They're not in either one. They're Orciny" (*City* 213).

The problem, however, is that this secret and rebellious third space simply does not exist. There is no Orciny. The concept was stitched together from old tales and archaeological bits and pieces by a New Age scholar; at present it was merely used to lure an enthusiastic student, the murder victim, into a rather profitable operation smuggling archaeological artifacts to an international corporation for R&D. She is killed because she stopped believing in the existence of Orciny (see *City* 320), and has now become a danger for the criminal master minds. Ultimately, Orciny, the third space, is an exploitable myth, but also a theoretical construct that fulfills ideological hopes and accommodates the recently fashionable academic paradigms.

The critique of recent theoretical constructs that underlies the debunking of Orciny can also be felt in some little jokes that may even go unnoticed. For example, one of the less gifted students writes her PhD thesis on the archaeological artifacts dug up in Ul Qoma, but then the problem with those findings is that they resist precise archaeological assessment and interpretation (see *City* 181). The title of her paper, however, is the inevitable: "Representing Gender and the Other in Precursor Age Artefacts." Miéville here joins some other authors that seem to have become rather disillusioned with the latest developments in literary theory and criticism, e.g., Ian McEwan, or A.S. Byatt, both of whom have expressed their views quite openly, sometimes in interviews, sometimes in their works. My favorite example, however, is Neal Stephenson's science fiction novel *Cryptonomicon*, in which he has a wonderfully funny passage on the work of a young literary scholar who gained academic fame by deconstructing beards; now, "on the strength of her beard work, three Ivy League schools are fighting over who will get her" (77). In his interview with Joan Gordon, Miéville repeatedly stressed his dissatisfaction with postmodern theory, in particular the rejection of grand narratives and the hegemonial practice of "colonizing lots of techniques and implying that anything like those techniques is therefore 'postmodernist'" (Gordon, "Interview").

The other possible third space is *Breach*. This is a multi-purpose term that refers equally to an illegal action, i.e., a transgression, the institution that sanctions the action and punishes the transgressor, and the location where this institution resides. You breach, and then you are taken by Breach and brought into Breach. The institution is beyond all usual governmental powers, but it can only take action when a breach has actually occurred. The members are unknown—and unseen—and once you are taken into Breach you are gone. Transgressions can range from a voluntary, or possibly even involuntary, glance at "elsewhere" to a step over the invisible boundary into the foreign territory.

The narrator recalls a frightening situation, when an Ul Qoman truck went out of control and killed a Besź pedestrian.

> In seconds the Breach came. Shapes, figures, some of whom perhaps had been there but who nonetheless seemed to coalesce from spaces between smoke from the accident, moving too fast it seemed to be clearly seen, moving with authority and power so absolute that within seconds they had controlled, contained, the area of the intrusion [*City* 81–82].

The Breach also serves as a kind of bogeyman for children, and as such it is included in the internal control training. The kids play Breach, transgressing chalked lines and chasing each other in the local version of cops and robbers (see *City* 46). And, indeed, Breach exists in the cracks and empty spaces that cannot be attributed to either city. It is simultaneously everywhere and invisible, because the inhabitants are conditioned not to see it. Thus, the third space is exactly the opposite of a contact zone. It serves to maintain the division, if necessary by force; it rigidly polices transgressions and has, as an almost supernatural force, become an integral part of the mental setup. It is also easily recognizable as a highly imaginative re-construction of behaviors and features that are part and parcel of the alienated urban life in a globalized but also rigidly divided world.

The City and the City is a marvelous construction, possibly a new variety of magic realism, in which reader hesitation is increased by the very lack of anything magical and by the uncanny feeling of "having been here before," which now turns a seemingly realist setting into an alien and familiar world that is far stranger than a land of fairies and dragons. Miéville has approached and challenged the problems of multicultural environments in several novels, and I want to turn briefly to an alternative conceptualization that seems to be radically different from *The City and the City*, but in the very difference ultimately touches upon similar themes and phenomena.

Perdido Street Station

Perdido Street Station is something between science fiction and fantasy with lots of weirdness in between. After all, Miéville describes his work as "weird fiction." The novel is set in a city that Miéville has revisited several times since, New Crobuzon, and in the imagery of these books he once more turns a common perspective on the city on its head. If, as suggested at the beginning of my paper, one of the most common concepts of the city is the image of the organic community, this one seems to be built on a real organism, albeit one that died a long time ago. In Bonetown, one of the poor districts, the "Ribs" of a gigantic fossilized creature rise a hundred feet into the air, and "Fifty feet below [...], archaeologists had found vertebrae the size of houses; a backbone which had been quietly reburied after one too many accidents on-site. No limbs, no hips, no gargantuan skull had surfaced. No none could say what manner of creature had fallen here and died millennia ago" (Miéville, *Perdido* 29). The city is a city of waste, of debris and filth, of rotting buildings and decaying quarters. But it is still a rather busy place. It could be described as a London Below without a London Above. It is quite impossible to give any kind of outline of the story, and it would be a pity to try, as the book has to be relished as an extended voyage into a brilliantly twisted mind creating a marvelously twisted world. But I do want to offer a short scene which I think is rather significant for Miéville's way of manipulating the reader by unexpected turns. It is the description of two lovers, Isaac and Lin, getting up in the morning. This is the first time we meet them, and we know nothing about them. I have cut it from five pages to a few lines.

> He lay hugely in the bed without opening his eyes. [...]. Lin clapped twice. She knew when Isaac woke. [...] He groaned and rolled over. "Termagant!" he moaned after her. "Shrew! Harridan! All right, all right, you win [...]." Lin made an obscene gesture at him without turning around. She stood with her back to him, nude, at the stove [...]. Lin was hairless. Her muscles were tight under her red skin, each distinct. She was like an anatomical atlas. Isaac studied her in cheerful lust. [...] Isaac and Lin sat naked on either side of the wooden table [...] A dark-skinned man, big and nude and detumescing, gripping a knife and fork, unnaturally still, sitting opposite a khepri, her slight woman's body in shadow, her chitinous head in silhouette. Light glinted in Lin's compound eyes. Her headlegs quivered. She picked up half a tomato and gripped it with her mandibles. [...] As Lin gathered her notes and sketches to go, Isaac tugged her gently onto him, on the bed. He kissed her warm red skin. She turned in his arms. She angled up on one elbow and, as he watched, the dark ruby of her carapace opened slowly while her headlegs

splayed. The two halves of her headshell quivered slightly, held as wide as they would go. From beneath their shades she spread her beautiful, useless little beetle wings [...]. The air between them charged. Isaac's cock stiffened [...] [*Perdido* 8–13].

And so it goes on in a rather drastic depiction of the two lovers about to have sex. Of, course, this scene is absolutely weird, and the sexual attraction between a human and sf's most traditional alien, the bug-eyed monster, is not easy to pull off successfully. However, Miéville manages to present these two characters as convincing lovers in an environment that does not readily accept such forms of misalliance—they are the underdogs, the rebels against norms and conventions, a very awkward Romeo and Juliet, and their fate is fully captivating. But then *Perdido Street Station* extrapolates the multicultural, multi-ethnic or multiracial city and turns it into a habitation not so much of different species but of different classes, phyla or even kingdoms. Within the cities there are humans, various kinds of birds with various levels of intelligence, the Khepri (humanoid beetles), Vodanoi (fat and frog-like aquatic beings), Grindylow (telepathic fishpeople), Cactacae (humanoid cacti), Remades whose bodies have been mutilated in one or the other way as a kind of legal punishment, a spider god named Weaver, and a steam-punk artificial swarm intelligence emerging from the junkyards of the city. These are merely some of the more imaginable alien life forms. There are also vampires, thanatoids, and slake moths, and in *Perdido Street Station* only the latter pose a real problem as they feed on human dreams and ideas and leave only empty shells of vegetable bodies. By the way, Hell has an embassy in New Crobuzon (as the sea has an embassy in London in *Kraken*), and in the course of the novel a rather courteous, but ultimately unproductive meeting with His Infernal Excellence, the ambassador from Hell, takes place (see *Perdido* 241). As he refuses to help against the slake moths, Weaver is invoked next, and compared to him the devil's emissary seems to have been the less scary alternative (see *Perdido* 237). The text thus produces a totality of otherness including not only all the well-established varieties of fantastic humanoids and artificial intelligences but also members of very different biological orders. But here, in the face of all the differences—differences that result from biological facts and thus are not easily reduced to social constructions—common interests and desires are negotiable. The world is weird and the dangers are terrifying, but the possibilities for solidarity among the animate and even non-animate inhabitants are striking. The lines of conflict in this world do not follow the common visual distinctions of biological markers but the division between those in power and the disempowered, between the aggressors and the victims. *Perdido Street Station* is in many ways an inversion of *The City and the City*—or vice versa, as it was written first. In the latter novel, sameness is divided rigorously, and this status quo is maintained by equally strong internal and external control mechanisms. And of course, even with all the weird and awkward aspects, it is a world that ultimately also resembles ours. In *Perdido Street Station*, extreme differences are brought together up to the point where the faint-hearted might easily be shocked. But here, these differences can ultimately be overcome by affection and love, but also for the pursuit of a common cause. The group that Isaac brings together to fight the terrifying slake moths consists of humans, khepri, garuda, vodanoi, a remade, the Construct Council and the Weaver, and "they can contribute separate skills, perspectives, and motives, their dialectic mateship cross-pollinating and resulting in the hybrid vigor of their group" (Gordon, "Hybridity" 470). Once more the world is weird, but it also contains the seed of a utopian vision. The protagonists live in a world of waste, but they do create their own contact zone, albeit a contact zone that also would not quite fit Mary Louise Pratt's classroom.

Notes

1. Calvino is quoted from an internet source without pagination. My references indicate the chapters.
2. I want to thank Elizabeth Ho for sending me the abstract of her paper.
3. In an interview with Joan Gordon, Miéville suggests that "the postmodern fascination with hybridity and miscegenation too often blurs into a fetishistic and sometimes quite self-indulgent celebration of marginality for its own sake" (Gordon, "Interview"). I do not see this as a full rejection of postcolonial concepts and theory but rather as a rejection of the dogmatism that is occasionally involved in academic schools and fashions.
4. Vere Gordon Childe (1892–1957) was a famous Marxist archaeologist who excavated Skara Brea on the Orkney Islands and later became director at the Institute of Archaeology in London.

Works Cited

Adams, Douglas. *Life, The Universe and Everything*. London: Pan Books, 1982. Print.
Ariely, Dan. "Can Beggars be Choosers." 30 Nov. 2011. Web. 25 Sept. 2012.
Bear, Greg, *Strength of Stones* [1981]. New York: ibooks, 2002. Print.
Brians, Paul. "Notes on Salman Rushdie *The Satanic Verses*." 13 Feb. 2004. PDF document. Web. 25 Sept. 2012.
Calvino, Italo. *Invisible Cities* [Italian original 1972]. Transl. William Weaver. *Scribd*. Web. 15 Feb. 2013.
Choo, Chun Wei. "IT2000: Singapore's Vision of an Intelligent Island." *Intelligent Environments: Spatial Aspects of the Information Revolution*. Ed. Peter Droege. Amsterdam: Elsevier, 1997. 49–65. Print.
Coover, Robert. *Ghost Town* [1998]. New York: Grove Press, 2000. Print.
Droege, Peter. "Tomorrow's Metropolis: Virtualization Takes Command." *Intelligent Environments: Spatial Aspects of the Information Revolution*. Ed. Peter Droege. Amsterdam: Elsevier, 1997. 1–17. Print.
Gaiman, Neil. *Neverwhere* [1997]. New York: Harpertorch, 2001. Print.
Gordon, Joan. "Hybridity, Heterotopia, and Mateship in China Miéville's *Perdido Street Station*." *Science Fiction Studies* 30.3 (2003): 456–76. Print.
_____. "Reveling in Genre: An Interview with China Miéville." *Science Fiction Studies* 30.3 (2003): 355–73. Web. 19 Sept. 2013.

Ho, Elizabeth. "Mapping the New Europe in China Miéville's *The City & the City.*" Abstract for a paper read at the international conference "Interrogating Cosmopolitan Conviviality: New Dimensions of the European in Literature." Bamberg, May 24–25, 2012.
Johnson, Steven. *Emergence: The Connected Lives of Ants, Brains, Cities, and Software* [2001]. London: Penguin, 2002. Print.
Joyce, James. *Ulysses* [1922]. New York: Vintage, 1986. Print.
Miéville, China. *The City and the City* [2009]. London: Pan Books, 2011. Print.
_____. *King Rat* [1998]. London: Pan Books, 1999. Print.
_____. *Kraken*. London: Pan Books, 2010. Print.
_____. *Perdido Street Station* [2000]. New York: Del Rey, 2003. Print.
_____. *Un Lun Dun* [2007]. London: Macmillan, 2008. Print.
Novak, Marcos. "Cognitive Cities: Intelligence, Environment and Space." *Intelligent Environments: Spatial Aspects of the Information Revolution*. Ed. Peter Droege. Amsterdam: Elsevier, 1997. 386–419. Print.
Pratchett, Terry. *Reaper Man*. London: Corgy, 1992. Print.
Pratt, Marie Luise. "Arts of the Contact Zone." *Profession* (1991): 33–40. Print.
Pynchon, Thomas. *The Crying of Lot 49* [1966]. London: Picador, 1979. Print.
_____. *V.* [1963]. London: Picador, 1975. Print.
Stephenson, Neal. *Cryptonomicon* [1999]. London: Arrow Books, 2000. Print.
Sue, Eugéne. *The Mysteries of Paris* [French original 1842–1843]. Project Gutenberg. Web. 25 Sept. 2012.
Vanderbeke, Dirk (in cooperation with Christoph Gossel). "The City as a Superorganism." *"The Mighty Heart" or "The Desert in Disguise?" The Metropolis Between Realism and the Fantastic*. Ed. James Fanning, Anne Hegerfeldt, Jürgen Klein, and Dirk Vanderbeke. Tübingen: Stauffenburg Verlag, 2007. 162–83. Print.
Winterson, Jeanette. *Passion* [1987]. New York: Grove Press, 1988. Print.

III. THE FANTASY OF POLITICS

Fantastic Body Politics in Joe Abercrombie's *The First Law* Trilogy

GEROLD SEDLMAYR

> "I've been trying to get through this damn book again." Ardee slapped at a heavy volume lying open, face down, on a chair.
> "*The Fall of the Master Maker*," muttered Glokta. "That rubbish? All magic and valour, no? I couldn't get through the first one."
> "I sympathise. I'm onto the third and it doesn't get any easier. Too many damn wizards. I get them mixed up one with another. It's all battles and endless bloody journeys, here to there and back again. If I so much as glimpse another map I swear I'll kill myself" [*LAK* 474].

Introduction

With *The First Law* trilogy, first published between 2006 and 2008, Joe Abercrombie renegotiates fantasy as a genre. This becomes obvious in the just-quoted passage from the third volume, *Last Argument of Kings*, which, clearly, serves as a meta-commentary. Quite readily and unanimously, both of the characters in this scene, Ardee and Glokta, utter their contempt for epic romances, epic histories or, indeed, epic fantasies. And yet, paradoxically enough, the trilogy itself does feature wizards, and in the course of the 1,500-plus pages, some of them might even be mixed up by the reader. As a matter of fact, "[i]t's all battles and endless bloody journeys, here to there and back again," at least if considering the books' surface structure only.

In truth, however, if Abercrombie's is an epic fantasy itself, it is one aiming at subverting the ideology inherent in the traditional epic hero story. In *Decon-*

structing the Hero, Margery Hourihan characterizes this traditional hero story as follows:

> In Western culture there is a story which has been told over and over again, in innumerable versions, from the earliest times. It is a story about superiority, dominance and success. It tells how white European men are the natural masters of the world because they are strong, brave, skilful, rational and dedicated. It tells how they overcome the dangers of nature, how other "inferior" races have been subdued by them, and how they spread civilization and order wherever they go. It tells how women are designed to serve them, and how those women who refuse to do so are threats to the natural order and must be controlled. It tells how their persistence means that they always eventually win the glittering prizes, the golden treasures, and how the gods—or the government—approve of their enterprises. It is our favourite story and it has been told so many times that we have come to believe that what it says about the world is true [Hourihan 1].

Abercrombie takes crucial elements of this story—in terms of character, for instance, the strong male warrior hero, the wise old man who acts as a guide, the beautiful maid waiting at home as reward—and disrupts their conventional generic value and meaning.

In the following, the trilogy will first be defined as an immersive fantasy. In a second step, it will be argued that the subversive potential of Abercrombie's story ultimately depends on his depiction of the body and that this depiction in itself must be considered in the politico-economic terms offered by late capitalism. Subsequently, notions of power in the trilogy will be related to images of violated bodies, before ultimately reconnecting these arguments to the issue of genre.[1]

Thinning: *The First Law* as a Hybrid of Immersive and Portal-Quest Fantasies

In order to attain more precision when it comes to genre, the taxonomy offered by Farah Mendlesohn in *Rhetorics of Fantasy* will be used, all the while keeping in mind her own avowal that "[t]axonomy [...] needs to be understood as a tool, not as an end in itself" (xv). It will be proposed that *The First Law* trilogy must be read primarily as an *immersive fantasy* which, however, dialectically engages with and uses elements of another subgenre, namely the *portal-quest fantasy*, the latter serving as the major vehicle of the sort of master narrative sketched by Hourihan. Regarding definition, it must first be said that, quite basically, "[t]he immersive fantasy is a fantasy set in a world built so that it functions on all levels as a complete world" (Mendlesohn 59). In an immersive fantasy, hence, from the beginning, the reader is thrown into a full "secondary world." There is no portal whatsoever through which the characters move from one world to another, from a known environment to an unknown one, like the wardrobe in C.S. Lewis' *The Lion, the Witch and the Wardrobe,* Rowling's platform nine and three-quarters at King's Cross station in the *Harry Potter* books or, indeed, the border of the Shire in Tolkien's *The Lord of the Rings* (for the latter see Mendlesohn 31–32). Hence, the readers do not discover the world *along with* their characters, simply because the characters already know their world—although they may of course not know all aspects of it. This has consequences for the rhetoric employed in immersive fantasies. Rather than featuring omniscient narrators that explain the world for us and thereby present an objective, *true* view of affairs, immersive fantasies commonly rather employ character-focused (often homodiegetic) narration. In Mendlesohn's terms, "we must sit in the heads of the protagonists, accepting what they know as the world, interpreting it through what they notice, and through what they do not" (59). This in turn implies that we, as readers, are forced to create the world presented to us from the bits and pieces of information that we get from the characters in a rather impressionistic way, a cognitive technique that Mendlesohn calls "syntactic bootstrapping, the construction of a world from pieced-together hints and gradual explanations, the understanding of a world by the *context* of what is told" (75).

In *The First Law* trilogy, Abercrombie employs multiple focalization, one model for this certainly being George R.R. Martin's narrative style in the *A Song of Ice and Fire* series. To be more precise, the reader observes and gets to know this particular secondary world through the eyes of six different point-of-view characters: two Northmen, a woman from the South, and three characters from the Union, which is a state on the large central island, Midderland; two of these are soldiers and one is a torturer in the service of His Majesty's Inquisition. Briefly, this is the plot: it becomes clear very soon that Midderland is threatened both from the North and the South. Two power-hungry rulers try to extend their influence to the Union. Under the guidance of a Gandalf-like wizard, Bayaz, the point-of-view characters ultimately contribute to saving Midderland by fighting these invasions off. This sounds very much like the Fellowship's battle against Sauron, and it certainly is, yet then again, it is not.

In order to both explain this paradox and also come to the subject proper, namely the body and body politics in the trilogy, one other aspect of immersive and portal-quest fantasies has to be mentioned, namely the aspect of thinning. In his entry on "thinning" in *The Encyclopedia of Fantasy*, John Clute claims that

> Even in HIGH FANTASY—which tends to be ringfenced from time's arrow—the SECONDARY WORLD is almost constantly under some threat of lessening, a threat frequently accompanied by mourning [...] and/or a sense of WRONGNESS. In the

structurally complete fantasy, thinning can be seen as a reduction of the healthy LAND to a PARODY of itself, and the thinning agent—ultimately, in most instances, the DARK LORD—can be seen as inflicting this damage upon the land out of envy [942].

This "lessening" of the world can be observed to happen on various levels. One of these levels pertains to a long-established *topos* in fantasy literature: very early on, the reader learns that the magic, slowly but relentlessly, is leaking from the world (see e.g., *TBI* 30). In the capital of the Union, Adua, whose inhabitants believe themselves to occupy the center of civilization and commerce, hardly anyone still believes in magic.

It is only through its interdependence with another level of lessening, though, that the *topos* of the waning of the miraculous attains topicality and is given political clout: in *The First Law*, thinning, very literally, affects the bodily level first and foremost. As has been mentioned before, one of the point-of-view characters is a torturer, and Abercrombie is so considerate as to not spare us any details regarding Sand dan Glokta's profession. In the following scene, Glokta is interrogating the head of a very powerful merchant guild, Sepp dan Teufel.

> Glokta curled his fist round the smooth grip of the cleaver, the blade scraping against the wood as he pulled it slowly towards him. He stared down at Teufel's hand. *What beautiful fingernails he has. How long and glossy. You cannot work down a mine with nails like that.* Glokta raised the cleaver high.
> "Wait!" screamed the prisoner.
> Bang! The heavy blade bit deep into the table top, neatly paring off Teufel's middle fingernail. He was breathing fast now, and there was a sheen of sweat on his forehead. *Now we'll see what kind of a man you really are.*
> [...] Glokta lifted the cleaver again. "Confess."
> "You couldn't ..."
> Bang! The cleaver took off the very tip of Teufel's middle finger. Blood bubbled out onto the table top. [...]
> Bang! The tip of Teufel's index finger jumped in the air. His middle finger was down to the first joint. Glokta paused, wiping the sweat from his forehead on the back of his hand. [...]
> [Practical] Severard shook his head. "That's excellent work, Inquisitor." He flicked one of the discs of flesh across the table. "The precision ... I'm in awe" [*TBI* 49].

As this passage illustrates, in this trilogy, thinning assumes a literal—bodily—nature. It is not an exaggeration to claim that these books primarily are about bodies, about mutilated, violated, hurt bodies, bodies in pain, dying bodies. Two of the most prominent point-of-view characters, Inquisitor Glokta and the Northman Logen Ninefingers, are themselves maimed right from the beginning of the trilogy, while the others are being disfigured in the course of the novels. Glokta, who, in his former life, had been a young handsome man, popular with the women, winner of the most prestigious fencing contest in the Union, and had had a promising military career before him, has ended up as a cripple. During the last war with the Gurkish Empire in the south he was captured, tortured and imprisoned for years. Most of his teeth are missing, his leg constantly hurts, he cannot control his bowels anymore; in short, he leads a life of pain and social exclusion. As the reader learns from Glokta by being granted access to his thoughts: *"Eight years since the Gurkish released me, yet I am still their prisoner, and always will be. Trapped in a cell no bigger than my own crippled body"* (*LAK* 281). Logen Ninefingers, the Northman, who is known as the "Bloody Nine," is similarly isolated; he is the "most feared man in the North." No one, except his closest companions, wants to associate with him. His body is littered with scars. In fact, these function as the physical markers of his inner life and his past: "There were plenty more memories, all crowding in and cutting at him. The stump of his finger after the battle at Carleon, burning and burning and making him crazy. [...] Logen felt them now on his scattered skin, all of his scars, and he hugged his arms around his aching body" (*BTAH* 54).

Late Capitalism and the Fantastic Fragmented Body

Of course, mutilated and metamorphosed bodies have always been common in fantastic literature. More so, their presence has always also had a very definite social and political significance. As Rosemary Jackson has remarked:

> "Fantastic" character deformation suggests a radical refusal of the structures, the "syntax" of cultural order. Incoherent, fluid selves exist in opposition to precious portraits of individuals as whole or essential. They break the boundaries separating self from other, leaving structures dissolved, or ruptured, through a radical open-endedness of being. The fantastic makes an assault upon the "sign" of unified character and this has far-reaching consequences in terms of interrogating the process of character construction [Jackson 86–87].

In this sense, for example, Gregor Samsa's transformation in Kafka's *The Metamorphosis* may be read as an attack against a certain closed conception of the self that has been established in Western modernity since the late eighteenth century. What is it, however, that makes Abercrombie's treatment of the body *contemporary*, especially when considering that his images of bodiliness are caught in the generic structures of an epic romance? "[W]hat happens," to borrow one of Fredric Jameson's questions, "when plot falls into history" (*Political* 117)? In order to answer these questions, it is necessary to read the trilogy in terms of a "negative hermeneutic" (Jameson, *Political* 117) with reference to the understanding of romance narratives, and so to emphasize that all inquiries pertaining to the body, including a political reading of body imagery, are closely connected to the issue of genre. For reasons to be explained in the following, one important related question to ask is: if we agree that romances, in various ways, act as taproot texts for contemporary genre fantasy, "what, under wholly altered historical circumstances, can have been found to replace the raw materials of magic and Otherness which medieval romance found ready to hand in its socioeconomic environment" (*Political* 117)?

Indeed, the whole bulk of Western fantastic literature from the late eighteenth century up until today can be characterized as being a reaction against an advancing secularization of the world. If you like, it is a literature written to—at least temporarily—stop magic's leaking from the world, with Tolkien's whole venture, including its ecocritical aspects, being surely one of the most prominent examples. However, what seems quite particular for our own time— a time that might be labeled by terms such as "late capitalism" or "postmodernism"—is a specific cultural and political prioritization of the body. As Jean Baudrillard claimed in his lucid analysis of consumer culture, first published in 1970, an analysis that has lost nothing of its relevance: "In the consumer package, there is one object finer, more precious and more dazzling than any other [...]. That object is the BODY" (129). As a result of the sexual liberation in the Sixties, as a consequence of the coming into being of a media society that relentlessly propagates new and apparently universal ideals of beauty and of youthfulness, including the formation of tailored hygienic and dietetic practices, "the body," Baudrillard claims, "has today become an *object of salvation*. It has literally taken over that moral and ideological function from the soul" (129). We could claim, then, that the body is one of *the* central receptacles of a postmodern sort of magic today. The magic that metaphysics once held has leaked into the physical.

Significantly, this "sacralization of the body" (Baudrillard 132) goes hand in hand with the radical insertion of the body in an economic logic: the body has become one's capital. It is a prime carrier of meaning, and therefore value, in today's Western consumer societies. However, and this is probably the most important point here, what is called the body cannot be granted any more "reality" than, say, the "soul." Within the late-capitalist system, the body has lost its corpo-reality (*Leiblichkeit*), it has been reduced to a sign, a signifier without any stable signified. Thereby, the body, being our new currency, largely lacks any of the intrinsic use-value it once might have had; instead, its meaning exhausts itself in a dubious sort of exchange value. In Baudrillard's words: "Bodies and objects form a network of homogeneous signs which may [...] exchange their significations (this is, properly speaking their 'exchange value') and 'show each other off [...] mutually'" (134).

This, in turn, implies that the body, precisely because it is part of a political and economic sign system whose elements only attain meaning by their being *different* from other elements, can never attain wholeness, can never be or represent an essence. To put it more bluntly, the magic surrounding bodies is a hoax. Despite its glittering surface, the body in late capitalism has always already been a mutilated, a disfigured body. It is fantastic precisely because it purports to be whole and essential while in fact *it is not*.[2] Today, we increasingly define our bodies by way of mediated, simulacral fantastic bodies; bodies which are always already fragmented as a result of their being subjected to a late-capitalist economic logic.

What is of interest for the present purpose is that certain *forms* of heroic fantasy seem to serve as vehicles of that late-capitalist conception of the body that thinkers like Baudrillard criticize, especially when they feature heroes whose "exterior persona either reflects an interior, ontogenetic reality, or is the essential collection of characteristics that constitute their subject totally: whereupon there is no interior to reflect" (Miller 193). It shall be argued, however, that Abercrombie attempts to write against these forms by subverting them from within. His depictions of the deformed, dismembered, mutilated body in pain are so numerous that they lose their *extraordinariness* in the course of the narrative. Within the intratextual universe of Abercrombie's novels, fragmented bodies become the norm and thereby help to point out that—within our own, the extratextual, world—they might quite easily also be the norm, if we just cared to look a little closer.

Hence, what makes Abercrombie's novels more political than many other fantastic slasher novels and films is the fact that, throughout, fragmented bodiliness seems to be connected to a capitalist world order. In Abercrombie's secondary world, as in our own, while magic is leaking out, economics seem to fill the vacuum. During the siege by the Gurkish of a town held by the Union, Glokta makes clear to the commanding general that the city has to be defended at all costs.

> Glokta felt his hand bunching into a fist on the parapet. "We must make the Gurkish pay for every stride of ground." *We must make them pay for my ruined leg.* "For every inch of dirt." *For my missing teeth.* "For every meagre shack, and crumbling hut, and worthless stretch of dust." *For my weeping eye, and my twisted back, and my repulsive shadow of a life.* He licked at his empty gums. "Make them pay" [*BTAH* 338–9].

Although it seems to be, Glokta's "Make them pay" is not metaphorical. Indeed, many of the Gurkish attackers will ultimately pay with their lives, yet none of these casualties of course can buy back Glokta's teeth or repair his twisted back. The body's exchange value is vastly overrated, especially when comparing it to the exchange value of money. The beleaguered city can withstand the besiegers for such a long time only because it has been granted a huge amount of money by a mysterious banking house, Valint and Balk. Only by way of this money can the walls be repaired and bodies bought, namely those of mercenaries, while it allows the destruction of enemy bodies.

As is revealed in the end, this mysterious banking house belongs to none other than the novels' ever-present guide figure, the wizard Bayaz. As he confesses to Glokta, by way of his money and his magic, he has managed to influence basically every important political event in the Union for hundreds of years (see *LAK* 582–83). What is worse: most of the wide-ranging decisions taken or actions accomplished by the point-of-view characters have also been pre-arranged by the wizard. Jezal, for example, has only become king of the Union because Bayaz has carefully arranged his ultimate ascension from a time even before Jezal's birth. In the first book, Jezal can only win the prestigious fencing contest, because Bayaz magically remote-controls his body. In fact, all of the characters, without their realizing it, are mere pawns in a game that Bayaz plays very cunningly. As he tells Glokta quite frankly: "People like to watch the pretty puppets, Superior. Even a glimpse of the puppeteer can be most upsetting for them. Why, they might even suddenly notice the strings around their own wrists" (*LAK* 579).

Power Politics, Superficial Bodies and the Sterility of Violence

In an unpublished interview with Christina Schneider, Abercrombie said about Tolkien's *The Lord of the Rings* that, ultimately, it is difficult "to understand why Sauron is what he is and does what he does. [...] He doesn't seem a particularly appealing guy to follow. I don't know why anyone would pick his side" (Schneider 3). To make up for this lack, in *The First Law* trilogy, Abercrombie tries to give Sauron a face and a body, so to speak. Bayaz, in all his bodiliness, however, is not so much an incarnation of "pure" evil, precisely because the trilogy does not allow easy distinctions between those time-worn categories, good and evil, right and wrong. After all, if we were still prepared to use the term "evil" freely, we would have to admit that all of those characters we have come to sympathize with are *also* evil to a large degree. As Bayaz himself unashamedly proclaims: "Evil? [...] A word for children. A word the ignorant use for those who disagree with them. I thought we grew out of such notions long centuries ago" (*BTAH* 324). What Bayaz stands for, then, is power, a power that is both invisible—you rarely become aware of the strings around your wrists—and decidedly material. His actions illustrate, to borrow a phrase from Judith Butler, "the productive and, indeed, materializing effects of regulatory power" (9–10). In other words, the idea of power that the wizard Bayaz incorporates is one that strictly depends on an economics of power that is both beyond traditional moral distinctions and beyond the comprehension of the individual *actant*.

In this context, it is quite crucial to note that Bayaz is not a point-of-view character. He cannot be, since he is also beyond any notion of individuality. This is not to say, though, that he incorporates some lost essence, some unfathomable truth. As we know from Jameson, one aspect of the logic of late capitalism is its generation of "depthlessness" (Jameson, *Postmodernism* 12). Accordingly, although we get glimpses of Bayaz's history, the sort of power he stands for is as depthless as late capitalism itself. Bayaz does not care about insides, because, for him, everything is exchangeable, everything is ultimately an outside. You simply need to cut a body open or let it explode, you will not find anything but blood and guts, mere surfaces, as this demonstration of Bayaz's magic illustrates: "Like a bottle dropped from a great height, the nearest Practical burst apart. There was no thunderclap, only a gentle squelching. One moment he was moving toward the old man, sword raised, entirely whole, the next he was a thousand fragments. Some unknown part of him thudded wetly against the plaster next to Jezal's head" (*TBI* 505).

This also helps to explain the paradoxical fact that the present era of the Magi, who had once been merely the disciples of the old, all-powerful, superhuman but now dead and mythicized rulers, is referred to by the librarian of the old University as an enlightened age. As he makes clear, the fall of the "Master Maker," Kanedias, signified "[t]he end of the age of myth, the beginning of the age of reason. Bayaz, the Magi, they represent order. The Maker is a god-like figure: superstition, ignorance, I don't know" (*TBI* 343). Although undoubtedly offering a fantasy world in a partly quasi-medieval, partly quasi–Renaissance setting, the trilogy offers more parallels to our own, the "primary," world than at first meets the eye. As mentioned above, in Adua, the capital of the Union, hardly anyone still believes in magic in the fairy-tale sense; for most of the people in the so-called civilized parts of the world, belief in magic is superstition. And yet, magic is present. However, in Abercrombie's creation, magic—as represented by Bayaz—is merely a code word for *modern* power in the Foucauldian sense: "I am First of the Magi. I am the last authority and I say ... I am righteous. [...] Power makes all things right. That is my first law, and my last. That is the only law that I acknowledge" (*LAK* 610). And it is this—namely that "magic" is shorthand for the sort of (meta-subjective) power that structures and characterizes modernity (and postmodernity)—which in turn accounts for the centrality of the body in these novels.

According to Jan-Philipp Reemtsma, as a consequence of the Enlightenment, which had moved the human subject into the center of things, the frame that is provided by the individual's own body has come to take the place of the larger metaphysical framework which once, in pre-modernity, had spanned the whole cosmos. This transfer, however, did not happen without a cost. If the modern body has come to function as the symbolic guarantee of our own integrity—after all, the inviolability of the body is regarded as a human right—and if bodily integrity thereby also compensates for the centrifugal tendencies of a highly differentiated society, then "[a]ssaults on this form of compensation can have disastrous consequences" (Reemtsma 73). In the words of Bryan S. Turner: "The dominant concerns and anxieties of society tend to be translated into disturbed images of the body. [...] Body metaphors illustrate the fact that we use the body as a convenient way for talking or thinking about the moral and political problems of society" (1). Seen in this light, Abercrombie's relentless provision of images of violated bodies is indicative of a very modern—or indeed postmodern—sort of crisis.

Unsurprisingly, then, the only body that remains largely unharmed throughout the whole trilogy is Bayaz's. In the scene alluded to above, the one in which Bayaz magically explodes one of the Practicals that had tried to hunt down Logen and Ferro, he is disturbed while bathing. When Jezal, the point-of-view character in this scene, a young, arrogant upper-class captain, witnesses the mage emerge from the bathroom, Bayaz is totally naked: "'What the fuck is this?' [Bayaz] roared, striding into the centre of the room, water dripping from his beard, down through the grizzled white hairs on his chest, off his slapping fruits. It was a strange sight to see. [...] Ridiculous, and yet no one was laughing" (*TBI* 505). Exposed and uncovered, Bayaz only appears to be a weak "naked old man" (*TBI* 505). In fact, his unashamed patriarchal power, as symbolized by the explicit wholeness of his body, not least his "slapping fruits," exposes the others' superficiality. Significantly, not only does the Practical burst apart into "a thousand fragments" (*TBI* 505), the spectacle has a considerable effect also on the bystanders: Jezal "felt faint, and queasy, and awfully hollow inside" (*TBI* 505–6). Hence, in a weird way, the wholeness of Bayaz's body functions as a sort of "positive" foil for the potential hollowness and vulnerability of the central protagonists' bodies and selves. When formerly handsome Jezal, shortly before reaching the Edge of the World, sees himself in the mirror for the first time after having been maimed in a fight, he has to realize that his "face was a ruin. The pleasing symmetry was gone forever. [...] [H]is noble chin was twisted at a slovenly angle. The scar began on his top lip as no more than a faint line, but it split in two and gouged brutally into the bottom one, [...] giving him the appearance of having a permanent and unsightly leer" (*BTAH* 491). Although Jezal is intent on giving a lie to the old dictum that the outside mirrors the inside—"Perhaps he was an uglier man, but he was a better man too" (*BTAH* 491)—the reader soon learns that his resolution, whether honest or not, will have no value whatsoever. Most of his actions as king of the Union, at least those with a political impact, will have been manipulated by Bayaz (see e.g., *LAK* 34, 193, 269). Like the others, Jezal is a puppet on a string. Of the heroism traditionally pertaining to epic romances, not much remains.

To once again come back to the scene in which naked Bayaz demonstrates his power: there is nothing of the awe-inspiring, sublime sort of effect that the reader might experience for example when being presented with Gandalf's confrontation with the Balrog in Moria. The First of the Magi simply makes the Practical burst apart, no big show, not some "thunderclap," just "a gentle squelching" (*TBI* 505). The event itself, of course, is exceptional, but instead of feeling awe and wonder, the reader—along with Jezal—is probably taken aback by its ostentatious "ordinariness" rather than elevated. In other words, Abercrombie's very graphic depictions of bodiliness go along with a "casualization" (Mendlesohn 75) not only of the fantastic but also of violence. In an essay on the depiction of violence in Oliver Stone's *Natural Born Killers* and Quentin Tarantino's *Pulp Fiction*, Tony Bartlett argues that the "cinematic act," even in those cases in which violence is made extremely explicit, "appears [...] undecidable (and, therefore, non-accountable), between real violence (depth) and pure phantasy/comedy (surface)" (7). Arguably, although they miss the visual quality of cinema, this argument also holds for novels, and it is maybe even the case that the generic features of the *fantasy* novel stress the superficial, "phantastic" quality of *imagined* violence in an even clearer manner than other fictions do. Nonetheless, as Bartlett argues via René Girard, in a time in which sacrificial solutions to critical situations have lost their metaphysical meaning and therefore their legitimation, crises—and an outbreak of "real" violence as a reaction to them—can only be contained by presenting spectacles of *imagined* generative violence. By implication, this means that spectacles of imagined violence are themselves symptomatic of real-world crises: "From a Girardian perspective one could say that in as much as cinema [as well as other 'expressive art'] offers even a phantasmal sacrificial resolution then it must immediately be part of a generalized sacrificial crisis of the society in which it exists" (9). Precisely because such "phantasmal sacrificial resolution[s]" are merely imagined, however; precisely because they are ultimately unable to penetrate surfaces, they cannot simply be repeated, but have to be intensified in order to be successful. As Bartlett writes: "The function of cinema in this sense"—or of popular novelistic art, for that matter—"would also explain why the face of violence in movies [or novels and 'epic fantasy romances'] gets progressively more monstrous: it must continually outdo a crisis of violence it itself helps to unfold" (9).

As had been argued before, the more the reader is bombarded with images of violence in Abercrombie's trilogy, the less is she likely to be affected. As images of violence lose their extraordinariness, the concept of heroic sacrifice is exposed as sham: "[Dogman] remembered all those men gone back to the mud. Harding Grim. Tul Duru Thunderhead. Rudd Threetrees. Forley the Weakest. And what for? Who was better off because of it? All that waste" (*LAK* 632). Hence, Abercrombie's fantasy is political precisely because it helps to point out the sterility of violence in modernity. Although the trilogy is constructed according to a circular pattern (Logen's fall in the first and last chapter), this is not the traditional regenerative cycle of life—death—life. There is no proper development. The sort of meta-personal power represented by Bayaz has simply managed to stabilize itself. While the characters have altered physically, it is highly questionable whether their alteration also bears an inner—a "moral"—quality. When we meet Glokta for the first time, he is a torturer. When we meet him for the last time, he still is a torturer, although with a lot more power. If anything, his insight into the workings of this kind of world—a thoroughly modern world—is even more sober than in the beginning. As he says to the former Arch Lector Sult, a man who is about to be painfully questioned: "freedom is far overrated in any case. We all have our responsibilities. We all owe something to someone. Only the entirely worthless are entirely free. The worthless and the dead" (*LAK* 659).

Concluding Remarks

I hope it has become clear that a worldview such as that expressed in Abercrombie's trilogy at least complicates the potentially conservative ideology transported by traditional fantasies. Structurally, this is attained by activating the subversive potential of elements belonging to immersive fantasies against the holistic rhetorical tendencies at the heart of the portal-quest genre. Hence, while we are granted direct insight into the characters' inner lives, it is doubtful whether this insight can guarantee "authenticity" and "fullness." Rather, Abercrombie's point-of-view narrative technique serves to stress the relativity of the characters' perspectives, which correlates with the vulnerability and openness of their bodies. Hence, precisely at the point at which the reader agrees to immerse herself in the narrative, the hollowness she encounters will reveal the constructedness of the traditional hero story, many of whose elements Abercrombie has incorporated in his text. To put it differently, "thinning" not only affects events on the level of the story, especially when it comes to the wholeness of the characters' bodies, it also affects the body of the text itself.

Instead of providing a "proper" closure, therefore, the conclusion of *The First Law* trilogy can offer merely a parody of restoration. Although the enemies have been defeated, the price that has to be paid by the winners is disproportionately large. The magic that Bayaz uses to destroy his powerful opponents bears a very clear resemblance to weapons of mass destruction in our world: its effects are uncannily like those of an atomic bomb, and one of the point-of-view characters even dies from them. If the "real reward" in quest fantasies "is moral growth and/or [...] redemption" (Mendlesohn 4), then our "heroes" are not properly rewarded. They are conscious about their shortcomings, but they seem to be equally conscious about the fact that they will not be able to alter them for the better. Last but not least, traditional portal and quest fantasies are vehicles of an ideology that holds that "[t]here can be only one understanding of the world: an understanding that validates the quest" (Mendlesohn 13). Very often, a wise guide figure—like Aslan or Gandalf—functions as the medium of this very truth, a guide figure via which crucial information is downloaded into the text. However, while Bayaz's narratives in *The First Law* trilogy are as "uninterruptable [and] unquestionable" (Mendlesohn 13) as those of a Gandalf, their "truths" are not versions of some higher authorial truth, at least not in a metaphysical sense. We know, in other words, that something is crucially wrong with what Bayaz tries to tell the protagonists and, by extension, us.

In conclusion, Abercrombie's fantasy novels very successfully engage in deconstructing the coherence of what Hourihan calls Western cultures' favorite story. Significantly, they begin their work of deconstruction on the level of the body, whose coherence and quasi-sacral status is targeted throughout. The textual bodies of epic fantasies, just like the glossy bodies of late capitalism, are highly vulnerable constructs, whose political trajectories are worth a closer inspection.

Notes

1. I would like to thank my students at my former university, the University of Würzburg, for always giving me valuable input during seminars on fantasy. I would especially like to thank Christina Schneider and Johannes Beck, who both wrote their final theses on Abercrombie's *The First Law* trilogy.

2. In order to illustrate, allow me to quote from Laurie Penny's aptly titled *Meat Market: Female Flesh under Capitalism*: "The 'fragmented parts of the body' that Baudrillard describes are a key feature of advertorial eroticism: disembodied parts, particularly of women, are fetishised as symbols of a sexuality that they cannot access. Shampoo suds run down naked torsos in soft-focus; lingerie is stretched over moronically thrusting groins; and everywhere, on book-covers and cereal packets and boxes of sanitary towels, disembodied legs in stilettoed high heels emblematise a cutesy feminine imperative that edges to replace genuine erotic impulse in as sincere a manner as that in which O'Brien in George Orwell's 1984 vowed that the party would destroy the orgasm. To paraphrase Orwell, if you want a vision of the future of feminism, imagine a high heel coming down on a woman's face—forever" (Penny 9–10). Similar claims could of course be made about the role of the male body in advertising and elsewhere.

Works Cited

Abercrombie, Joe. *Before They Are Hanged*. Book Two of *The First Law*. London: Gollancz, 2007. Print. [*BTAH*]
_____. *The Blade Itself*. Book One of *The First Law*. London: Gollancz, 2006. Print. [*TBI*]
_____. *Last Argument of Kings*. Book Three of *The First Law*. London: Gollancz, 2008. Print. [*LAK*]
Bartlett, Tony. "The Party's Over (Almost): Terminal Celebration in Contemporary Film." *Contagion: Journal of Violence, Mimesis, and Culture* 5 (1998): 1–13. Print.

Baudrillard, Jean. *The Consumer Society: Myths and Structures* [French original 1970]. Trans. Chris Turner. London: Sage, 1998. Print.
Butler, Judith. *Bodies That Matter: On the Discursive Limits of "Sex."* London: Routledge, 1993. Print.
Clute, John. "Thinning." *The Encyclopedia of Fantasy*. Ed. John Clute and John Grant. London: Orbit, 1997. 942. Print.
Hourihan, Margery. *Deconstructing the Hero: Literary Theory and Children's Literature*. London: Routledge, 1997. Print.
Jackson, Rosemary. *Fantasy: The Literature of Subversion*. London: Routledge, 1981. Print.
Jameson, Fredric. "Magical Narratives: On the Dialectical Use of Genre Criticism." *The Political Unconscious: Narrative as a Socially Symbolic Act* [1981]. London: Routledge, 2002. 89–136. Print.
_____. *Postmodernism, Or, The Cultural Logic of Late Capitalism*. Durham, NC: Duke University Press, 1991. Print.
Mendlesohn, Farah. *Rhetorics of Fantasy*. Middletown, CT: Wesleyan University Press, 2008. Print.
Miller, Dean A. *The Epic Hero*. Baltimore: The Johns Hopkins University Press, 2000. Print.
Penny, Laurie. *Meat Market: Female Flesh under Capitalism*. Winchester: Zero Books, 2010. Print.
Reemtsma, Jan-Philipp. *Trust and Violence: An Essay on a Modern Relationship* [German original 2008]. Trans. Dominic Bonfiglio. Princeton, NJ: Princeton University Press, 2012. Print.
Schneider, Christina. "Joe Abercrombie in Interview with Christina Schneider." 2012. Unpublished manuscript (27 pages).
Turner, Bryan S. "Social Fluids: Metaphors and Meanings of Society." *Body & Society* 9.1 (2003): 1–10. Print.

The Fantasy of Politics: The Past and the Future of Object-Related Fantasy

SLADJA BLAŽAN

The New Role of Fantasy in Contemporary Culture

At the 2012 annual meeting of the German Association for Research in the Fantastic (*Gesellschaft für Fantastikforschung*), a red thread began shimmering through and became increasingly more discernible as the days advanced. Most keynote speakers, as well as some panelists, seemed to be addressing an urgency to recognize the new hybridization of the genre of fantasy. Historical changes and various cultural developments had led to an infiltration of reality into fantasy and vice versa. John Clute, who at the time was compiling a new *Encyclopedia of Science Fiction*, attested that this work led him to the conclusion that "the world is a different place now" in comparison to the time when the first and now famous edition was published. It is, Clute claimed, particularly the academic treatment and common perception of fantasy and science fiction that has changed, which consequently calls for a revision of now outdated theories of the same. Previously considered an antagonistic genre, the acceptance of fantasy has reached an unprecedented level as literature and culture have diligently worked towards integrating them into what has become the mainstream.

Another exemplary keynote speaker, the German scholar of fantasy, Dieter Petzold, took his talk in a suspiciously similar direction, even if coming from a slightly different standpoint. He came to the conclusion that what we call fantasy nowadays can no longer be squeezed into the tight corset that used to define this genre. Postmodernism has reached popular culture; consequently, the ironic stance demands sophisticated readers flexible enough to oscillate between fantasy and realism. A new and more forceful infiltration of genres is noticeable, which Petzold exemplified with Brian Stableford's more recent encyclopedia *The A to Z of Fantasy Literature* and its sheer endless list of entries attempting to define types of fantasy. According to Petzold, the hybridization vogue and the resulting inability on the side of the scholars to squeeze fantasy into ordered and precise taxonomies proves that fantasy has reached the mainstream. The list of speakers with similar claims is long. What is important for my argument is that both of these scholars assume that this is an anticipated and logical development that emerged in relation to current cultural and political world events. In what follows, I will take a closer look at this conjecture between fantasy and politics.

Fantasy—"a natural human activity"

Before addressing this seemingly organic but specifically contemporary change in the perception of fantasy, I would like to go back to the beginnings of the fantasy genre and recall how some of the first discussions of this literary field inevitably included reality. Fantasy today, according to the often-quoted *Encyclopedia of Fantasy* edited by John Clute and John Grant, is "a self-coherent narrative. When set in this world it is impossible in the world as we perceive it" (338). This distinction between the familiar set of rules and codifications constructing "this world" and the one that is located outside of it has been fantasy's trademark since the early beginnings of this genre. However, one could also claim that a necessary *connection* between the two worlds has been just as prominently highlighted and kept at the center of attention among scholars of fantasy since the early stages. If we return to early texts attempting to define this genre, we will see that modern fantasy began not as a rejection but as a defense of the real. As early as 1883, George MacDonald in "The Fantastic Imagination" points out the importance of laws familiar to man "in this world" for the creation of a fantastic story:

> The laws of the spirit of man must hold, alike in this world and in any world he may invent. It were no offence to suppose a world in which everything repelled instead of attracted the things around it; it would be wicked to write a tale representing a man it called good as always doing bad things, or a man it called bad as always doing good things: the notion itself is absolutely lawless. In physical things a man may invent; in moral things he must obey—and *take their laws with him into his invented world* as well [233–34, my emphasis, S.B.].

Only the establishment of a relation between the two "worlds" allows the writer to become a creator. And the now famous lecture that for many scholars marks the beginnings of the fantasy genre, "On Fairy-Stories" by J.R.R. Tolkien (originally presented in 1939), is nothing but a promotion of the psychological usefulness of fantasy, as the same may provide a forum for "recovery, escape, and consolation" (75), once again, "in this world." Escape in this equation in no way implies escapism, often wrongly used as an argument against fantasy. On the contrary, Tolkien writes about the possibility of escaping an arresting situation via fantasy or even fantasy's applicability to the preservation of sanity, as fantasy in some cases might be the only access to reality.[1]

The functionality of fantasy has, thus, been a steady companion to the genre since its early beginnings. While the creation of a separate *world* has always been an essential element, this did not exclude the existence of points of connection between the two worlds that are necessarily created by the writer and the reader alike. With regard to J.R.R. Tolkien one could even argue that his theory of fantasy constitutes a defense of the real. In fantasy "man [the reader] becomes a sub-creator," Tolkien observes (60). It is his "visions of fantasy" that allow for a "freedom from the domination of observed fact" (74). He continues:

> Fantasy is a natural human activity. It certainly does not destroy or even insult Reason; and it does not either blunt the appetite for, nor obscure the perception of, scientific verity. On the contrary, the keener and the clearer is the reason, the better fantasy will it make. If men were ever in a state in which they did not want to know or could not perceive truth (facts or evidence), then Fantasy would languish until they were cured. If they ever get into that state (it would not seem at all impossible), Fantasy will perish, and become Morbid Delusion [74–75].

Needing both worlds in order to perceive fantasy, the reader can assume the position of an observer, who, locating herself within the fantastic realm, can take a step outside of the real and recover a functional sense of perspective because fact or evidence, reason and truth will remain necessary categories. Widening this perspective, we could say that the observer of world events also depends on fantasy, as only an imaginary external perspective onto the machinations of the world will make such a broad scope perceivable. In other words, in certain situations, indeed, only fantasy allows access to reality.

Cycles and Encyclopedias

A book that makes excessive use of this quality of fantasy is Reza Negarestani's *CYCLONOPEDIA: Complicity with Anonymous Materials,* an uncomfortable and extraordinarily inaccessible piece of writing that nevertheless managed to inspire a whole symposium at the New School in New York in 2012, as well as various blogs, lists and fanzines (see Keller et al.). Published in 2008, it was even catapulted to one of the best books of the year 2009 by *Artforum.* I would like to argue that one of the reasons for its popularity in spite of its unreadability and problematic style is its specific convergence of fantasy with reality, with the purpose of constructing a narrative in the service of addressing world politics. This particular combination seems to be answering the current demand for fantasy embedded within a realistic setting. As expected, this type of topical salmagundi has been difficult to classify. The cover description given by the publishers already oscillates between genres:

> At once a horror fiction, a work of speculative theology, an atlas of demonology, a political samizdat and a philosophic grimoire, CYCLONOPEDIA is a work of theory-fiction on the Middle East, where horror is restlessly heaped upon horror. Reza Negarestani bridges the appalling vistas of contemporary world politics and the War on Terror with the archeologies of the Middle East and the natural history of the Earth itself.

China Miéville marks *CYCLONOPEDIA* as "a founding text of some new mo(ve)ment" (12), whereas Jeff and Ann VanderMeer feature Negarestani on their webpage *Weird Fiction Review* as "the most original weird fiction writer to appear in recent years." According to Jeff and Ann VanderMeer's definition in their publication under the same title, the new weird is "a type of urban, secondary-world fiction that subverts the romanticized ideas about place found in traditional fantasy, largely by choosing realistic, complex real-world models as the jumping off point for creation [sic] of settings that may combine elements of both science fiction and fantasy" (xvi). The new weird is, thus, a type of fantasy that allows for the inclusion of real-world paradigms into traditional fantasy settings or the other way around. It is this definition that led the VanderMeers to include a chapter from *CYCLONOPEDIA* in their anthology *The Weird*.

CYCLONOPEDIA, indeed, in many ways circles around real-world paradigms without dispensing with fantasy. The plot, if it was to be reduced to one sentence, could be described in the following manner: oil is the only entity that can settle the dust in the Middle East. Moistened by oil, dust particles unite together and spread everywhere; consequently, oil rules the earth by spinning world narratives. Here is a representative example from the chapter "The Dead Mother of All Contagions":

> Xero-data, or dust, swarms planetary bodies as the primal flux of data or the Mother of all Data-streams in the Solar system. Each particle of dust carries with it a unique vision of matter, movement, collectivity, interaction, affect, differentiation, composition and infinite darkness—a crystallized data-base or a plot ready to combine and react, to be narrated on and through something. [...] Earth as a rebel disciple of the Sun is shelled with dust particles from within and without. For this reason, there is no fiction more original—in terms of schizophrenia, collectivity of writers, movements of different plots, composition, rich inauthenticity and jargons—than the Earth itself, the Earth composed of dust particles and fluxes [Negarestani 88].

But how can the earth narrate itself? The answer is: through oil. The narrative begins with a preface that consists of diary (or blog) entries by Kristen Alvansen, a young American woman who, in the beginning, lures the reader into expecting a detective story as she discovers a strange manuscript in her hotel room in Istanbul called *Cyclonopedia*, written by a writer called Reza Negarestani. Kristen Alvansen is also the name of an American artist who is associated with the writer Reza Negarestani and prominently features him on her webpage, further blurring the line between fact and fiction. Similar postmodern elements of metafiction will be retained throughout the text, adding yet another turn of the screw to the already tight generic debate. The manuscript discovered by Alvansen turns out to be an analysis of the work of Hamid Parsani, a former archeology and mathematics professor at Tehran University, who was expelled for "insufficient scholarship" (9), upon which he disappeared. Alvansen decides to follow up on the clues given in the manuscript and ventures out on a quest for Dr. Parsani (or his ideas). The rest of the text is presented as excerpts from Parsani's study, written either by himself or collected by his "secret students" or "former friends," as he himself grew increasingly more interested in "topics usually entertained only by unhealthily-minded teenagers" (11).

Far from discovering a coherent plot, Alvansen, and by implication the reader, is only able to identify more "plot holes," which are characterized in the book through a presence rather than absence. "Plot holes are psychosomatic indications of at least one more plot densely populating itself in the holes it burrows through and digs out" (Negarestani 61). It is these plot-holes that will keep reappearing throughout the text, taking the reader from "bacterial archeology" (7) through "diabolic particles" (74), "warmachines" (112), "dust enforcers" (113), "catalytic spaces" (180) and "schizotrategies for openness" (194), with oil remaining at the center of this critical theory/science fiction/fantasy/Ph.D. thesis/detective story-potpourri. Parsani explains: "Emerged under such conditions, petroleum possesses tendencies for mass intoxication on pandemic scales (different from but corresponding to capitalism's voodoo economy and other types of global possession systems)" (17). Certainly, to present oil as a pandemic cosmic entity designed to keep humans under its sway or even as the lubricant of world narratives might be an adage likely to be overheard at any social gathering and, thus, not necessarily worth highlighting. But going the extra step of providing the narrative that helps imagine this exact scenario in a world that functions according to its own laws—which, as explained by MacDonald, can never venture too far away from earthly laws—is reserved for the genre of fantasy. In this way, fantastic elements, indeed, allow an access to the current socio-political reality concerning the Middle East, the traffic with oil and the so-called "War on Terror." Parsani's study offers further points of analysis:

> The release of these multiplicities disguised as one within each dust particle is equal to the arrival of the alien not from without but from within. As in the case of a spore about to break open and release its bacteria, this emergence of new life forms and collective particles might be apprehended as an insider takeover, the rise of a new people [Negarestani 90].

The now established "()hole complex" that ungrounds and subverts the earth is the "zone through which the Outside gradually but persistently emerges, creeps in (or out?) from the Inside" (91). The holes that consequently emerge are "political" because the holes are connected through the narration lube—oil. Reading through the plot holes is to follow the narration lube. In this way, the oil becomes the narrator, not dependent on humans even regarding story-telling devices. With its chasmic point of view, oil can tell its own story. Negarestani calls this "hidden writing" (60).

Cosmic Fantasy

As is true for many writers of fantasy and science fiction alike, Negarestani's writing is strongly influenced by H.P. Lovecraft. Particularly Lovecraft's famous concept of "cosmic horror" features as a direct model for the above explained acts of hidden writing.[2] One of the most striking features of Lovecraft's cosmicism is its objectification of evil, which, in his stories, literally materializes, the most famous example of which might be found in "The Call of Cthulhu" (1926), where Cthulhu refers to one of the Great Old Ones who lived long before man existed and is understood to be the epitome of evil (referenced in Negarestani 49).[3] In this short story, the statuette of Cthulhu initiates a succession of investigative moves that lead to the awakening of the evil force. The development of this and most of Lovecraft's narratives is not dependent on characters and their thoughts and actions. Commonly led by curiosity, they only serve the purpose of unveiling the catastrophic or even apocalyptic effects of certain non-human agents, to which they are eventually or potentially subjected. As *pars pro toto*, they are presented as an element of the world or universe without agency, as it is the "awesome grandeur of the cosmic cycle wherein our world and human race form transient incidents" (Lovecraft, *Dunwich* 15). The objects, in this way, seem more alive than the protagonists, whose existence appears accidental. Shifting his focus away from the anthropocentric view, Lovecraft established a type of fantasy that produced numerous epigones and even led Fritz Leiber, Jr., to call him a "literary Kopernikus" (44). Shifting the focus away from humans and their subjective perspective dominated by psychological interpretations introduced a new paradigm, one that turned towards objects and non-human actors as well as an external perspective. Individual stories, in this way, were replaced by stories that can affect not only the earth but the whole cosmos. Negarestani is one of the many writers who follow in this tradition. Alvansen's discovery of Dr. Parsani's study and her desire to follow up on its clues is not too far away from the narrator's discovery of the papers of his late granduncle, George Gammell Angell, a prominent professor of Semitic languages, and the nephew's subsequent research in "The Call of Cthulhu." Both are discovering cults and seeming mythologies with global effects. Parsani explains this connection himself: "The Middle East stalks the world as petrol. Is there anything more Lovecraftian than the building of a new pipeline, winding its blobbing flutes?" (Negarestani 72). It is this Lovecraftian move away from subjectivist viewpoints and corresponding narrative techniques that Negarestani is following up on with *CYCLONOPEDIA*. The materialist approach to fantasy and particularly to what is marked as evil within this genre builds the framework for a focus on the omnipresence and the omnipotence of oil. But what kind of a political message is being sent out by the radicalism of this non-human agent without any recourse to ontological presence?

The shared anti-humanism of object-related fantasy is not unproblematic. In *CYCLONOPEDIA* central objects or materials appear as "Inorganic Demons or xenolithic artifacts":

> These relics or artifacts are generally depicted in the shape of objects made of inorganic materials (stone, metal, bones, souls, ashes, etc.). Autonomous, sentient and independent of human will, their existence is characterized by their forsaken status, their immemorial slumber and their provocatively exquisite forms. Their autonomy alone marks their outsideness to the human and to its ecology, the planetary biosphere; this is why they are frequently associated with alien life forms and defined by the prefix xeno- (outside) [223].

Placing inorganic artifacts outside of "the human" and, more importantly, of "its ecology" automatically erases any responsibility on the side of humankind. This is not an uncommon narrative strategy. By associating inorganic material as a sentient entity with alien life forms, Negarestani draws from a long tradition of object-related horror texts, two of which are referenced extensively in the text: William Friedkin's film *The Exorcist* (dust flows unearthed next to the statuette of Pazuzu initiate forms of demonic possession) and John Carpenter's film *The Thing* (infestation of civilians by an animate object).[4] Following the effects of objects seems to necessarily take a fantastic turn. The scientist Parsani is outraged in his manuscript but cannot help but make the connection himself: "Before penning his article [on the film *The Thing*], Parsani had protested, 'Why would I need to read science fiction when I make my living by studying and interacting with the Middle East, which doesn't make sense even to something like science fiction?'" (123).

As it turns out, to study the Middle East in the context of the War on

Terror and oil in its whole complexity did not produce a comprehensive and logical narrative. Even science fiction, or rather speculative fiction in general, seemed too constricted when embarking on this venture. But science fiction and fantasy do come as close as possible, and, thus, are necessary frameworks for this topic, in Parsani's conclusion. In other words, the real is weird enough to be fantastic. The more we/the reader/the inquisitive characters in Lovecraft's and Negarestani's work learn about the world, the more do we/they expose its unmitigated *weirdness*.

However, this observation becomes obsolete when humans are excluded from the economy of action, participation or even motivation. If characters can do nothing but passively observe the animated objects spread their evil powers, where does this leave the responsible subject? Objects appear as truly subject-independent, not even allowing for an illusion of agency regarding moral issues and regulatory reactions on the side of the humans. In *CYCLONOPEDIA*, just like in the largest part of Lovecraft's oeuvre, humans do not even imagine themselves as agents. Instead, thinking about oil, Dr. Parsani asks himself in his papers: "The question is: How long can the cavernous sentience ride in this modern vehicle?" (Negarestani 72). Thus marked as simple bystanders, humans can only speculate about the timing of their impending demise. Even the oil is not "ungrounded" by the human agent (48); it is alive and makes its way out on its own terms. "Things leak into each other according to a logic that does not belong to us and cannot be correlated to our chronological time" (49). The non-human agent, oil, which tells its story itself and offers the reader a "blobjective point of view" (71), continues to ride the "plot holes" (61) as an ancient and enigmatic manifestation absolutely external to human prerogatives. "The blob (petroleum) [...] surpasses even tentacle-headed monstrosities in sentience and foreignness" (49). The subtitle, *Complicity with Anonymous Materials*, does not mark a silence but an inability on the side of the humans to influence the movements of the oil with its geopolitical value, which autonomously keeps creeping through all modern societies.

Speculative Realities and the Fantasy of Politics

Apart from its relation to the work of Lovecraft, Negarestani's work relates to the work of a new circle in current continental philosophy of a group of scholars and artists who gather around the leading ideas of "speculative realism," many of which are expressed in the journal *Collapse*.[5] Not necessarily to be subsumed under a new school of theory, speculative realism collects a few thinkers who insistently reject theories that conceptualize the world in terms of human subjectivity. Instead, they prefer philosophies that rely on the non-human factor and seek to filter out principles of intelligibility encoded in physical reality. Quentin Meillassoux's rejection of so-called correlationism that focuses on the world before perception, or Graham Harman's object-oriented philosophy that focuses on the autonomous existence of things, are the most prominent examples. Far from revolutionary, the movement rather inscribes itself in a wider field of philosophies that turn toward non-human factors, such as Bruno Latour's actor-network theory, post-humanism or Bill Brown's thing theory. However, unlike thing theory's focus on how inanimate objects constitute human subjects, speculative realism returns to a pre–Kantian model and the nature of subject-independent objects.[6] Exploring this anti-anthropocentric stance leads to a depiction of realism that allows for speculation, which in turn is not commonly associated with realism. This is one of the reasons why philosophers associated with speculative realism do not shy away from fantasy in order to explore this conjecture. When Meillassoux writes about the absolute real as something "capable of existing whether we exist or not" (28), it is hard not to feel reminded of the Great Old Ones in Lovecraft's work. In fact, this intrusive association recently led Graham Harman to publish a book on Lovecraft as an object-oriented thinker. The publishers introduce his book *Weird Realism: Lovecraft and Philosophy* as a study that will reveal that "as Hölderlin was to Martin Heidegger and Mallarmé to Jacques Derrida, so is H.P. Lovecraft to the Speculative Realist philosophers" (Harman, *Weird Realism* vi). In this way *CYCLONOPEDIA* and, in a wider sense, speculative realism are reclaiming the space of the real by demonstrating that reality does not exhaust reality. Fantasy offers an additional perspective.

Which brings me to the politics of fantasy, or, more precisely, to the new role of fantasy in contemporary society. I would suggest that even if it is far from being an exploration of the genre of fantasy, Jacqueline Rose's study, programmatically called *States of Fantasy*, marks a first step towards acknowledging a new appreciation and integration of fantasy into socio-political narratives. Central to her study is the thesis that "there is no way of understanding political identities and destinies without letting fantasy into the frame" (4). Of course, Rose's argument is following up on the power of psychic investment and not the genre of fantasy, but her argument has been expanded since the first publication of the book in 1996 as it truly addresses a current concern. Her idea that "[f]antasy is not therefore antagonistic to social reality, it is its precondition or psychic glue" (3), led scholars such as Donald Pease to analyze the role of fantasy within the image repertoire of the Cold War in his book *The New American Exceptionalism*. Similarly, Ramón Saldivar suggests that race and history today require a new "imaginary" for thinking about "the nature of a just society and the role of race in its construction," which he calls "historical fantasy" (574). Saldivar really does make a claim for a new genre or "a realm of twenty-first century *fantasy*" on Jacqueline Rose's original proposal (574).[7] In following her argument, he attempts to introduce a "new world fantasy" that emerged in what has been called ethnic novels and the reality of which is "not simply gratuitous, nor merely virtual; it might well be quintessentially postmagical, post-postmodern and postracial" (596). Engaging with the genre of fantasy, ethnic writers have found *new* ways of escaping the tight corset of prescribed identity. Saldivar's curious definition of fantasy as dealing with "latent forms of daydream, delusion, and denial" (594), which he uses in order to distinguish a new generation of (ethnic) writers, who use fantasy in order to focus on socio-politically effective topics, is misleading. I hope that it is clear by now that fantasy has never had the function of mere escapism, nor is the functionalizing of fantasy as access to real-world problems new. Even the convergence of fantasy with reality within ethnically and racially marked writing has been present in North American literature throughout the nineteenth and twentieth centuries, making significant contributions to what came to be called Western popular culture. Ethnic topics, commonly culturally marginalized and in direct opposition to white mainstream popular culture, have been inscribed and inscribing themselves into the very same fields via science fiction and fantasy for a long time, the most obvious example of which would be Afro futurism that developed around the charismatic persona of Sun Ra.[8] More in the vein of Pease's argument, Saldivar's analysis demonstrates not a new type of fantasy suitable for the twenty-first century but the new acknowledgment of fantasy: "this linking of the imaginary and the real through historical fantasy is what makes group identifications, family relationships, and even the desire for love between individual persons seem both inevitable and unachievable at one and the same time" (592).

What is new is not the genre but the approach. We are facing a new generation of writers (ethnic or not) who do not consider the genre of fantasy as a hermetic entity reserved for aficionados and the odd scholar off the beaten track. Instead, their familiarity with the genre of fantasy turns it into a useful tool for reading the world. The writers of the new weird and ethnic novels exemplify this turning point, but cannot claim exclusivity; David Foster Wallace would certainly qualify for this category, to name only one writer outside of these circles. Having grown up immersed in the culture of science fiction and fantasy, various contemporary writers simply use the language and the image repertoire of speculative fiction as a means of expression in order to address their discontent with current society. As Jacqueline Rose puts it succinctly: "The modern state enacts its authority as ghostly, fantasmatic authority. But it would be wrong to deduce from this [...] that the state is any the less real for that" (9). To turn this equation around, the new fantasy writers might be writing about real-world problems, but it does not mean that their writing is any less fantastic for that. Instead, writers like Negarestani demonstrate how the fantastic supplies fiction with a laboratory for testing terms like globalization, world economy and political domination.

But what is the political impact of this type of writing? Unfortunately, works such as *CYCLONOPEDIA,* with their focus on real-world object-related fantasy, miss a chance of placing the human within this equation and thus, rather than providing a framework for criticism, offer a downright exculpation narrative. Specific references to reality fail to offer potential for social realism. If new theories in literature and philosophy seem to implicate that we have moved beyond the materiality of reality in opposition to fantasy, exposing the omnipotence of real fantastic objects irretrievably uncouples politics from being. It is not clear where this new interest in object-related fantasy is going to turn; future developments in fantasy fiction, which has recognized that fantastic elements can be a key to an intelligible representation of the world, will show if there is real potential for political narratives within this field. For now, what is at stake is not the politics of fantasy, but the fantasy of politics.

Notes

1. Similarly, Freud writes about fantasies being "protective fictions" and marks fantasy as a defense mechanism (see Freud 250).
2. On the role of "cosmic horror" in Lovecraft's oeuvre, please see Zachrau.
3. Another good example would be H.P. Lovecraft's "The Colour Out of Space," which focuses on a meteorite that infiltrates and contaminates its environment.
4. Some other "inorganic demons" (224) mentioned in *CYCLONOPEDIA* are the "mask in Kaneto Shindo's *Onibaba,* [...] the cube in Clive Barker's *Hellraiser,* the Frostmourne sword in *Warcraft 3,* the lamp in *Aladdin,* the Turin Shroud or the Chains of Saint Peter" (223).
5. The phrase refers to a group of authors who developed related ideas at an April 2007 conference at Goldsmiths College, comprising Graham Harman, Iain Hamilton Grant, Ray Brassier, and Quentin Meillassoux. See also issues of the journal *Collapse* devoted to the theme, in particular all of *Collapse* 2 (Mar. 2007).
6. On thing theory, see Brown. On speculative realism, see Brassier et al. and Bryant, Srnicek and Harman.
7. Saldivar uses the phrase "speculative realism" in his title but does not in any way reference the movement in philosophy. The phrase is not defined in the text apart from an introductory remark: "With this coinage, I want to retain the contradictory impulse suggested by the forcible joining of the gravitas of history with the spectral quality of fantasy" (585).
8. Various scholars have already pointed this out: Ingrid Thaler has made the same claim for the writings of Octavia Butler, Jewelle Gonmez and Nalo Hopkinson in *Black Atlantic Speculative Fictions.* Most importantly, continual focus on exchange and interaction—instead of on specific cultural practices and differences—between mainstream cultures in the U.S. and so-called marginalized ethnic or racialized cultures has been pointed out by various scholars, perhaps most famously by Paul Gilroy in *The Black Atlantic,* where he marked the Black Atlantic as the center of "fractal patterns of cultural and political exchange and transformation" (15), or in Toni Morrison's *Playing in the Dark* and "Unspeakable Things Unspoken." In the context of fantasy, see also Nalo Hopkinson's anthology *So Long Been Dreaming: Postcolonial Science Fiction and Fantasy.*

Works Cited

Brassier, Ray, et al. "Speculative Realism." *Collapse* 3 (2007): 307–449. Print.
Brown, Bill. "Thing Theory." *Critical Inquiry* 28.1 (2001): 1–22. Print.
Bryant, Levi, Nick Srnicek, and Graham Harman, eds. *The Speculative Turn: Continental Materialism and Realism.* Melbourne: re-press, 2011. Print.
Clute, John, and John Grant, eds. "Fantasy." *Encyclopedia of Fantasy Online.* London: Orbit, 1997. Web. 2 May 2013.
Freud, Sigmund. *Extracts from the Fliess Papers (1892–9).* The Standard Edition of the Complete Psychological Works. Vol. 1. London: Hogarth, 1966. Print.
Gilroy, Paul. *The Black Atlantic: Modernity and Double Consciousness.* London: Verso, 1993. Print.
Harman, Graham. *Weird Realism: Lovecraft and Philosophy.* New York: Zero Books, 2012. Print.
Hopkinson, Nalo, ed. *So Long Been Dreaming: Postcolonial Science Fiction and Fantasy.* Vancouver: Arsenal Pulp, 2004. Print.
Keller, Ed, Nicola Masciandaro, and Eugene Thacker, eds. *Leper Creativity: Cyclonopedia Symposium.* New York: Punctum, 2012. Print.
Leiber, Fritz, Jr. "Ein literarischer Kopernikus." *H.P. Lovecrafts kosmisches Grauen.* Ed. Franz Rottensteiner. Frankfurt: Suhrkamp, 1997. 44–59. Print.
Lovecraft, Howard Phillips. *The Dunwich Horror and Others.* Ed. S.T. Joshi. Sauk City, WI: Arkham House, 1984. Print.
MacDonald, George. "The Fantastic Imagination." *A Dish of Orts: Chiefly Papers on the Imagination, and on Shakespeare.* Kent, 1883. Gaslight (Mount Royal College, Calgary). Web. 2 May 2013.
Meillassoux, Quentin. *Après la finitude: Essai sur la nécessité de la contingence.* Paris: Seuil, 2006. Print.
Miéville, China. "Fiction by Reza Negarestani." *World Literature Today* 84 (2010): 12. Print.
Morrison, Toni. *Playing in the Dark: Whiteness and the Literary Imagination.* Cambridge: Harvard University Press, 1992. Print.
_____. "Unspeakable Things Unspoken: The Afro-American Presence in American Literature." 1998. *Feminist Literary Theory and Criticism.* Ed. Sandra M. Gilbert and Susan Gubar. New York: Norton, 2007. 266–77. Print.
Negarestani, Reza. *CYCLONOPEDIA: Complicity with Anonymous Materials.* Melbourne: re-press, 2008. Print.
Pease, Donald. *The New American Exceptionalism.* Minneapolis: University of Minnesota Press, 2009. Print.
Rose, Jacqueline. *States of Fantasy.* Oxford: Clarendon, 1998. Print.
Saldivar, Ramón. "Historical Fantasy, Speculative Realism, and Postrace Aesthetics in Contemporary American Fiction." *American Literary History* 23.3 (2011): 574–99. Print.
Stableford, Brian. *The A to Z of Fantasy Literature.* Lanham, MD: Scarecrow, 2005. Print.
Thaler, Ingrid. *Black Atlantic Speculative Fictions: Octavia E. Butler, Jewelle Gomez, and Nalo Hopkinson.* New York: Routledge, 2010. Print.
Tolkien, J.R.R. "On Fairy-Stories." *The Tolkien Reader.* New York: Ballantine Books, 2001. 31–87. Print.
VanderMeer, Ann, and Jeff VanderMeer. "The Gallows-Horse." *Weird Fiction Review.* N.p., 19 Dec. 2011. Web. 13 Jan. 2014.
_____, and _____. *The New Weird.* San Francisco: Tachyon, 2008. Print.
_____, and _____, eds. *The Weird: A Compendium of Strange and Dark Stories.* London: Atlantic Books, 2011. Print.
Zachrau, Thekla. *Mythos und Phantastik: Funktion und Struktur der Cthulhu-Mythologie in den phantastischen Erzählungen H.P. Lovecrafts.* Frankfurt: Peter Lang, 1986. Print.

Tolkien's Baits: Agonism, Essentialism and the Visible in *The Lord of the Rings*

Dirk Wiemann

The world of Tolkien studies seems to be as polarized as J.R.R. Tolkien's world itself: ever since the first publication of *The Lord of the Rings*, a struggle has been going on between those who deride Tolkien as retrogressive and those who come to his defense by trying to demonstrate the productive qualities of his work. In the fifties, this controversy was played out in terms of literary merit, with Philip Toynbee or Edmund Wilson ridiculing Tolkien's works as "dull, ill-written, whimsical and childish" (Toynbee quoted in Zimbardo and Isaacs 31) and "juvenile trash" (Wilson 314), and C.S. Lewis or W.H. Auden emphasizing the aesthetic depth and moral profundity of that heroic and religious quest narrative for the modern age. Today, the frontline is primarily defined by the ideological thrust that critics identify in Tolkien. And against a host of commentators who insist that the moral absolutism of *The Lord of the Rings* is "paternalistic, reactionary, anti-intellectual, racist, fascistic, and perhaps worst in contemporary terms, irrelevant" (Scheps 49), there is an even more articulate and variegated camp of defenders who read Tolkien as an advocate of such politically desirable causes as gender equity (Burns, esp. 128–51), queerness (Rohy; Smol), hybridity (McFadden), ecological justice (Brisbois; Campbell) and a deeply democratic interest in the "empowerment of the marginalized" (Chance 62).

More often than not, however, Tolkien's detractors appear far more convincing than his many defenders. One cannot, for example, disprove the charge of racism—the naturalizing, dehumanizing representation of the enemy side—with the claim that "nothing could be more contrary to the assumptions of racism than a Hobbit as a hero" (Rearick 874), when hobbits themselves are introduced as little xenophobic philistines with a deep mistrust of everything foreign. Nor can one summon up the figure of Éowyn to demonstrate how Tolkien allows for female agency (see Benvenuto 46–53; Michel 68–76) when all that agency is enabled only by Éowyn's temporary erasure of her femininity (see Porter 91). Though it cannot be disputed that there are numerous moments where Tolkien's text encourages appropriations for critical projects of all kind, the text as a whole invariably operates on the principle of re-containing these "progressive" moments in its relentlessly dichotomous order. Like little dots of color on a vast black and white canvas, they are only residual elements and more importantly, narrative baits that lure the contemporary reader into complicity with a text that, in the final instance, refuses to yield to non–Manichaean interpretations.

"Tal-Elmar"

A particularly telling case in point is the posthumously published narrative fragment titled "Tal-Elmar" which, according to Christopher Tolkien, marks "a departure from all other narrative themes within the compass of Middle-earth" (quoted in Tolkien, "Tal-Elmar" 422) since it offers something unique: a look at the world from the perspective not of a hobbit, elf or man of the West, but of a "wild man," a member of a "decaying, half-savage people" (Tolkien 434) whose habitat is in the vicinity of "the mouths of Anduin and the Langstrand" (422). At some unspecified point in time in the early years of the Second Age, the protagonist and focalizer, Tal-Elmar, is witness to the arrival of a fleet of Númenoreans whose mission it is to conquer and colonize that area. Interestingly, the fragment grants some insight into the legend-based knowledge that the "half-savage people" have about those invaders: they describe them as cannibals who sacrifice their captives "with torment on the black stones in the worship of the Dark" (427). From the perspective of the "swart folk," these intruders appear as "cruel and lawless and the friends of demons. Thieves are they. For our lands are ours from of old, which they would wrest from us with their bitter blades. White skins and bright eyes are no warrant for such deeds" (425).

It would be tempting to read "Tal-Elmar" as a text in which Tolkien for once grants a voice and an own consistent world-view to the otherwise muted Others of his universe, similar perhaps to the way in which Shakespeare, according to Stephen Greenblatt, invests Caliban with an "opaque" linguistic world in its own right that "compels us to acknowledge the independence and integrity of Caliban's construction of reality" (31). For in the perspective of the "wild men," the Manichaean order of Tolkien's "magnificent pagan universe" (Žižek,

"Brunhilde's Act" 39) gets fully inverted so that the heroes of *The Silmarillion* and *The Lord of the Rings* now appear as demonic worshippers of the "Dark," while their racialized Others interrogate the very ethical binarism that persistently organizes their othering: white skins and bright eyes as attributes of marauders and brutal conquerors. Of course this is more than a mere inversion inasmuch as the stark divisions of Tolkien's world, instead of emanating from some irreconcilable essences, now appear as thoroughly de-essentialized products of reciprocal stereotyping representations. Does an apocryphal text like this introduce another Tolkien, one whose narratives could be read as underpinned by an anti-foundationalist subtext? Does it not confirm all those who read Tolkien as "progressive?"

Almost, but not quite: even this unfinished fragment tends towards a closure that would re-contain all such possibilities. For Tal-Elmar is not *really* a "wild man" but has always been an outsider to their community: too slender and tall, too light-complexioned, too fair-haired, too bright-eyed. Deep down, he is himself a Númenorean: "one of alien race, whom fate has cast away among an ignoble people" (423). And this is a matter of genetics: his paternal grandmother was a captured Númenorean, and her "blood" seems to run purely in his veins. This is why he has always been visited by strange dreams in the unheard language of Númenor, and why he inexplicably feels that the incoming conquerors are his "kin," even when they pronounce the death sentence on the whole community in which Tal-Elmar was born and bred: "Here the Men of the West have resolved to make their homes, and the folk of the Dark must depart—or be slain" (437). The narrative, in short, opens as a story of moral and ethical transvaluation but moves towards a reconfirmation of the dominant moral code of Tolkien's universe. The text breaks off in midair, but it is obvious that its telos is the revelation of an authentic, indeed "original identity" (Frye 149) and a side-taking in a polarized world whose stark divisions are heavily re-enforced as historical necessity.

Had Tolkien finished this tale, had he fully elaborated and "decorated" it, who knows, perhaps he would have achieved what he manages with most of his major works, especially *The Lord of the Rings*: to enlist his reader with apparently non-essentialist, non-foundationalist and non-dichotomizing baits into the same kind of militant side-taking that he obviously had prepared for his hero, Tal-Elmar. Any attempt to "redeem" Tolkien critically has to work through this effect: how the critical bait first works and then gives way to the allure of an irreducible binarism that enforces a Manichaean, militant reading. Instead of trying to de-essentialize and de-antagonize (in short, to de–Tolkienize) Tolkien, would it not be more fruitful and also more honest to first acknowledge head-on that the embarrassment of Tolkien's Manichaeism cannot be wished away, and then to ask why Tolkien's writings retain their irresistible allure: perhaps not although but (more embarrassment!) *because* they make a militant of their reader.

From here it would be viable to speculate whether it could be precisely this insistence on (and of) antagonism that endows these texts with a productive politicizing potential in a post-political era in which, in most parts of the world, politics has been superseded by policing (for the distinction see Rancière, *Disagreement* 29). It could be argued that Tolkien's texts are particularly germane to contemporary political praxes and theoretical attempts to restore "the political" as a site of "dissensus" distinct from "politics" as the realm of deliberation, governance, and compromise. It is in this vein that Fredric Jameson observes that, as a response to the actual end-of-history hegemony of a purely procedural and managerial politics, a militant, "genuinely theoretical political theory" has begun to emerge that endorses "the political" as a field of intervention "re-cast in the agonistic structure of Schmitt's 'friend and foe' and finding its ultimate figure in war" ("Symptoms" 406). Instead of being dissolved either into some abstract "de-antagonised" "System" that cannot be seen through or into some idealized "non-adversarial democratic politics" (Mouffe, "Agonistic Public" 101), the political proper "is the battleground where different hegemonic projects are confronted, without any possibility of final reconciliation" (Mouffe, "Artistic Activism"). When conceived this way, the political is clearly more at home in a starkly divided Middle-earth than in a contemporary Europe governed by the principles of "para-politics," that is, "the attempt to depoliticize politics (to translate it into police logic): one accepts political conflict, but reformulates it into a competition, within the representational space, between acknowledged parties/agents" (Žižek, *Ticklish Subject* 190). The effect of this "para-politics" is "to de-antagonise politics by way of formulating the clear rules to be obeyed so that the agonic procedure of litigation does not explode into politics proper" (Žižek, "Afterword" 71). Obviously, therefore, "para-politics" rests on a set of institutions and discourses that systematically contain "genuine" politics by way of "translating" antagonism into something else, namely competition. Theorists like Mouffe or Žižek engage in a project of undoing that translation by substituting the notion of some unresolvable agonism at the heart of the social for the hegemonic figure of consensus-oriented deliberation. Hence the struggle over what democracy is gets staged in these writings *also* as a struggle over how democracy gets represented (it being understood that representation involves a constitutive power).

From such a vantage point, Tolkien's Manichaeism ceases to be an embarrassment, but, rather to the contrary, becomes an asset to be endorsed. *The Lord of the Rings*, then, offers a paradoxical kind of escapism: the escape not to some pastoral, harmonic idyll but to the dichotomous constellation of "the political" in which the antagonist can be clearly identified, so that agency becomes thinkable again as passionate participation and side-taking in "the agonistic struggle among adversaries" (Mouffe, "Artistic Activism"). In this vein, a truly political reading of Tolkien would not elaborately contain or wish away, but, to the contrary, heartily acknowledge the Manichaean subtext—not only as that on which Tolkien's work is essentially premised (and without which it would tumble as anticlimactically as Sauron's tower), but more provocatively as that which one is looking and longing for in his books. More than that, the book would be readable now as a powerful medium through which the radical figure of agonism may infiltrate the largely "para-political" cultural formation of the post–1989 world.

A viable hypothesis then would be that *The Lord of the Rings* gratifies, or at least speaks to, a desire—perhaps nostalgic, perhaps proleptic—for the political as an agonistic "battlefield." Yet even if this approach can more or less easily assent to the constitutive Manichaeism at the heart of Tolkien's work, it is by no means fully immune to those difficulties that riddle queer, feminist or otherwise politically informed readings of Tolkien: true, unlike those well-meant misreadings it does not have to disavow the rigid binarisms structuring Tolkien's text, but it has to be wary not to swallow Tolkien's agonism as yet another bait. For agonism in Tolkien comes with a further absolute which is definitely anathema to any anti-foundationalism worthy of the name: the inflexible essentialism of Tolkien that, as we have seen, overrides Tal-Elmar's acculturation in one sweeping gesture of identity-revelation. It is this essentialism that sets Tolkien's agonism at odds with the various agonisms of contemporary political theory. While the former is metaphysically grounded in (and in fact, emanating from) the given opposition of irreconcilable essences, the latter are firmly anti-identitarian and assume that subjects, both individual and collective, do not precede but are being produced, interpellated, sutured, framed, or constituted (and to some minuscule extent self-fashioned) in dynamic and power-structured exchanges with others, as exemplarily formularized in Gayatri Spivak's definition of the subject as effect:

> A subject-effect can be briefly plotted as follows: that which seems to operate as a subject may be part of an immense discontinuous network ("text" in the general sense) of strands that may be termed politics, ideology, economics, history, sexuality, language, and so on (each of these strands, if they are isolated, can also be seen as woven of many strands). Different knottings and configurations of these strands, determined by heterogeneous determinations, which are themselves dependent upon myriad circumstances, produce the effect of an operating subject [*In Other Worlds* 204].

Relations and encounters are therefore "ontologically prior to the question of ontology (the question of the being who encounters)" (Ahmed 7). Thus, in an apparently diametrical departure from anything Tolkienian, a "genuinely theoretical political theory" will endorse agonism but not conceive of it as a clash that derives from some given fixed identities of the involved antagonists. Even less will it posit agonism as a shadow theatre in which some metaphysical struggle between the polar principles of a "higher world versus a lower world" (Frye 150) is being fought out by proxy of human (or, for that matter, elvish, orcish, hobbit) actors. To the contrary, the agonism of "the political" unfolds not in some overdetermined universe, where an underlying order and concomitant "original identities" are gradually or abruptly revealed. Instead, its site is the contingent "open air of history" (Benjamin 261); hence the political is not about confrontations within the paradigms of a structured social body where each part has its appointed place by which it should abide, but about the fundamental "distribution of the sensible [which] determines who can have a share in what is common to the community based on what they do and on the time and space in which this activity is performed" (Rancière, *Politics* 12). Grasped as intervention into this "distribution of the sensible," the political opens a "division put in the 'common sense': a dispute about what is given, about the frame with which we see what is given" (Rancière, "Who Is the Subject" 176). Inasmuch as it inaugurates a "dissensus: putting two worlds in one and the same world" (176), the political inhabits "that irresolvable and productive paradox in which a future is claimed on behalf of peoples and rights that are not yet and may never be" (Honig 117). How can such anti-essentialism be possibly reconciled with Tolkien? Could one construct a reading position that holds these apparently incompatible agonisms together?

The paradoxical figure of dissensus itself could be a way out. Even while it is not founded on any pre-existing subject, political agency still requires a specific subject-effect: an emergent political subject, whether collective or individual, has to posit itself *as being* since "we need to posit the essence of the [agent] for political reasons" (Colebrook 567), albeit in an "ironic" way inasmuch as "we choose to use a concept which we know is flawed" (McLeod 195). Some degree of strategic essentialism appears unavoidable in an agonistic setting because it "offers the possibility of alliances in a 'war of position'" (Moore-Gilbert 202). Such "a *strategic* use of positivist essentialism in a scrupulously visible political interest" (Spivak, *In Other Worlds* 205) makes "use of the idea of essence alongside a recognition of the nonessential nature of essence" (Colebrook 559) and thereby opens a dissensus within the strategy itself. This is a complicated and potentially double-edged tool in the agonistic side-taking and subject-producing dynamics since "essences [...] are so useful that they can become dangerous" (Spivak, *Outside* 15): as soon as the fictional and provisional status of such a strategically invoked, non-essential "essence" is forgotten and gets "mistaken for a universal truth" (Moore-Gilbert 88), the agenda turns against itself and provides "a union ticket for essentialism" proper (Spivak quoted in Danius and Johnson 35).

If one could apply such a notion of strategic essentialism—one that does not forget about the strategic status of the essences it operates on—to a reading of Tolkien, it would be possible to outwit Tolkien's baits. Texts like *The Lord of the Rings* could then be reconciled to a viable political agenda that would tap the energies of agonism and "possible worlds" they inscribe without having to either disavow or succumb to the essentialist thrust of these texts. It should be clear that such a strategy can be lodged only with the reader. It requires a selective rearticulation of the potentials inscribed in the structured prefiguration of the text that, in a perhaps hyperbolically scrupulous reading, may be grasped as one vast enactment of the dynamics of strategic essentialism. I would like to put this possibility to the test by taking a closer look at only one of the many "baits" that Tolkien has planted into *The Lord of the Rings*, namely the issue of visuality.

Seeing Hobbits, Seeing Elves

It has often been remarked that *The Lord of the Rings* is "a text that hinges upon viewing: looks given, looks returned, looks frustrated, looks denied" (Battis 909). In that vein it could be argued that, early on, the whole quest gets motivated by a translation of narrative desire as visual desire expressed by Sam in a surrogate reader position: "Elves, sir! I would dearly love to see *them*. Couldn't you take me to see Elves, sir, when you go?" (Tolkien, *LotR* 62).[1] Yet once the hobbits leave the Shire, they enter a visual world that at times will gratify this scopophilic desire but more often than not will turn the protagonists into objects (rather than subjects) of the looks of others, some of them friendly, many hostile. Soon Sam himself, at the very moment of "seeing Elves," will undergo the awkward experience of objectification by an other's gaze: Galadriel's testing look, "which none could long endure" (*LotR* 348), leaves Sam feeling "as if I hadn't got nothing on, and I didn't like it. She seemed to be looking inside me" (348). Feminist and queer readings-into could thrive on such a passage in which the traditionally "male" penetrating gaze is displaced onto one of the few female characters of the narrative, who then virtually strips and reduces poor Sam to the status of "to-be-looked-at-ness" through which patriarchy produces feminine subjects (Mulvey 873): a perfect bait. For it cannot be disputed that an inversion of the patriarchal visual regime is dramatized here, but as the inversions in "Tal-Elmar" it is enacted only to be contained by the powerful persistence of essentialism: Galadriel's gaze does not stop short at the surface of bodies but like an x-ray pierces through appearances to the very heart of being ('looking inside me'), thus confirming the dimension of an existential core and a whole "depth model" (Jameson, *Postmodernism* 12) of the individual's authentic essence. Far from being "constituted" by the gaze, therefore, Sam is here being scrutinized and "seen through" as a subject that, independent of its appearance in the field of vision, is already in place. In a nutshell, this episode comprises the basic premises of the visual politics in *The Lord of the Rings*, where the gaze is always actively involved in power struggles but never productive. On these premises, Galadriel's gaze operates as a genuine agent in the "cold war" between the powers of Lórien and Dol Guldur: a permanent scopic clinch in which "the light perceives the very heart of the darkness, [whereas] its own secret has not been discovered. Not yet" (*LotR* 343).

This kind of vision as "seeing through" is deeply politicized and militarized because Middle-earth is a world that, for characters and readers alike, remains to a large extent in hiding and is therefore constantly suggestive of a concealed totality that no one gets to see. It is a world only partially available to the gaze, but precisely because of its always incomplete visual availability it constantly reconfirms the idea of its (invisible) totality:

> If the idea of hiddenness seems inextricably linked to visuality, it is also deeply intertwined with that of totality, for the experience of hiddenness is always one of incompleteness, a ratio between what is and what might be known. The degree to which we experience the world as hidden is therefore liable to be a function of the relationship between the totality of the world and our capacity to see it [Bull 168].

As in the cinematic tutor code, the reader is sutured into the narrative by way of participating in the wish of a wide range of characters (including Sauron) to see the whole picture, and cunningly the book seems to grant this—not least through the appended maps that, at closer scrutiny, prove to be punctured with gaps. This cartographic incompleteness corresponds to the conspicuously inefficient panoramic views from mountaintops and high towers that the book repeatedly offers. The most elaborate of these panoramas is filtered through the awareness of Frodo in his ring-enhanced vision from Amon Hen, "the Hill of the Eye of the Men of Númenor" (*LotR* 391):

> At first he could see little. He seemed to be in a world of mist in which there was only shadows: the Ring was upon him. Then here and there the mist gave way and he saw many visions: small and clear as if they were under his eyes upon a table, and yet remote. The world seemed to have shrunk and fallen silent. Eastwards he looked into wide uncharted lands, nameless plains and forests unexplored. Northward he looked, and the Great River lay like a ribbon beneath him, and the Misty Mountains stood small and hard as broken teeth. Westward he looked and saw the broad pastures of Rohan; and Orthanc, the pinnacle of Isengard, like a black spike. Southward he looked, and below his very feet the Great River curled like a toppling wave and plunged over the falls of Rauros into a foaming pit [...]. And Ethir Anduin he saw, the mighty delta of the River, and myriads of sea-birds whirling like a white dust in the sun, and beneath them a green and silver sea, rippling in endless lines [*LotR* 391].

This, it seems, is an enactment of the imperial "domination of reality by vision" (Said 240) in which space is telescoped into visually controllable territory. The anaphoric rendition of the act of seeing suggests totality as all four directions are included in this gaze. But Frodo's gaze from Amon Hen, however panoptic, does not really coincide with command or scopic mastery. For one, the visible world remains partly obscure even when available to the gaze: lands uncharted, forests unexplored, and the sea rippling off into infinity. Yet more than the world's reluctance to fully come out of hiding, it is the presence of *another*, more powerful, acquisitive and aggressive gaze that threatens to turn Frodo, hitherto the subject of vision, into its own object: "And suddenly he felt the Eye. There was an eye in the Dark Tower that did not sleep. He knew that it had become aware of his gaze. A fierce eager will was there. It leaped towards him; almost like a finger he felt it, searching for him. Very soon it would nail him down, know just exactly where he was" (*LotR* 392). The price for vision is the threat of exposure to the probing and hostile gaze of the other in a dialogue of looks, a potential reciprocity of seeing and being seen, that is repeatedly rehearsed in the course of the narrative, especially at those instances where hobbits give way to untrammeled scopophilia: earlier in the narrative, when Frodo is allowed to look into Galadriel's mirror, he already encounters the "Eye"; later on, when Pippin "looks like a greedy child" (*LotR* 578) into the Palantír, he likewise gets exposed to that same inquisitive eye of power. The subject-as-look is always also the subject-as-spectacle, so that the act of seeing necessarily involves a submission to the implied "presence of others as such" (Lacan 91). Homi Bhabha suggests that "in the objectification of the scopic drive there is always the threatened return of the look" (81). Even the sentry in Bentham's panopticon would still be subject to the gaze, this presence of others as such: because the gaze is not empirical but inscribed into the subject itself as the inescapable fantasy of being seen, and that fantasy is constantly reproduced by the subject itself. In the very act of looking, the subject gets simultaneously rendered as object of the cultural gaze and projected, as image, onto the screen on which the subject gets externally represented as spectacle to the effect of its "captation," which, then, ensures the subject's identity in the field of vision. Kaja Silverman politicizes these Lacanian categories by specifying that the screen is "the site at which the gaze is defined for a particular society, and is consequently responsible both for the way in which the inhabitants of that society experience the gaze's effects, and for much of the seeming particularity of that society's visual regime" (135). It is on this condition that seeing—both reproduction of and exposure to the gaze—turns into a production of subjectivity *and* intervention into economies of recognition.

The bait to read Tolkien in terms of visual culture theory has brought us this far: we could construe Tolkien's treatment of visuality not only as a virtually post-foundationist foray into "the vast, uncharted expanse of the look itself" but more pointedly as a politically empowering agenda of redistributing the sensible by "reconstituting it, shifting it, widening it, so that all subjects gain a visibility that cannot diminish them" (Battis 922; 923): a veritable politics of recognition. But it is only another bait. For the visual field in Tolkien, energized as it is with all those scopic duels and reciprocities of looks, is not productive of subjects. What holds for Sam holds for Frodo as much as it does for every other actor on that stage: they all, as subjects, always precede their entrance into the visible world, which then operates only as the arena where they reveal (or conceal) themselves. Thus the subject Frodo is wholly underived of the visual dynamics on Amon Hen; it is instead always already there, fully constituted elsewhere and only temporarily forgotten as it were. As a subject that remembers its ontological independence from the visual field, Frodo is free to decide to go back into hiding by putting off the ring: "*Suddenly he was aware of himself again. Frodo [...]: free to choose, and with one remaining instant to do it in*" (*LotR* 392; my emphasis). One remaining instant to do *what* in? To bring one's irreducible essence into hiding again. For what is being hidden by Frodo's act of removing the ring is identity proper: that deep substratum of selfhood, the authentic "you" underneath the "veil" of the "flesh" that Sauron—like Galadriel a visual great inquisitor—tries to strip aside. Later on, while trudging towards Mordor, Frodo constantly feels "the Eye: that horrible growing sense of a hostile will that strove with great power to pierce all shadows of cloud, and earth, and flesh, and to see you: to pin you under its deadly gaze, naked, immovable. So thin, so frail and thin, were become the veils that still warded it off" (*LotR* 616).

Can the essentialism of that "you" be construed as strategic? After all, there are other instances in the narrative where other characters deliberately choose to offer themselves as objects of Sauron's look—instances where to come out of hiding spells out a challenge. Thus when Aragorn reveals himself to Sauron in another ocular duel played out with the help of the Palantír of Orthanc, he stakes a claim to recognition that appears to involve some measure of strategic self-presentation:

> It was a bitter struggle, and the weariness is slow to pass. I spoke no word to him, and in the end I wrenched the stone to my own will. That alone he will find hard to endure. And he beheld me. Yes, Master Gimli, he saw me, but in other guise than you see me here. [...] Now in the very hour of his great designs the heir of Isildur and the Sword are revealed; for I showed the blade re-forged to him [*LotR* 763].

Again the bait is looming large as Aragorn deliberately steps forth into the enemy's field of vision in the strategically chosen "guise" of the king. The visual field, as Kaja Silverman proposes, is a site of a limited agency inasmuch as the subject-as-spectacle can *to some extent* determine its appearance in (or disappearance from) the visible world. Whereas Frodo as a sovereign subject makes the crucial decision to withdraw from the visual field, Aragorn deliberately presents himself to Sauron as the heir of Isildur. True, this self-presentation involves a degree of dressing-up for the occasion by the demonstrative use of royal insignia; these, however, are far from accidental but to the contrary the phenomenal tokens of an underlying essential core of royalty that demands to be acknowledged. In this ocular duel, the king is not constituted as a subject through his engagement in the visual field, but is already fully established before he enters it. Therefore, like all those other visual clinches, this one too confirms how seeing is not productive in Tolkien: Aragorn performs an act not of self-fashioning but of self-revelation in which an authentic core—as in "Tal-Elmar" a genetic deep structure hitherto latent and "in hiding"—is finally made phenomenally manifest. Moreover, the power to demand recognition appears as a privilege of those aristocratic subjects who have always already been "endowed with value" ("mit Wert belehnt"; Schaffer 19), even if they have kept this endowment undercover for strategic reasons. What first appears as strategy is thus again revealed as "a union ticket for essentialism."

And yet, the option remains to diagnose in Tolkien a deep "ambivalence about essentialist and anti-essentialist narratives" (Saler 187). For the constant evocation and assertion of deep-structural core identities is in fact counterpoised by the equally persistent reminder to the fictional status of precisely those identities. In a world where characters recurrently are brought to marvel whether they "walk in legends or on the green earth in the daylight" (*LotR* 424), everyone is potentially reducible to an actant in a "tale" that is not written by those "inside it." Agency, then, can be derived only from the correct interpretation of "what sort of tale we've fallen into" (*LotR* 696): a subjectivity that proceeds from the insight that what "seems to operate as a subject" is indeed the effect of the "text" into which it is embedded. To some extent such metafictional devices ironicize the essentialist thrust of the book by alerting the reader to the "fictionalism" (Saler 176) from which Middle-earth paradoxically derives all its virtually empirical reality effects, including its agonistic essentialism which now, far from referring to some actual essences "out there," appears itself as grounded on the effects of the novel's representational strategies and thus reconcilable with the post-substantialist theoretical interventions of agonistic thinkers like Mouffe or Žižek. In this vein, in *The Lord of the Rings*, we do not encounter subjects but subject-effects. Only that these "effects" are so effective that not only they themselves but along with them the readers are prone to forget their effect-status. It is against this forgetfulness, that is: against its own alluring reality effects, that the narrative intermittently recalls that even the "green earth" itself is "a mighty matter of legend even if you tread it under the light of day" (*LotR* 424), so that the very materiality of the world is a narrative construction in the last resort, and yet functions simultaneously as solid reality. Against Tolkien's own claims, *The Lord of the Rings* could thus be read as one vast allegory, not of some geopolitical confrontation but of the mechanisms and potentials of strategic essentialism as such, deploying but also reflecting the ambivalences inherent to that program: to allow the reader, on the one hand, to indulge in the illicit pleasures of a "useful" but "dangerous" essentialism and a concomitant militancy, while at the same time constantly signaling that such readerly "commitments are dependent on various forms of coding" (Spivak, *Outside* 16).

Notes

1. Quotations from *The Lord of the Rings* will subsequently be taken from this edition in the following way: *LotR* page numbers.

Works Cited

Ahmed, Sara. *Strange Encounters: Embodied Others in Post-Coloniality*. London: Routledge, 2000. Print.
Battis, Jes. "Gazing upon Sauron: Hobbits, Elves, and the Queering of the Postcolonial Optic." *Modern Fiction Studies* 50.4 (2004): 908–26. Print.
Benjamin, Walter. *Illuminations: Essays and Reflections*. Intr. Hannah Arendt. Trans. Harry Zohn. New York: Schocken, 1968. Print.
Benvenuto, Maria Raffaella. "Against Stereotype: Éowyn and Lúthien as 20th-Century Women." *Tolkien and Modernity*. Vol. 1. Ed. Frank Weinreich and Thomas Honegger. Zurich: Walking Tree, 1996. 31–53. Print.
Bhabha, Homi K. *The Location of Culture*. London: Routledge, 1994. Print.
Brisbois, Michael J. "Tolkien's Imaginary Nature: An Analysis of the Structure of Middle-earth." *Tolkien Studies* 2 (2005): 197–216. Print.
Bull, Malcolm. *Seeing Things Hidden: Apocalypse, Vision and Totality*. London: Verso, 1999. Print.
Burns, Marjorie. *Perilous Realms: Celtic and Norse in Tolkien's Middle-Earth*. Toronto: University of Toronto Press, 2005. Print.
Campbell, Liam. *The Ecological Augury in the Works of J.R.R. Tolkien*. Zurich: Walking Tree, 2011. Print.
Chance, Jane. *Lord of the Rings: The Mythology of Power*. Lexington: University Press of Kentucky, 2001. Print.
Colebrook, Claire. "Certeau and Foucault: Tactics and Strategic Essentialism." *South Atlantic Quarterly* 100.2 (2001): 543–74. Print.
Danius, Sara, and Stefan Jonsson. "An Interview with Gayatri Chakravorty Spivak." *Boundary 2* 20.2 (1993): 24–50. Print.
Frye, Northrop. *The Secular Scripture: A Study of the Structure of Romance*. Cambridge: Harvard University Press, 1976. Print.
Greenblatt, Stephen. *Learning to Curse: Essays in Early Modern Culture*. New York: Routledge, 1994. Print.
Honig, Bonnie. "Another Cosmopolitanism? Law and Politics in the New Europe." *Another Cosmopolitanism*. Seyla Benhabib et al. Oxford: Oxford University Press, 2008. 102–27. Print.

Jameson, Fredric. *The Political Unconscious: Narrative as a Socially Symbolic Act*. London: Methuen, 1981. Print.

_____. *Postmodernism, or, The Cultural Logic of Late Capitalism*. London: Verso, 1991. Print.

_____. "Symptoms of Theory or Symptoms for Theory?" *Critical Inquiry* 30.2 (2004): 403–408. Print.

Lacan, Jacques. *The Four Concepts of Psycho-Analysis* [French original 1973]. The Seminar of Jacques Lacan: Book XI. Trans. Alan Sheridan. Ed. Jacques-Alain Miller. New York: Norton, 1998. Print.

McFadden, Brian. "Fear of Difference, Fear of Death: The *Sigelwara*, Tolkien's Swertings, and Racial Difference." *Tolkien's Modern Middle Ages*. Ed. Jane Chance and Alfred K. Siewers. New York: Palgrave Macmillan, 2005. 139–53. Print.

McLeod, John. *Beginning Postcolonialism*. Manchester: Manchester University Press, 2000. Print.

Michel, Laura. "Politically Incorrect: Tolkien, Women, and Feminism." *Tolkien and Modernity*. Vol. 1. Ed. Frank Weinreich and Thomas Honegger. Zürich: Walking Tree, 1996. 55–76. Print.

Moore-Gilbert, Bart. *Postcolonial Theory: Contexts, Practices, Politics*. London: Verso, 1997. Print.

Mouffe, Chantal. "Agonistic Public Spaces, Democratic Politics, and the Dynamics of Passions." *Thinking Worlds: The Moscow Conference on Philosophy, Politics, and Art*. Ed. Joseph Backstein et al. Berlin: Sternberg Press, 2008. 95–104. Print.

_____. "Artistic Activism and Agonistic Spaces." *Art and Research* 1.2 (2007): n. pag. Web. 11 Jan. 2013.

Mulvey, Laura. "Visual Pleasure and Narrative Cinema" [1975]. *Film Theory and Criticism: Introductory Readings*. Ed. Leo Braudy and Marshall Cohen. New York: Oxford University Press, 1999. 833–44. Print.

Porter, Lynette. *Unsung Heroes of The Lord of the Rings: From the Page to the Screen*. Westport, CT: Praeger, 2005. Print.

Rancière, Jacques. *Dis-agreement: Politics and Philosophy*. Trans. Julie Rose. Minneapolis: University of Minnesota Press, 1999. Print.

_____. *Dissensus: On Politics and Aesthetics*. Trans. Steven Corcoran. London: Continuum, 2010. Print.

_____. *The Politics of Aesthetics*. Trans. and intr. Gabriel Rockhill. London: Continuum, 2008. Print.

_____. "Who Is the Subject of the Rights of Man?" [2004]. *Wronging Rights? Philosophical Challenges for Human Rights*. Ed. Akash Singh Rathore and Alex Cistelecan. New Delhi: Routledge, 2011. 168–83. Print.

Rearick, Anderson. "Why Is the Only Good Orc a Dead Orc? The Dark Face of Racism Examined in Tolkien's World." *Modern Fiction Studies* 50.4 (2004): 861–74. Print.

Rohy, Valerie. "On Fairy Stories." *Modern Fiction Studies* 50.4 (2004): 927–48. Print.

Said, Edward. *Orientalism* [1978]. New York: Vintage, 1994. Print.

Saler, Michael. *As If: Modern Enchantment and the Literary Pre-History of Virtual Reality*. Oxford: Oxford University Press, 2012. Print.

Schaffer, Johanna. *Ambivalenzen der Sichtbarkeit: Über die visuellen Strukturen der Anerkennung*. Bielefeld: transcript, 2008. Print.

Scheps, Walter. "The Fairy-Tale Morality of *The Lord of the Rings*" [1975]. *A Tolkien Compass*. Ed. Jared Lobdell. Peru, IL: Open Court, 2003. 41–53. Print.

Silverman, Kaja. *The Threshold of the Visible World*. New York: Routledge, 1996. Print.

Smol, Anna. "'Oh ... Oh ... Frodo!': Readings of Male Intimacy in *The Lord of the Rings*." *Modern Fiction Studies* 50.4 (2004): 949–79. Print.

Spivak, Gayatri Chakravorty. *In Other Worlds: Essays in Cultural Politics*. London: Methuen, 1987. Print.

_____. *Outside in the Teaching Machine*. New York: Routledge, 1993. Print.
Tolkien, J.R.R. *The Lord of the Rings* [1954–55]. London: HarperCollins, 1995. Print.
_____. "Tal-Elmar" [1996]. *The Peoples of Middle-earth: The History of Middle-earth*. Vol. 12. Ed. Christopher Tolkien. London: HarperCollins, 2002. 422–38. Print.
Wilson, Edmund. "Oo, Those Awful Orcs!" *The Nation* 182 (1956): 312–14. Print.
Zimbardo, Rose A., and Neil D. Isaacs, eds. *Understanding the Lord of the Rings: The Best of Tolkien Criticism*. Boston: Houghton Mifflin, 2004. Print.
Žižek, Slavoj. "Afterword: The Lesson of Rancière." Jacques Rancière. *The Politics of Aesthetics*. Trans. and intr. Gabriel Rockhill. London: Continuum, 2004. 67–79. Print.
_____. "Brunhilde's Act." *International Journal of Žižek Studies* 4 (2011): 1–44. Print.
_____. *The Ticklish Subject: The Absent Centre of Political Ontology*. London: Verso, 1999. Print.

About the Contributors

Sladja **Blažan** is an assistant professor in the English and American studies department at the University of Würzburg. She also taught at Free University Berlin and New York University, where she worked on a postdoctoral research project on romanticism. She received a Ph.D. in American literature and culture from Humboldt University Berlin. She is working on a book on spectrality and ghostliness in American literature published between 1760 and 1860 and her published books include *American Fictionary: Postsozialistische Migration in der Amerikanischen Literatur* (2006) and *Ghost Stories and Alternative Histories* (2007).

Andreas **Blüml** studied English literature, communication science and computer science at Ludwig-Maximilians-University Munich. He wrote an M.A. thesis on Peter Jackson's film version of J.R.R. Tolkien's *The Lord of the Rings*, parts of which were published by Reclam. He is a web designer but has stayed close to academia. In addition to literary studies, he has published about mobile application development and web design.

Sebastian **Domsch** teaches Anglophone literatures at the Ernst-Moritz-Arndt University in Greifswald. He has taught at the LMU Munich and the University of Texas at Austin. He is the author of books on Robert Coover, Cormac McCarthy, 18th-century literary criticism as well as video games and narratology. He has edited a collection on American 21st-century fiction and co-edited two other volumes. He is also one of the editors of the *Kritisches Lexikon für fremdsprachige Gegenwartsliteratur* (*Critical Dictionary of Non-German Contemporary Literature*).

Rainer **Emig** is chair of English literature and culture at Leibniz University in Hanover, Germany. His interests include literature and the media and literary, critical and cultural theory. Among his publications are *Modernism in Poetry* (1995), *W.H. Auden* (1999) and *Krieg als Metapher im zwanzigsten Jahrhundert* (2001) as well as the edited collections *Performing Masculinity* (with Antony Rowland, 2010), *Commodifying (Post) Colonialism* (with Oliver Lindner, 2010), and *Treasure in Literature and Culture* (2013). He is one of the editors of the *Journal for the Study of British Cultures*.

Christina **Flotmann** teaches literary and cultural studies at the University of Paderborn, Germany, where she is an assistant professor in the department of English and

American studies. Publications include *Ambiguity in Star Wars and Harry Potter: A (Post)Structuralist Reading of Two Popular Myths* (2013) and an edited volume, *Narrative in Drama*, co-edited with Merle Tönnies (2011). Her main research interests are contemporary popular fiction as well as Victorian literature and culture.

Stefanie **Fricke** is an assistant professor of English literature at Ludwig-Maximilians-University Munich. She published her dissertation *Ruinen alter Hochkulturen und die Angst vor dem eigenen Untergang in der englischen Literatur des 19. Jahrhunderts* (*Antique Ruins and the Fear of the Fall of the British Empire in 19th-Century Literature*) in 2009. Her research focus is 18th and 19th century literature and culture as well as modern popular culture. Apart from articles on Romantic and Victorian literature she has also published essays on Kazuo Ishiguro, David Lodge, Rose Tremain and U.S. war blogs.

Beatrix **Hesse** earned a Ph.D. with a dissertation on recurrent patterns of communication and interaction in Shakespeare's comedies. Her second book was *The Body in the Library and the Body on Stage* and concerned the development of the English crime play and its relationship to detective fiction. Further research interests include prose fiction of the late 19th and early 20th century and contemporary British drama. She has written on the supernatural tales of R.L. Stevenson and Henry James, and has published on Stevenson's uncanny tales in Scots and on Neil Blomkamp's film *District 9*.

Bärbel **Höttges** studied American studies, German literature, and film at the University of Mainz, the University of California, Irvine, and Columbia University, New York. She received an M.A. and a Ph.D. from the University of Mainz, where she is an assistant professor of American studies. Her focus is on ethnic studies as well as literature and religion, literature and film, and (life) writing and grief. She is the author of *Faith Matters: Religion, Ethnicity, and Survival in Louise Erdrich's and Toni Morrison's Fiction* (2007) and is working on a book on death and grief in American literature and culture.

Matthias **Kemmer** holds a master's degree in Japanese and American studies from the University of Würzburg, where he has taught courses on science fiction, horror and postmodernism. His research concentrates on moral philosophy, cultural pessimism, transgression, simulation, and liminal phenomena. His essay on liminality and hybridity in Stanley Weinbaum's sci-fi short stories appeared in *Liminale Anthropologien: Zwischenzeiten, Schwellenphänomene, Zwischenräume in Literatur und Philosophie* (2012). He is pursuing a degree in computer science at the University of Applied Sciences Würzburg/Schweinfurt.

Christian **Knirsch** studied English at the University of Mannheim and the University of Alabama, Tuscaloosa. His doctoral dissertation was on the veil as an epistemological metaphor in Anglo-American literature from Romanticism to postmodernism (*Der epistemologische Schleier*, 2012). Other publications include an article on transcendentalist thought as a continuation of Lockean empiricism in *COPAS* (2001) and an article on the neurological aspects in Siri Hustvedt's *The Blindfold* in *Filolog* (2011). His research interests include literary theory, postmodernism, science and literature, and popular culture.

About the Contributors

Gerold **Sedlmayr** is a professor of British cultural studies at TU Dortmund University. He is author of the monographs *Brendan Kennelly's Literary Works: The Developing Art of an Irish Writer, 1959–2000* (2005) and *The Discourse of Madness in Britain, 1790–1815: Medicine, Politics, Literature* (2011). His research interests and areas of publication include Romanticism, Irish studies, body studies, as well as British film and television.

Dirk **Vanderbeke** teaches English literature at the Friedrich-Schiller-University in Jena and at the University of Zielona Góra. His doctoral dissertation, *Worüber man nicht sprechen kann* (*Whereof One Cannot Speak*), explores the unrepresentable in philosophy, science and literature. His *Theoretische Welten und literarische Transformationen* (*Theoretical Worlds and Literary Transformations*) examines the debate about "science and literature" and science's role(s) in contemporary literature. He has published on a variety of topics, including Joyce, Pynchon, Milton, science fiction, and graphic novels.

Nicole **Waller** is a professor of American studies at the University of Potsdam. She is author of the monographs *Contradictory Violence: Revolution and Subversion in the Caribbean* (2005) and *American Encounters with Islam in the Atlantic World* (2011). Her areas of research and publication include Atlantic studies, Caribbean studies, colonial American literature, postcolonial studies, and Arab American literature and culture.

Dirk **Wiemann** is a professor of English literature at the University of Potsdam. He has published a monograph on *Genres of Modernity: Contemporary Indian Novels in English* (2008) and is the co-editor of *European Contexts for English Republicanism* (2013) and *Perspectives on English Revolutionary Republicanism* (2014), among others. His numerous articles focus on theatre and politics in the English Republic, Indian and British literature and film, and genre transformations in contemporary world literature.

Index

Abanes, Richard 121, 124, 133*n*11
Abercromie, Joe: *The First Law* trilogy 14, 165–78
Adalian, Joseph 58
Adams, Douglas: *Life, the Universe, and Everything* 156
adaptation 2, 11, 32, 57–58, 65, 68*n*13, 68*n*15, 68*n*17, 75, 87, 97, 99
aesthetics 2, 10–11, 13, 15, 38, 45, 49, 55, 58–59, 124–25, 191
Afghanistan 19, 88, 140–41, 143
Africa 68*n*10, 87, 100
African American 22, 59, 61–62, 66, 69*n*27, 103, 110–11
agency 65, 98, 111, 126, 168, 184–86, 192, 194, 196, 198, 201
agonism 7, 15*n*2, 194–97, 201
alterity 9, 77, 156
American Gods 153
American Idol (TV show) 22
America's Next Top Model (TV show) 19
Anansi Boys 153
anarchy 11, 46, 51, 53–55, 94–95, 125, 152
antagonism 7, 15*n*2, 179, 187, 193–94, 196
apocalypse 12, 17, 32, 97–98, 102, 110, 112, 119, 184
Ariely, Dan 155–56
Aristotle 4, 106
Armstrong, Ari 123
Armstrong, Karen 15*n*1
As I Lay Dying 68*n*16
Asia 40–41, 66, 87, 103
atheism 13, 80, 118, 127–28, 131
Attebery, Brian 3–5, 8, 95*n*1
Atwood, Margaret: *Oryx and Crake* 97
Auden, Wystan Hugh 191
Australia 131*n*2
Austria 153

authorial 79, 81, 115, 177
authority 10, 12, 20, 26, 54, 62, 77, 79, 80, 102, 105–8, 116, 130, 132*n*3, 132*n*7, 155, 159, 173, 188
authorship 46–47
avatar 11, 32, 35, 38–39, 100–6, 108, 110–13, 115–16

Babel (film) 156
Bakhtin, Mikhail 54
Baldur's Gate (computer game) 32
Barthes, Roland 11, 58, 137, 139–41, 147
Bartlett, Tony 175
Baudrillard, Jean 14, 158, 170–71, 177*n*2
Bear, Greg: *Strength of Stones* 150
Belfast 13, 155
belief (system) 8, 13, 15, 52, 64–65, 70*n*36, 121, 123, 129, 143, 173
Bell, Elizabeth 46
Bentham, Jeremy 113, 116*n*2, 199
Berlin 13, 155
Beyond: Two Souls (computer game) 99
Bhaba, Homi 199
Bible 63–65, 80, 118–21, 123–24, 129–31, 132*n*9
bildungsroman 10, 19
Bin Laden, Osama 140, 146–47
binary 102, 105–6, 108–10, 112, 139–40, 142–44
Blair, Tony 137, 140–42, 146–47
bloodlines 88, 90
body 14, 20, 23, 28, 46, 68*n*16, 75, 100, 104, 132*n*3, 139, 140, 144, 152, 154, 160, 165–67, 169–74, 176–77, 196
book burning 122, 132*n*7
The Book of Eli (film) 97–98
Borderlands (computer game) 35, 97
bourgeoisie 54, 87

209

Brassier, Ra 189*n*5
Braybrooke, David 116*n*2
The Brief Wondrous Life of Oscar Wao 6–7
Brooke-Rose, Christine 94
Brown, Bill 187
Bruno, Dave 123, 132*n*9
Burton, Tim 43, 46–48, 50; "The Nightmare Before Christmas" (poem) 47–48
Bush, George W. 137, 140–43, 147
Butler, Judith 172
Butler, Octavia 189*n*8
Byatt, A.S. 158

"The Call of Cthulhu" 184–85
Calvino, Italo: *Invisible Cities* 150, 154
Campanella, Tommaso 150
Canada 68*n*10, 131*n*2
capitalism 5, 14, 52, 169–71, 173, 177, 183
Card, Claudia 46
Cardwell, Sarah 65
Carey, Brycchan 147*n*1
Caribbean 7
carnivalesque 11, 54
Carpenter, John 185
Carroll, Rachel 61
categorical imperative (Kant) 114
Caucasian 11, 22, 40, 61, 92, 103
Cerebus 12, 72–84
Chambers, Joseph 119–20, 131*n*3
Childe, Vere Gordon 158, 162*n*4
Christianity 4, 11–13, 51–52, 60, 61, 65, 68*n*14, 70*n*36, 118–24, 126–31, 132*n*5, 132*n*6, 133*n*10, 133*n*11, 133*n*13, 133*n*15
Christmas 11, 43–55, 121, 127–28, 133*n*13
church 52, 61, 66, 70*n*36, 74, 127–30
city 13, 63, 73, 87–88, 92, 100, 150–61, 171, 182
The City and the City 13, 153–61; *see also* Miéville, China
civilization 67*n*7, 92–93, 97, 102, 112–13, 140, 166, 168, 173
class (character class) 31, 33–34, 39–41
class (social class) 4, 6–7, 10, 12, 21, 54, 57, 67, 86–87, 152, 174
Clery, E.J. 64
Clute, John 9, 167, 179–80
Cold War 94, 187, 198
Coleridge, Samuel Taylor: "The Rime of the Ancient Mariner" 3
Collins, Suzanne: *The Hunger Games* 10, 17–30, 97
"The Colour Out of Space" 189*n*3
comic (book) 7, 72–75, 77–83, 97
comic (mode) 4–5, 64, 82
commodity 23, 60, 63, 68*n*11, 68*n*12

communism 46, 107
"Composed Upon Westminster Bridge" 150
computer role-playing game (CRPG) *see* role-playing game
Conan the Barbarian 12, 72–75, 77
consumption 5, 17, 19–21, 23, 31, 45–46, 51–52, 99, 101, 120, 138, 170
contact zone (Pratt) 13, 157, 159, 162
Coover, Robert: *Ghost Town* 151
Cornwell, Neil 56*n*2, 56*n*4
counterculture 11, 43–45, 52, 55, 72
Croal, N'Gai 100
Crumb, Robert 72
Cruz, Omayra Zaragoza 57
The Crying of Lot 49 152
Cryptonomicon 158
Cukor, George: *My Fair Lady* 50
customization 11, 32–34, 41
CYCLONOPEDIA: Complicity with Anonymous Materials 14, 181–89

DC (publishing house) 72
DeLillo, Don: *White Noise* 154
democracy 8–9, 29, 57, 68*n*14, 140, 191, 194
Derrida, Jacques 142, 144, 187
Desmond, John 45, 55
Díaz, Juno: *The Brief Wondrous Life of Oscar Wao* 6–7
diegesis 12, 79, 112, 153, 167
discourse 2, 8, 10, 12, 78–79, 80, 84*n*1, 94, 98, 100–1, 106–10, 116, 137–39, 144, 147, 156, 158, 194
dnd (computer game) 32
Dobson, James 133*n*10
Dominican Republic 7
Douglas, Alfred: "Impression de Nuit: London" 150
Dragon Age (computer game) 32, 34, 40–41
Dragon Quest (computer game) 108
Dunn, George A. 60, 64, 68*n*11
dystopian fiction 10, 17–19, 29*n*1, 86

Eco, Umberto 44
ecology 87, 185, 191
economy 87–88, 90, 92, 99–101, 110, 153, 155–56, 166, 170–72, 183, 186, 189, 195
Edgeworth, Francis Ysidro 116*n*2
education 106, 119, 140
Eliot, Marc 46
Ellison, Ralph: *Invisible Man* 69*n*25
empire 93–94, 152, 169, 199
empiricism 9, 98, 106–7, 116*n*2, 199, 201
empowerment 161, 191, 200
Enlightenment 8–9, 87, 140, 173

Enslaved: Odyssey to the West (computer game) 97
escapism 41, 84, 86, 143, 181, 188, 194
essence 2, 4–5, 9, 14, 111, 140, 146, 157, 169, 171, 173, 191, 193, 195–97, 202–2
essentialism *see* essence
ethics 4, 12, 57, 67*n*7, 78, 81, 89, 91, 97, 101–2, 105–10, 113–16, 121, 124, 193
eucatastrophe 4
evangelicalism 121, 126, 128, 131*n*3, 132*n*10, 133*n*10
Everquest (computer game) 33
evil 6, 10, 13, 32, 41, 63, 73, 87, 105–6, 108, 116, 118–19, 121, 123, 124, 133*n*16, 137–48, 172, 184–86
The Exorcist (film) 185

factionalism 72, 75, 88, 105–8, 110–12, 119
Fallen Earth (computer game) 97, 104,
Fallout (computer game) 12, 32, 97–117
fan fiction 84*n*4
Faulkner, William: *As I Lay Dying* 68*n*16
feminism 49, 63, 68*n*11, 74–75, 79–80, 82, 101, 177*n*2, 195, 197
feudalism 60, 87, 94
Fimi, Dimitra 6
Final Fantasy (computer game) 108
Firchow, Peter E. 95*n*1
The First Law trilogy 14, 165–78
Fish, Stanley 126
Fiske, John 58–59, 67*n*5, 137–39, 143, 147
Foucault, Michel 14, 46, 99, 158, 173
Foy, Joseph, J. 61, 66
Freud, Sigmund 102, 189*n*1
Friedkin, William 185
fundamentalism 94, 119, 121, 140

Gaiman, Neil: *American Gods* 153; *Anansi Boys* 153; *Neverwhere* 151–52
A Game of Thrones (TV series) 86
gaze 156, 197–200
gender 4, 6–7, 10–12, 19, 31–41, 46, 50–51, 53, 57–60, 67, 72, 74–76, 81, 84*n*3, 86, 91, 100–3, 111, 158, 191
Genette, Gerard 112
genre 1–5, 8–9, 11, 14, 15*n*2, 18, 32–33, 57–58, 60, 61, 65–66, 67*n*1, 68*n*13, 70*n*39, 72, 74, 82, 84*n*1, 86, 89, 98, 102, 165–166, 170, 176, 179–83, 185, 187–88
Gerhard (artist) 73, 77
Ghost Town 151
ghoul 109–10, 113
Gilroy, Paul 189*n*8
Girard, René 175
Gish, Kimbra Wilder 120

Gonmez, Jewelle 189*n*8
good *see* evil
Gordon, Joan 159, 162*n*3
Gothic (genre) 11, 58, 60–61, 68*n*13, 68*n*16, 70*n*34, 86, 96*n*2
Goth(ic) subculture 3, 11, 43–44, 55
Granger, John 123–24
Grant, Iain Hamilton 189*n*5
Grant, John 180
Greenblatt, Stephen 192
Griesinger, Emily 123–24
Grossberg, Lawrence 57
Grossman, Lev 121, 128
Guins, Raiford 57

Haas, Lynda 46
Halloween 11, 48–49, 51–55, 120
happiness 61, 113–15, 116*n*2
Harman, Graham 187, 189*n*5
Harris, Charlaine: Sookie Stackhouse novels 11, 58, 65, 68*n*10
Harry Potter series 12–13, 17, 21, 29*n*1, 85, 118–36, 137–49, 167
Harvey, Linda 122, 132*n*6
Heavy Rain (computer game) 99
hegemony 8, 146–47, 158–59, 194
Heidegger, Martin 187
Hemingway, Ernest 77
hermaphrodite 75
heterosexuality 37, 50, 61, 93
Hispanic 103
historical novel 86
historicism 5–6, 87, 103, 107
historicity *see* historicism
Ho, Elizabeth 156, 162*n*2
Hobbes, Thomas 102
Hölderlin, Friedrich 187
homosexuality 11, 36–37, 40, 61, 66, 68*n*18, 68*n*19, 69*n*21, 69*n*22, 93, 103, 126, 191, 195, 197
Hopkinson, Nalo 189*n*8
Horne, Jackie C. 147*n*1
horror 4, 98, 182, 184, 185, 189*n*2
Hourihan, Margery 166, 177
Housel, Rebecca 60, 65, 68*n*11
Howard, Robert E.: *Conan the Barbarian* 12, 72, 74
humor 75, 77
The Hunger Games 10, 17–30, 97
hybridity 2, 103, 113, 156–57, 162, 162*n*3, 166, 179–80, 191

identity 10, 17, 19–21, 23–29, 30*n*7, 37–38, 44, 46, 59, 50, 63, 66, 88, 92, 105, 111, 188, 193, 195, 199–200

ideology 1–2, 4, 6, 13, 46, 49, 57, 59, 66, 67n5, 88, 91, 93, 94–95, 100, 110, 118, 126, 131, 133n11, 137–39, 141, 144, 146, 147, 158, 165, 170, 176–77, 195
immersive fantasy 14, 85, 87, 166–67, 176
imperialism *see* empire
"Impression de Nuit: London" 150
incest 90, 91, 93
independent publishing 72–73
industrialization 86–87
interactivity 12, 31, 40, 97–102, 104–5, 110, 112
interpretive community 126–27, 133n12
invisibility *see* visibility
Invisible Cities 150, 154
Invisible Man 69n25
Iraq 10, 19, 63, 88, 141, 143
Iser, Wolfgang 13, 124–25
Islam 68n10, 80, 140, 155
Islamism 65, 68n14, 140
Ivanhoe 86

Jackson, Peter 2, 6, 57
Jackson, Rosemary 3, 9, 169
Jacobs, Alan 123–24
Jacobs, Cindy 119
Jacob's Ladder (film) 99
James, Edward 6, 8
Jameson, Fredric 5, 7, 169, 173, 194
Jerusalem 13, 155
Johnson, Steven 150
Joyce, James: *Ulysses* 151
Judaism 90, 123, 152, 155,

Kafka, Franz: *The Metamorphosis* 169
Kant, Immanuel 114–15, 187
Keyes, Berit Haugen 54
Killinger, John 123–24
Kim, Sue 6
Kirkland, Robert: *The Walking Dead* (comic books) 97
Koukl, Gregory 123
Kraken 153, 161
Ku Klux Klan 49, 62, 69n24
Kuby, Gabriele 132n5
Kugelmass, Jack 52
Kurosawa, Akira 104

Lacan, Jacques 199
Lachowicz, Colleen 100
Land of the Dead (film) 109
Lanzendörfer, Tim 7
The Last of Us (computer game) 97
Latin America 7, 64
Latour, Bruno 187

Lawrence, Jennifer 22
Le Guin, Ursula K.: *A Wizard of Earthsea* 10, 85
Leiber, Fritz, Jr. 184
Lévi-Strauss, Claude 137–39
Lewis, Clive Staples 86–87, 89, 167, 191; Narnia novels 85, 87–89, 131, 167
liberalism 8, 15n2, 57, 68n10, 83, 107
Life, the Universe, and Everything 156
Lincoln, Abraham 111
Loach, Ken 2
Locke, John 108
The Lord of the Rings (novel) 3, 6, 14–15, 57, 85, 87–88, 98–99, 167, 172, 191–204; *see also* Tolkien, John Ronald Reuel
Lord of the Rings Online (computer game) 33, 40–41
Lost Highway (film) 99
Lovecraft, H.P. 184–87, 189n2, 189n3; "The Call of Cthulhu" 184–85; "The Colour Out of Space" 189n3
Lucas, George 146
Lynch, David 99
Lyne, Adrien 99
Lyotard, Jean François 94, 107, 115

MacDonald, George 180
magic 2, 14, 17, 32, 87–89, 95n1, 98–99, 118–19, 122, 129, 130, 132n3, 133n16, 146, 152, 159, 165, 168, 170–74, 176, 188
magic(al) realism 2, 159
Mallarmé, Stéphane 187
Manichaeism 15, 192–95
mapping 83, 87, 104, 109, 165, 198
Martin, George R.R.: *A Song of Ice and Fire* 12, 85–96, 167
Marvel Comics 72
marvelous (genre) 2, 7, 98
masculinity 12, 35, 59, 73–75
Mass Effect (computer game) 33–35, 37–38, 40–41
mass production 44, 51–52
Massively Multiplayer Online Role-Playing Game (MMO/MMORPG) *see* role-playing game
The Matrix (films) 97
McCarthy, Cormac: *The Road* 97, 111
McDonagh, Pierre 45
McEwan, Ian 158
McVeigh, Dan 123
media 10, 19, 22–29, 31, 35, 36–37, 39, 72, 77, 83, 97, 99–100, 139, 142, 156, 170–71
Meillassoux, Quentin 187, 189n5
Mendlesohn, Farah 6, 8, 67n1, 166–67
merchandise 21, 43–44

metafiction 12, 74, 76–77, 79, 81, 183, 201
The Metamorphosis 169
Metro 2033 (computer game) 97
Meyer, David J. 119, 133*n*10
Meyer, Stephenie: *Twilight* series 11, 17, 57–71
Middle Ages 4, 85–88, 94, 123, 133*n*13, 170, 173
Middle East 14, 88, 182–83, 185
Miéville, China 13, 150–63, 182; *The City and the City* 13, 153–61; *Kraken* 153, 161; *Perdido Street Station* 13, 153, 160–62; *Rat King* 153; *Un Lun Dun* 153
Might and Magic (computer game) 32
Mill, John Stuart 116*n*2
Miller, Laura 29*n*1
minority 45, 61–62, 113, 116*n*2
mode 2–5, 12, 38, 64–65, 74, 76–77, 79, 80, 82, 84*n*1, 98
money 12, 14, 21, 24, 54, 90, 156, 171–72
Moore, Clement Clarke: "A Visit from St. Nicholas" 47, 54
morals 12, 27–29, 53–54, 62, 65, 81, 97, 102, 105–16, 121, 124, 130, 139–44, 146–47, 151, 170, 172, 174, 176, 180, 186, 191, 193
Moria (computer game) 32
Morris, William: *The Well at the World's End* 96*n*2
Morrison, Tony: *Playing in the Dark* 189*n*8; "Unspeakable Things Unspoken" 189*n*8
Mouffe, Chantal 7–9, 15, 15*n*2, 194, 201
multiculturalism 156–57, 159, 161
Murphy, Derek 123, 133*n*16
Muslim *see* Islam
My Fair Lady 50
The Mysteries of Paris 151
myth 3, 15*n*1, 18, 54, 59–60, 72, 74, 77–79, 101–1, 111, 123, 137–41, 151, 158, 173, 185
mythology *see* myth

Narnia novels 85, 87–89, 131, 167
Nash, Mark 132*n*6
nation 7, 17, 22, 61, 68*n*10, 86, 101–2, 111, 141
Natural Born Killers (film) 175
naturalization 2, 4–5, 139–40, 145, 191
Neal, Connie 123
Negarestani, Reza: *CYCLONOPEDIA: Complicity with Anonymous Materials* 14, 181–89
Neverwhere 151–52
New Age 52, 121, 158
"The Nightmare Before Christmas" (poem) 47–48
9/11 (terror attacks) 13, 141–42, 144
Nissenbaum, Stephen 11, 54

Norris, Mike 119–20, 132*n*3
Northern Lights trilogy 10
NPC (non-player character) 36, 40, 103–5, 108–9, 112, 116

Obama, Barack 137, 146–47
occult 13, 119–21, 128–31, 132*n*6
O'Donoghue, Stephanie 45, 55
"On Fairy Stories" 4–5, 180–81
ontology 106, 114–15, 151, 185, 195, 200
open world (game world) 12, 102, 104
Oryx and Crake 97
othering 12, 41, 100, 193

paganism 11, 51–52, 192
Page, Ellen 99
para-politics 194–95
parody 12, 47–48, 64–65, 73–79, 82, 168, 176
The Passion 152
pastoral 61, 66, 194
patriarchy 4, 11, 47, 51, 53, 59, 87, 91, 93, 174, 197
Patterson, Steven W. 147*n*1
Pease, Donald 187–88
Peeters, Benoît 150
Penny, Laurie 177*n*2
Perdido Street Station 13, 153, 160–62; *see also* Miéville, China
performance 50–52, 54, 103
Petzold, Dieter 179–80
Pinocchio (film) 46
Plato 150
Playing in the Dark 189*n*8
Pong (computer game) 99
post-apocalypse *see* apocalypse
postcolonialism 13, 95, 157, 162*n*3
postmodernism 50, 80–82, 86, 93, 151, 158–59, 162*n*3, 170, 173–74, 179, 183, 188
Pratchett, Terry: *Reaper Man* 151
Pratt, Mary Louise 157, 162
producerly (Barthes) 58, 65, 138, 147
Protestantism 60, 121
Pullman, Philip: *Northern Lights* trilogy 10
Pulp Fiction (film) 175
Pygmalion 50
Pynchon, Thomas: *The Crying of Lot 49* 152; *V.* 151–52

queerness *see* homosexuality
quest 14, 19, 24, 32, 36, 93, 104–5, 109, 112, 116, 142, 166, 176–77, 183, 191, 197

Rabin, Nicole 61, 66
race 6–7, 10, 11, 12, 21, 31–33, 37, 40–41, 51,

58–59, 62, 67, 86, 92, 102–3, 166, 184, 187, 193
racism 40–41, 49, 62, 109, 110–11, 191–92
Rage (computer game) 97
Rancière, Jacques 7–9, 15, 194, 196
Rashômon (film) 104
Rat King 153
Ratzinger Joseph (Pope Benedict XVI) 121, 126, 132n5
readerly (Barthes) 11, 58–59, 76, 102
realism 2–3, 5, 7, 12, 14, 29, 40, 76–79, 82–84, 98–101, 104, 110, 124, 151–54, 159, 180, 182, 186–87, 189
Reaper Man 151
reception 58, 62, 81, 124, 126, 131n2
Red Sonja 72, 75
Reemtsma, Jan-Philipp 173–74
referentiality 12, 76–78, 80, 82
religion 7, 10, 12–13, 51–52, 69n22, 72, 75, 78, 80, 83, 86, 88, 91–95, 110, 118, 121–31, 140, 142, 150, 191
Renaissance 85, 88, 173
Resident Evil (computer game) 100, 111
response theory 13, 124
rhetoric 13, 62–63, 67n1, 137–39, 147, 166–67, 176
"The Rime of the Ancient Mariner" 3
The Road 97, 111
Rogue (computer game) 32
role-playing game (RPG) 5, 11–12, 31–42, 97–117
romance 5, 11, 18, 24, 36–37, 40, 59, 67, 86, 165, 169–70, 174–75
Romero, George A. 109
Rose, Jacqueline 187–88
Rousseau, Jean-Jacques 102
Rowling, Joanna K.: *Harry Potter* series 12–13, 17, 21, 29n1, 85, 118–36, 137–49, 167
Run Lola Run (film) 104
Rushdie, Salman: *The Satanic Verses* 8–9, 157
Russell, Bertrand 116
Russia 131n2

Saldivar, Ramón 187–88, 189n7
Sandel, Michael J. 114
Sarkeesian, Anita 101
The Satanic Verses 8–9, 157
Satanism 13, 119, 121, 125, 131, 147
satire 22, 47, 72–73, 74, 75, 77, 82, 101, 120, 157
Schnoebelen, William 121
Schuiten, François 150
Schulzke, Marcus 106
Schwartz, Daniel 132n7

science fiction 3, 7, 31–33, 35, 41, 86, 98, 150, 158, 160, 179, 182–86, 188
Scotland 86–88
Scott, Walter: *Ivanhoe* 86; *Waverley* 86
selfhood 10, 138, 200
Selick, Henry 46–48, 50
Sells, Laura 46
sexuality 12, 46, 59, 60–61, 63, 66, 69n21, 69n22, 91, 93, 103, 177n2
Shakespeare, William 192
Shaw, George Bernard: *Pygmalion* 50
Sherer, Moshe 106
Sidgwick, Henry 116n2
Silent Hill (computer game) 99
The Silmarillion 193
Silver, Anna 58–59
Silverman, Kaja 199–200
Sim, Dave: *Cerebus* 12, 72–84
Skyrim (computer game) 36, 99, 103
slavery 21, 62, 69n27, 70n36, 89, 92, 97, 103, 105, 108, 110–11, 140
socialism 87, 95n1
A Song of Ice and Fire 12, 85–96, 167
Sookie Stackhouse novels 11, 58, 65, 68n10
South Africa 155
Southern (U.S. American) 61, 63, 68n16
spectacle 64, 70n34, 174–75, 199–200
speculative realism 14, 186–87, 189n6, 189n7
Spencer, Glen 121
Spencer, Kathleen L. 69
Spivak, Gayatri 195–96
Stableford, Brian 180
Star Wars 13, 78, 137–49
Star Wars Galaxies (computer game) 33
Stephenson, Neal: *Cryptonomicon* 158
Stone, Oliver 175
Strength of Stones 150
subculture 11, 43–45, 56
subject-as-spectacle 199–200
subject-effect 195–96, 201
subjectivity 105–7, 115, 124–25, 173, 186, 199, 201
Sue, Eugène: *The Mysteries of Paris* 151
Sun Ra 188
Superman (comics) 83
supernatural 2–3, 64–65, 67n1, 69n32, 70n34, 86, 89, 92, 98, 122, 159
Survivor (TV show) 19
Swift, Jonathan 150
sword and sorcery 4, 72–74, 77, 85

"Tal-Elmar" 192–97, 201
Tarantino, Quentin 175
technology 17, 19, 87–88, 98–100, 112, 122, 128

Index

TERA (computer game) 35
Thailand 131n2
Thaler, Ingrid 189n8
Thatcher, Margaret 77
theology 6, 57, 72, 74, 76–80, 182
The Thing (film) 185
thing theory 187
third space 157–59
Third World 7, 19, 156
Thomson, Judith J. 114
Tim Burton's A Nightmare Before Christmas (film) 11, 43–56
Todorov, Tzvetan 2, 67n1, 86, 98, 109
Tolkien, Christopher 192
Tolkien, John Ronald Reuel 2, 5–7, 12, 14–15, 31, 41, 86–89, 93, 150, 167, 170, 191–204; *The Lord of the Rings* 3, 6, 14–15, 57, 85, 87–88, 98–99, 167, 172, 191–204; "On Fairy-stories" 4–5, 180–81; *The Silmarillion* 193; "Tal-Elmar" 192–97, 201
Torah 74, 80
Toynbee, Philip 191
True Blood (TV series) 11, 57–58, 60–68
Tuleja, Tad 53
Turkey 153
Turner, Bryan S. 174
Twilight series 11, 17, 57–71
Tykwer, Tom 104

Ultima (computer game) 32–34
Ulysses 151
uncanny 2, 98, 150, 159
underground comix 72–73
United States 7, 11–12, 17, 19, 21–22, 32, 36–38, 50–52, 58–62, 64, 66, 68n10, 68n14, 69n25, 69n27, 72, 88, 100, 102, 107, 111–12, 115, 122, 131n2, 140, 142, 157, 183, 188, 189n8
"Unspeakable Things Unspoken" 189n8
urbanity *see* city
utilitarianism 113–15, 116n2
utopia 4–5, 13, 86, 157–58, 162

V. 151–52
vampire 11, 57–71, 104, 161
VanderMeer, Jeff and Ann 182

Vaughan, Brian: *Y—The Last Man* (comic books) 97
Victorianism 59–60, 86
violence 5, 12, 18–20, 27, 46, 65, 75–76, 101, 105, 110, 113, 172, 175–76
visibility 6, 9, 15, 125, 150, 152–55, 157, 159, 172, 191, 196–201
"A Visit from St. Nicholas" 47, 54
visuality *see* visibility

The Walking Dead (comic books) 97
The Walking Dead (TV series) 98, 102
Wallace, David Foster 188
Walt Disney Corporation 43–47
War on Terror 14, 182–83
Waverley 86
weird fiction *see* weirdness
weirdness 13, 151, 153–55, 160–62, 174, 182, 186, 188
The Well at the World's End 96n2
West, Marsha 121
Westman, Karen E. 147n1
White, T.H. 95n1
White Noise 154
Wilson, Edmund 191
Winterson, Jeanette: *The Passion* 152
Winthrop, John 150
Wiœniewska, Dorota J. 47
witchcraft 13, 41, 87, 89, 118–21, 124, 132n4, 133n10
A Wizard of Earthsea 10, 85
Wordsworth, William: "Composed Upon Westminster Bridge" 150
World of Warcraft (computer game) 33, 39, 99, 104
World War II 154
writerly (Barthes) 11, 58, 60, 65

xenophobia 88, 192

Y—The Last Man (comic books) 97

Ziv, Avner 106
Žižek, Slavoj 158, 194, 201
zombie 41, 95, 98, 100, 109

www.ingramcontent.com/pod-product-compliance
Ingram Content Group UK Ltd.
Pitfield, Milton Keynes, MK11 3LW, UK
UKHW041958140426
5217IPUK00015B/867